RUFUS JONES SPEAKS TO OUR TIME

THE MACMILLAN COMPANY
NEW YORK · BOSTON · CHICAGO
DALLAS · ATLANTA · SAN FRANCISCO

MACMILLAN AND CO., LIMITED
LONDON · BOMBAY · CALCUTTA
MADRAS · MELBOURNE

THE MACMILLAN COMPANY
OF CANADA, LIMITED
TORONTO

Rufus Jones

Rufus Jones
SPEAKS TO OUR TIME

AN ANTHOLOGY

EDITED BY

HARRY EMERSON FOSDICK

NEW YORK

The Macmillan Company

1951

FIRST PRINTING

The Editor makes grateful acknowledgment for the use of quoted material from Rufus Jones' books to:

The Estate of Rufus M. Jones for *Social Law in the Spiritual World* (Winston, 1904).

The Friend (London) for excerpts from Volume 60 (1920), Volume 65 (1925), Volume 68 (1928), Volume 51 (1911).

Stanford University Press for *Spirit in Man* (1941).

George Allen & Unwin, Ltd., for *Nature and Authority of Conscience* (Swarthmore Press, 1920) and for *Quakerism: A Religion of Life* (Headley Brothers, 1908).

Harper & Brothers for *Faith and Practice of Quakers* (Methuen, 1927) and for *The Church's Debt to Heretics* (Doran, 1924).

The International Missionary Council for "Secular Civilization and the Christian Task," Jerusalem Meeting of the Missionary Council, 1928.

The Beacon Press for *Re-Thinking Religious Liberalism* (1935).

The American Friend for excerpts from Volume 9 (1921).

Joseph E. Rowntree and the Yorkshire Friends Service Committee for the pamphlet, "Our Social Task and the Life Which It Demands."

The Survey Associates for "The Quaker Peace Position," *The Survey*, Volume 34, 1915, and for an article from the August, 1942, issue of *The Survey Graphic*.

The University of Pennsylvania Press for "The Church as an Organ of Social Ideals" in *Religion and the Modern World* (1941).

The Estate of Rufus M. Jones and the Macmillan Company for quotations from the following books: *Spiritual Energies in Daily Life* (1922), *Pathways to the Reality of God* (1931), *Inner Life* (1916), *Trail of Life in the Middle Years* (1934), *Preface to Christian Faith in a New Age* (1932), *Eternal Gospel* (1938), *A Call to What Is Vital* (1948), *Testimony of the Soul* (1936), *Luminous Trail* (1947), *New Quest* (1928), *World Within* (1918), *Studies in Mystical Religion* (1909), *Radiant Life* (1944), *Fundamental Ends of Life* (1924), *Flowering of Mysticism* (1939), *New Eyes for Invisibles* (1943), *New Studies in Mystical Religion* (1927).

INTRODUCTION

R UFUS JONES cannot be put into print. He wrote fifty-seven books and uncounted articles and editorials, but even so he himself has never been published. To be sure, one of his friends said about his writings, "While we are reading them, we feel him near and talking to us in person"; but the man who said that, along with thousands of others who would say the same, had first known Rufus Jones himself. That was a kindling, stimulating experience. He was a radiant person. He possessed the "inner light" about which he wrote. "To meet him," said one of his colleagues, "was to feel set up for the day."

Nevertheless, while so luminous a personality cannot be printed, his writings do reveal him. This anthology is a labor of love and gratitude on the part of one who first met Rufus Jones through his books and was immeasurably helped. A young man, just entering on his ministry, confused by the theological wrangles of his time, and struggling to find a footing for his faith, the editor of this anthology ran upon "Social Law in the Spiritual World." That book opened the door to a new era in my thought and life and, re-reading it recently, I perceived afresh how much of my message has been rooted in the rich soil which that book provided. Years afterwards Rufus Jones became my friend. I understand what one of his students meant when he said, "He lighted my candle." Everything that was in his books was in the man—and very much more! Now, when I read his writings, a uniquely radiant personality is talking to me.

Rufus Jones has fallen on sleep, and if he is to speak to this oncoming generation, which desperately needs his message, it must be through his books. But many of them are out of print. Can an anthology rescue from forgetfulness the essential gist of this man's gospel, make freshly audible to his friends his living voice, and bring to those who never knew him his vital ideas of life's significance? His friends have thought it worth the trying. Samuel Butler's saying—"My books are me"—is far from true in the case of Rufus Jones; he was much more than his books. Yet they do express his mind and heart, and this anthology is the endeavor to provide in very condensed form his essential message.

For those who have not known the man himself, a brief sketch of his life may make his writings more vivid and understandable. He was born into a Quaker home on a farm in Maine, January 25, 1863. It was a home, he wrote, "in which religion was a vital part of the air we breathed. I was not 'christened' in a church but I was sprinkled from morning till night with the dew of religion. We never ate a meal which did not begin with a hush of Thanksgiving; we never began a day without a family gathering, the reading of a chapter in the Bible, followed by a period of silent worship when we talked with God, not far away, but very near. This was a Quaker home, the product of generations of deep inward religious life."

To many moderns such a picture of family piety suggests dourness and repression. In Rufus Jones' account of it in "A Small-Town Boy," however, one finds about the gayest, happiest, most humorous and, at the same time most worthwhile story of healthy boyhood ever written. Religion in that Quaker home was, at it was ever afterwards to Rufus Jones, real, adventurous, exciting. When he recalled what the Biblical characters meant to him as a boy he said that their deeds "were more a part of me than movie actors or baseball heroes ever can be to a modern youth."

There was apparently in the boy, as there always was in the man, something that shone. When a distinguished Friend, who later became the first President of Bryn Mawr College, visited the humble home in Maine, his eye lighted on the lad, and then he looked again. Before he left, he put his hand on the small boy's head and solemnly announced that Rufus would some day be a "bearer of light and a purveyor of truth." Meanwhile, Rufus himself has said that the sound he loved best was the swish of his scythe in the wet morning grass, and next best the sound of his ax in the winter woods. He grew up, like all Maine farmboys, used to household duties and hard work in the out-of-doors. He was a natural leader, and the boys of the community gathered around him. All the games, pranks, competitions, fights and celebrations that made country life in a pioneer settlement far more exciting than the corner of Broadway and 42nd Street, Rufus and his cronies enjoyed. He was no saint. He "played hookey" from school; he heard the profanity and smut that no boy escapes; and as he came into his teens he had his inward struggles, feeling that he was "helplessly drifting down the stream." But always there was the deep, stabilizing influence of the Quaker Meeting—"three miles from home, through a fascinating woods, full of imaginary animals"— where even a boy "grew confident that there was a mutual and reciprocal intercourse with the Beyond." And there was the school, where Rufus thrived, until the evening gatherings at the country grocery store elected him to read the news, or even Mark Twain and Artemus Ward, because he did it so well. And back of all these was the home. Once when Rufus had run away from his proper job at weeding a turnip patch to spend a day swimming and fishing, he returned at night expecting punishment. He got it, but in an unlooked-for way. His mother led him to his room, put him in a chair, and then kneeled down and prayed: "O God, take this boy of mine and make him the boy and man he is divinely designed to be." Then she kissed him and went out, leaving him "in the silence with God." As Rufus afterwards exclaimed in recalling the incident, "That was an epoch!"

Anyone who thinks of such a community as South China, Maine, seventy-five years ago, as isolated, does not understand the Quakers. The leading man in the town was Rufus' uncle, Eli Jones. He was a traveling Friend; he had visited England, Ireland, Norway, Denmark, France, Germany, Liberia, Syria and Palestine. He was a vivid speaker—"He knew how to preach for a boy," wrote Rufus. "I sat on the edge of my seat and drank it all in." Indeed, John Bright, the English reformer and orator, once heard Eli Jones preach in London, and wrote in his diary that it was the greatest sermon he had ever heard in his life. "Uncle Eli" became, as Rufus said, "my hero and one of my major inspirations." So at sixteen years of age, Rufus faced his family with a crisis. He was determined to have an education. How it could be financially arranged was difficult to see, but faith, hope and love did it, and the boy entered the Friends' Boarding School—now Moses Brown School—in Providence, Rhode Island, to prepare for college. The awakening of his mind, the broadening of his intellectual horizons, which he has vividly described, must here be left to the imagination. He found himself, and went on to Haverford College, a small institution then with only eighty students, but "it was for me," wrote Rufus, "probably the best educational center that could have been found in America." There, through the mediation of Professor Pliney Earle Chase he discovered his vocation. Reading Emerson's essay on "The Over-Soul," at Professor Chase's suggestion, was an "epoch moment" in his life. Back of Emerson's mysticism he sought out "Plotinus and Proclus, Jacob Boehme, and George Fox—freshly interpreted—and the mystical contributions of the Orient. It threw open the windows of my soul." From then on he never doubted his major mission—"to be an interpreter of this religion of the inward way."

This mission in the end carried Rufus Jones into more varied fields of activity than anyone could then have dreamed, and we can only briefly survey them here.

He became *the leading historian of mysticism*. A year after graduation from Haverford he went to Europe, mastered French and German, visited leading continental experts in his chosen field, and began laying the foundation in philosophy and psychology on which to build his future work. Later at Heidelberg, Oxford and Harvard he improved the tools of his scholarship, and in coöperation with the Rowntree family, well-known English Friends, brought into ever clearer focus his purpose to interpret the history of the mystical experience. Then in 1905 the door of opportunity opened. Joseph Rowntree made financially possible the ambitious undertaking of which Rufus Jones had long been dreaming, and during the next sixteen years he and William Charles Braithwaite brought out seven volumes—two on the history of mysticism and five on the history of Quakerism—of which he wrote five.

These major works of historical scholarship represent only a small part of Rufus Jones' labors in the interpretation of what William James called "a religion of veracity rooted in spiritual inwardness." All his books are suffused with the "practice of the presence of God," and while this anthology breaks up Rufus Jones' message into thirteen different areas, each one of them is saturated with the conviction that "the soul is most like God of anything in the universe, and just as the wrist or the temple reveals the throbbing pulse beat of the human heart, so the soul of man is where the moral and spiritual will of God palpitates and breaks through."

Rufus Jones also became *a great teacher of philosophy*. He taught philosophy at Haverford College for forty-one years, from 1893 to 1934, and was professor emeritus until his death in 1948. Whatever else he did—and his doings pretty much covered the earth before he was through—his teaching was central. "I have always felt," he said, "that I was at my best in a class-room, and there is no question that I am happiest when I am teaching a class of youth." He was a scholar; he was out to find the truth, no matter where the road to it led; the London *Times* spoke of him as "the greatest spiritual philosopher living in America since William James." But, as a teacher, he remained, as he always did, distinctively Rufus Jones, human, practical, loveable, humorous, picturesque. One can easily imagine an erudite lecturer on ethics discoursing on the conventionalized behavior of those who passively accept the prevalent moral patterns of their environment, but what Rufus Jones said in his class on ethics was this: "There are plenty of individuals who find themselves moving along certain courses of life as a log from the Maine forest finds itself moving into the onward sweep of the current of the Kennebec River. Neither the individual nor the log has asserted any autonomy, and neither one is captain of the voyage of venture."

It requires but little imagination to understand why thousands of his former students look back to his classroom with endless gratitude. "I endeavored," he said, "to make the lecture periods occasions for facing seriously and above all else, honestly, the difficulties confronting the modern world and to blaze a trail which would make life rich, meaningful and thrilling."

Rufus Jones became *a reformer in the Society of Friends*. When he began his work the Quakers needed a reformer. The preceding two or three generations had seen a typical but nonetheless pathetic deterioration of the Society—a process of cooling, hardening, stiffening, as lava once molten turns to rigid forms. A movement which had revolted against the stereotypes of secondhand religion adopted stereotypes, became too centrally concerned about minor legalisms of garb and speech and habit. The Quakers had started out to be a "peculiar" people, open to the fresh inspiration and leadership of the spirit, but their peculiarities became externalized, institutionalized, legalized. In his later years Rufus Jones looked back with half-incredulous amazement on the situation he had known in earlier years: "We can hardly imagine that state of mind that would lead a Monthly Meeting to disown a high-minded Friend because he owned a piano. It is difficult for us to believe the fact that 100,000 Friends were dropped from membership for marrying out of Meeting."

Moreover, the Society was rent by controversy. Small in number though the Friends were they could not stay together. Both in matters of theology and of legalistic requirement they differed widely, and disrupting schisms threatened the spirit and mission and very existence of the Friends.

Rufus Jones' ministry of reconciliation is one of the most notable achievements of his life. From 1893 to 1912 he was editor of the *Friends Review* and its successor, the *American Friend*. He traveled far and wide to speak at Quaker meetings in the United States and England—all kinds of Quaker meetings, representing all the varied points of view—calling the Friends back to the vitalities of their faith, making great matters seem great and small matters small, and with his invincible geniality, charm and goodwill drawing together what was falling apart. To be sure, he met opposition. He was honest, direct, candid, at times hard-hitting. He was always charming but he was never soft. His life story was not smooth and easy. While all Quakers now honor him, saying as the Friends Service Council in London did when he died, "No American Friend since John Woolman has had so widespread an influence in the world," at the beginning many of them made his going hard. It is not untypical that at one meeting a member prayed immediately before Rufus Jones spoke: "Thou knowest, O Lord, that now we are about to hear a great many things that are not so." At one Quaker college in the Middle West the president, after Rufus' first lecture, advised his students that they were hearing unsound doctrine and should let it pass through one ear and out the other. At that, Rufus put his foot down, and before the next lecture the president publicly apologized.

Before his end came, however, all this was past history. He could say then, "I was plainly justified by results for the part I took in that long and painful struggle for Quaker unity in America." In celebration of Rufus' eightieth birthday a dinner was given him in Philadelphia and he could then look back with humor on the old controversy: "The first time I attended the Biennial Conference a leading Hicksite minister whispered to me and said, 'I have read every one of thy editorials and there has not been one that I have not agreed with.' 'Is that so?' I said. 'Thee is the only person in the world who can say that.' During those almost twenty years I was a constant target for sharp-shooting archers. The *Evangelical Friend* printed a number of articles in red ink, to make them more fiery and emphatic. Every week I had my list of verbal catapults, all of which I duly answered. My dear friend, David Scull, said to me one day in this period of constant battle, 'I hope thee will be favored to keep humble.' 'Well,' I said, 'everything is being done that can be done to keep me in that humble frame of mind.' "

Rufus Jones became *an outstanding leader in the extension of Quaker Service around the world*. He was a doer of the word, not a hearer only. A philosopher and a mystic, he achieved practical results in organized humanitarian service such as most philosophers and mystics would not dream of undertaking. The American Friends' Service Committee, whose worldwide usefulness is now a matter of popular renown, was in large measure the result of his vision, inspiration and leadership. Clarence E. Pickett, for twenty years the Committee's Executive Secretary, says of him: "Rufus Jones is more responsible than any other person for the founding of the American Friends' Service Committee. Whatever life and spirit it may have brought into the world is a tribute to his labor, his humor, his wisdom, and his rare spirit."

It all began during the First World War. As soon as the war started in 1914, British Friends organized the Friends' Ambulance Unit and reorganized the Friends' War Victims Relief Committee which had been founded after the Franco-Prussian war. American Friends were deeply interested in the work of these two committees. Funds were collected and sent to England and in 1915 Rufus Jones selected four young American Friends to join the work of the Friends' Ambulance Unit.

When America entered the war in April 1917, the American Friends' Service Committee was organized, with Rufus Jones as chairman, to provide some form of constructive service for young Friends and others who could not conscientiously serve in the army. The Friends were anxious about their position; their pacifism must mean not negative passiveness but positive peace-making. Said the Yearly Meeting in 1917: "We are united in expressing our love for our country and our desire to serve her loyally. We offer our services to the government of the United States in any constructive work in which we can conscientiously engage."

Grayson Murphy, one of Rufus Jones' former students at Haverford

College, was appointed Chief of the American Red Cross in France. Commissioners of the Red Cross studied the work of the English Friends' War Victims Relief Committee and, as a result, a tri-partite arrangement was made. The Service Committee sent men and a few women to the already established British work in France. Says Rufus Jones: "This (American Unit) was to become a bureau of the Civilian Department of the Red Cross and at the same time was granted permission to merge with the English Friends to form the Anglo-American Mission of The Society of Friends." So began a worldwide campaign of philanthropic service which in the end won the Nobel Peace Prize for the Quakers.

Rufus Jones was at first Chairman, and then Honorary Chairman of the American Friends' Service Committee, from 1917 to his death in 1948. He saw the work expand until its usefulness circled the globe. The story of this extraordinary adventure in the practice of the Sermon on the Mount cannot be told here. Rufus Jones, in his book, *A Service of Love in Wartime,* has pictured what was done during the First World War, but when that ended, doors of opportunity stood so wide open, calls of need were so insistent, the Quaker conscience was so aroused, and the testimony of unselfish care for enemy and friend alike had proved itself so cogent, that the work expanded by leaps and bounds. It is typical of the Committee's strategy that when, in the early 1920's, Herbert Hoover faced the problem of starving German children, the Quakers spent over $12,000,000 in answer to his call, and at one time furnished at least one meal a day to 1,200,000 German children.

The Committee's spirit was dramatized in 1938 when, amid the Jewish calamities in Germany, Rufus Jones led a delegation which went to Berlin and faced the Gestapo at Hitler's headquarters. "We represent no sects," they said, "and we have no interest in propaganda in any form. . . . We do not ask who is to blame for the trouble which may exist. . . . We do not come to judge or criticize but to enquire whether there is anything we can do to promote human welfare and to relieve suffering." Those who suppose that the Quakers were or are discouraged because such attempts to implement the Christian ethic did not solve the international problem or prevent the Second World War, do not understand the Quakers. The *war* did not solve the world's problem either, but left more and worse problems than were here before. The Quakers have a long view; they are sure that in the end neither the spirit that causes war, nor the processes which war involves, nor the results which follow it, can ever solve mankind's problems—only the spirit which the New Testament teaches and which Christ incarnates. To that conviction Rufus Jones' life was dedicated, not in theory alone but in such effective, organized, practical, worldwide, humane service that he became, as another put it, "the nearest thing the Friends have to an international spokesman."

Rufus Jones became *an interpreter of vital religion to multitudes in many countries and in all the churches*. He had a global mind. He was one of the delegation which toured the Orient and brought back an influential report on "Rethinking Missions." His concern knew no boundaries of nation, race, denomination or religion. He founded the Wider Quaker Fellowship, not to glorify Quakerism, but to include in one companionship the tens of thousands of men and women who share what the Quakers stand for—a vital, first-hand experience of God, an "open" religion of immediate access to the Spirit's fresh revelations, not a "closed" religion of petrified ecclesiasticisms and static theologies. And he wrote and spoke constantly with one mastering motive: to make religious experience an inward personal possession, an "inner light," a vital resource of power and peace and a sound mind.

In no anthology is it possible to reproduce the effect of Rufus Jones' personal approach to a listening audience. He was one of the most welcome preachers in the college chapels of America, but the qualities commonly associated with popular speakers do not first occur to one who would explain his wide acceptance. He was not "eloquent," certainly not "oratorical." His grip on an audience was far more intimate. He was natural, genuine, direct, human. He spoke from experience to experience. He possessed the spiritual vitality he pled for, and he shared it. What he himself said, thinking of Phillips Brooks, was true of him—"You listen to a hundred persons unmoved and unchanged. You hear a few quiet words from the man with the kindling torch and you suddenly discover what life means, forever more."

To be sure, he used humor. No one who ever knew Rufus Jones will forget his stories. Religious temperaments differ and some great souls have been of the solemn sort, but Rufus Jones belonged to the tradition of St. Francis of Assisi. He was radiant, enthusiastic; his very presence brought elevation of spirit; gaiety was native to him, and humor was part of his persuasive equipment as a speaker. If he addressed an audience of school children, one might expect him to begin with his story of the embarrassed commencement orator who started off by saying: "When I look down into the faces of these dear boys and these dear girls, it makes me think of the time long ago when I was a little boy and a little girl." After that, one may be sure that he had his audience. If he was pleading for intrepid character, one might expect him to say: "One of our countrymen was building a stone wall, as everybody did when I was a boy. A neighbor came by and asked the old farmer why he was building such an odd-shaped wall, wider than it was high. Without looking up from his work, the farmer said: 'So if it blows over, it'll be higher than it wuz before.' " After that, intrepidity ceased being an abstraction and became visually imaginable. If he was asking his audience to stop blaming circumstance and to tackle their own characters, one might look for some such story as this: "Many years ago a man from another state was driving through Maine with an old-fashioned four-wheeled carriage. He stopped a local farmer and asked him if there wasn't any end to the hill on the road—'I have been driving up this old hill for two hours.' 'Hill, stranger,' said the farmer, 'there ain't no hill here. You've just lost off your own hind wheels.' "

Such use of humor was part of Rufus Jones' power of visualization, putting into story, parable, simile, metaphor, any truth he was speaking of. When, however, one has analyzed as best one can such factors in his persuasiveness, one comes back to the spirit of the man himself. He possessed vital religion; he knew at first-hand what inner fellowship with the "Beyond" could mean; and in his addresses and writings he was sharing an experience that was the realest fact in his life. He was, indeed, for multitudes "one among a thousand, an interpreter."

Of necessity this sketch of Rufus Jones' career is brief, partial, incomplete. Those who would know him more fully should read his own autobiographical books—"A Small Town Boy," "Finding the Trail of Life," "The Trail of Life in College," "The Trail of Life in the Middle Years," and a biography of him, "Rufus Jones, Master Quaker," by David Hinshaw. His life— "by reason of strength, four-score years"—becomes the more impressive, the more one knows about it. His home background, his early joys and hardships, his precarious venture to secure an education, the death of his first wife and his only son, his discovery that he "must be, else sinning greatly, a dedicated spirit," his battle with ill-health, his personal griefs and social controversies, the beauty of his family life and the multitude of his friendships, and at last his achievements, concerning which a colleague writes, "At first sometimes his proposals seemed incredible and impossible, but I have never known anyone who lived to see as large a proportion of his dreams fulfilled"—all this makes a fascinating story.

This anthology, however, has been compiled not primarily because of any nostalgic retrospect, but because Rufus Jones has a message for these present times and for the future. An astonishingly small portion of what he wrote is dated. Most of it is timeless. He deals so constantly with ultimates and universals that what he said yesterday is relevant today. Moreover, while Rufus Jones did live yesterday, his thought was always dealing with tomorrow. He was an historian but he studied what *had been* for the sake of what *might be*. In him the future tense was dominant, he was a forward-looker; to the end of his days he was saying, "Forward, march!" As he closed his address at his eightieth birthday dinner he said: "I do not for a minute forget that I am on Pisgah and looking over a sweep of vision which another than myself must bring to realization. It will be young Joshuas, not eighty-year-old veterans, that will lead on to new goals. But *there*, in front of us, is the land to be won."

In one of Rufus Jones' books, "The Church's Debt to Heretics," he describes the kind of heretic for whom he thinks the church should be endlessly grateful:

Men and women who believed in their inmost souls that they had a heavenly vision, a divine revelation of the way forward, and that it was given to them to be the bearers of the truth. They were ready for the uttermost sacrifice in behalf of the cause to which they were devoted. The capricious innovator, the freakish disturber, the hysterical champion of novelties, the unhappy rebel against whatever is, need not occupy us. We are interested here rather in discoveries of fresh thought, the recipients of new illumination, gifted leaders of unwon causes, prophets of neglected or forgotten truth, profound interpreters of the deeper significance of life.

That represents admirably the ideal of Rufus Jones.

The editor of any anthology of the writings of such a man must ask for sympathy. It was not difficult to select the thirteen categories which constitute the structure of this book. Within these major areas, I am confident, will be found the main emphases of Rufus Jones' message. But to choose which passages should be used and which elided—*that* was a task, and no man's decisions can altogether coincide with the preferences of another. If some reader's favorite books are not quoted as fully as the reader desires, I hope he will remember that it is because I thought that elsewhere Rufus Jones had proclaimed the same truth more forcibly. Some of our author's writings are not suited to the purpose of an anthology. One cannot easily make brief, intelligible excerpts, for example, from his elaborate treatises on the ancient mystics; the sweep of biography and historical background is too vast to be handled by extracts. In another area an even more frustrating problem presented itself. Rufus Jones' venturesome endeavor to express in worldwide social service the impetus which his Christian faith had brought to him was *done*, rather than *written*. Throughout his books one feels the undercurrent of his social interest; the economic and political tensions and perils of the world were always in the background of his thought; but his thought about them habitually issued in deeds rather than words. His writings, therefore, do not fully represent all that he stood for in the domain of social problems; they center in the spiritual inspirations which moved him rather than in the social solutions they moved him to. Here, again, the *whole* man is not in his books. One must supplement what he wrote by the remembrance of what he did, if one would grasp the dynamic and practical effectiveness of his ideas.

As for the rest, I have done the best I could, rejoicing in the passages which clearly raised their hands, asking to be used, but sad at the exclusion of many others of equal worth. I hope that one effect of this anthology will be to send the reader directly to Rufus Jones' books. That would be its crowning service. His message is amazingly timeless, but that means that it is amazingly timely. If in this confused, chaotic world we could find his trail of life and follow it, we could reproduce the experience which an early Quaker gratefully described: "I felt the evil in me weakened and the good raised up."

HARRY EMERSON FOSDICK

CONTENTS

⇛ I ⇚

Where Is God?

I

A VISITOR on the Maine coast had a noble impulse to start a Sunday School on one of the islands lying within sight of his summer habitat. This particular island was a tiny one, so small in fact, that the surrounding ocean could be seen from every part of it. A few families had planted themselves on its inhospitable rocks somewhat as the local swallows plant their adobe nests on the eaves of the farmer's barns. Here among the scrubby trees and blueberry bushes, amid boats and nets and fish and lobster pots, in the undying noise of the shingle on the shore and the unceasing break and tumble of the surf, the little children of the island played and toiled. There was no place to which they could go where they could escape the sea. It resounded in their ears when they awoke in the morning and it was the last sound they heard as they dropped off to sleep at night. From every rock and knoll and hillock of their small domain they could see it, and taste and smell its salty tang. It was the almost exclusive source of their daily food. Their first adventure and their only excursions from home were out on the swells of its heaving bosom.

The kindly visitor collected all the children and gathered them around him in friendly fashion for their first lesson. Before he tried to tell them of invisible realities he thought he would begin with visible and familiar things. "How many of you," he asked, "have ever seen the Atlantic Ocean? Please raise your hands the way I do, for I have seen it." To his surprise not a hand went up. They looked stolidly at him, not knowing in the least what he was talking about. The Atlantic Ocean was as foreign to their minds as the South Pole would have been if he had asked how many of them had seen that. They had been born by the shore of the Atlantic Ocean, they had lived by it and enjoyed its beauty, they had boated on it and had bathed in it, but nobody had ever named it to them before, or interpreted it to their minds. It was their constant environment, and yet they had never once discovered that there was such a thing as the Atlantic Ocean, rolling unexplored in front of their eyes.

This simple event may not inaptly, I think, be treated as a parable of life. There are persons all about us who never dream that their little island of spirit, over which they exercise control and dominion, is ringed about and

3

surrounded by an inner world of Spirit, from which they draw their central being and to which they owe all the functions of their reason, all their enjoyment of beauty, all their capacity of love, all their certitude of truth, all their power to expand life in ideal directions, and all their transcendent hopes and faiths. To be isolated and insulated from that More of Life to which we belong would carry with that isolation and insulation such a contraction and shrinkage that one would become only the minimal fraction of self, like Balzac's famous character who diminished in size whenever he made a self-centered choice, until at length he became as invisible as an atom is! And yet it is possible to live sundered from that environing Life of the Spirit and to be wholly unaware and unconscious of the near presence.

Like a sick child that knoweth not his mother while she blesses
And presses on his burning brow the coolness of her kisses,
But casts his fevered eyes around, "My mother, where's my mother?"
As if such tender deeds and words could come from any other.
At length, with sudden start, the fever gone, he sees her bending o'er him;
Her face all pale with watchful love, the unwearied love she bore him.

Somewhat so it is with all of us most of the time in reference to the enveloping Life of God. We live outward and are busy with "things." The whirl and eddy of external events, the turmoil and bustle of secular affairs, keep our attention strained. We are always hurrying to go somewhere else from there. How can we bring our minds into parallelism with the currents of the Spirit? How can we feel "the bubblings of the Stream that feeds the world"? How can we know the "tides of that mystic ocean whose rim no foot has trod"? . . .

I saw a flying fish once, in an excessive and over-enthusiastic flight, leap clear out of his normal element and land high up on the deck of our ship. It was the surprise of his young life, and he was instantly disillusioned. His wings and his fins became useless. He frantically flopped about and panted for the life he missed. I picked him up and dropped him over the side of the ship into his native element. He knew what to do the moment he struck it—he corresponded with it and refreshed his life with its resources. While he was in it he had no need to seek it—"Does the fish soar to find the ocean?"—but having lost it he came back into it with a new thrill of being.

It often happens with us "amphibious" beings—made for two worlds—that some shock that occurs in our lower world of things wakes us up with a start and gives us a sudden sense of the Upper World to which we belong or at least might belong, and which was there all the time while we lived in unconsciousness of it. "Dear, soothing, healthy, restoration-hours," Walt

Whitman wrote, "after the confining years of paralysis, after the long strain of war and its wounds and death." How much we all need these soothing "restoration-hours"—these moments when the soul is healed and restored. Few things—no things that I know of—are so completely and effectively restorative as the discovery that this World of the environing Spirit is verily closer to us than breathing and is charged with the resources of Life for which we pant.

From *Spiritual Energies in Daily Life,*
pp. 180–185.

→⟫⟪←

MOST persons would "listen on their knees" to anyone who would make God absolutely real to them, so that they could say as John did, "We have beheld His glory." The world is weary of traditional religion, of formalism and hollow words, but most hearts are hungry for that true thing by which life is actually renewed.

To speak of the quest for God as the serious business of our age is in no way to question the reality of the revelation with which this Christian era began. Every serious man to-day realizes how profoundly all our thought of God is grounded in the Person of Christ and in the truth which His first interpreters declared as facts of their own experience. But nobody else's experience can ever be a substitute for my own. The truth for me must be the truth I know, not the truth which I hear reported as once known by men of an earlier day. "Each generation," as George Macdonald has said, "must do its own seeking and finding. The fathers having found is only the warrant for the children's search."

To admit that God *was* known in experience, but can now be known only by report, is to cast the deep taint of doubt upon all that is reported of Him. It means either that He has changed so that He cannot show Himself now, or that from the nature of the case man has become incapable of having a revelation of Him, however much God wills to show Himself. On the contrary, the revelation in the first century is the supreme warrant for our faith that God is essentially self-revealing and that man can find Him and know Him and become His organ of manifestation. The nearer we get to the original record and its real meaning, the less is it possible for us to stop *satisfied* with a record. The more profoundly we are impressed with its truth, the more compulsion we feel to possess the experience which flowered into these immortal documents. The belief, then, in the reality of a primitive revelation, far from checking our own quest for God, is just the flame which kindles us with assurance in our own personal quest—a quest which gives life its highest significance. . . .

How shall we start to find Him, or to prove that He can be found? Where are we to look for Him? Many have fancied that He could be found at the end of a syllogism; logic could prove His existence and compel all persons who submit to the laws of this exact science to admit it. The argument is very simple. In its simplest form it proceeds from cause to effect. Here is some object. It must have been caused or made. Therefore there must be a First Cause or Maker. This argument is open to all sorts of objections. To pass by some of the profoundest ones, it will be enough to point out here that the most we can legitimately infer from the argument of causation is that back of every event there is an infinite chain of causes. It does not lead us, and never can lead us, to an Absolute Being. If we say that the law of causality leads us to God, we must at once ask what caused Him and what was the cause of that cause. A God who was discovered by the causality argument would, too, of necessity be a finite god, however powerful he might be, and we should have no good ground for saying *he* rather than *it*! Since Kant's time, it has been recognized that there is no logic which can carry us from a finite fact or event to an Absolute Being.

Logic next tries the argument from *design*. Things in our world are adapted to ends. They seem made for uses and functions. Now design and adaptation presuppose a designer. As the watch implies a watchmaker, so the eye, with its fine adjustment to ether vibrations, implies a creative artist. With purpose everywhere in creation we must acknowledge a Being who planned it. Used in the right way there is no doubt that the argument from ends, or teleology, carries conviction and proves all materialistic views inadequate; but the argument from design to a personal God does not convince anyone who is not already convinced.

In the first place, what *we* call design is the result of an infinite number of selections. Through a series of uncounted years by survivals of the fittest those beings that adjusted to the environment lived and those that did not are not here to show their lack of design. Everything that survived of necessity had design and adaptation. Then again, design after all is through and through *subjective*. It depends on our personal interests whether we find design or not. If one wishes to make music, a harp is admirably designed for his purpose. If, however, he wishes to cut a walking-stick, the harp which is in his hand lacks design for the end in view. The most that can be proved from design is the fact that man is a being who finds designs and ends and purpose everywhere in *his* world.

Even if he leaps from design to a designer the most he could infer would be that there is, or was, a great Artist who has forced his thought into the stubborn matter of the world, but the Artist Himself will be forever outside and His character will remain unknown.

Finally, logic gives us what is known as the ontological argument, which is hoary with age and sacred because it has supported the faith of many saintly souls. In its simplest form it runs as follows: I find in my thoughts the idea of a perfect Being; now perfection involves existence, for a being who did not exist would not be as perfect as a being who did exist; therefore this perfect Being, the idea of whom is in my thoughts, must have real existence. As in both the former arguments, there is also a profound truth involved in the heart of this argument, but as it stands it is not a valid argument. The most we can say is that if we think of a perfect Being, we must *think of Him as existing*. Whether He really does exist or not must be settled in some other way. The logical chain has always proved too weak to carry us from a finite—whether it be an event, or a design or an idea—to an infinite and absolute Reality. If we have no method of "proving" except the method of logic, then it is true that "nothing worthy proving can be proven, nor yet disproven." ...

If our search for God is to have a happy issue we must *first* resist the tendency to narrow "knowledge." We must rather insist on raising it to its highest terms. We must include under the *knowledge-process* our entire capacity for dealing with reality. Secondly, we must look for God where He *could* be found—not in the wide stellar spaces, not "in eagle's wing or insect's eye," not at the end of a logical syllogism. If He is to be found at all we must look for Him in the spiritual realm. We must go at once where spirit manifests itself. All attempts to find God apart from and dissevered from personal life have failed, and of course always will fail. He is surely not less personal than we are. He will at least be as genuinely spiritual as we mortals are!

There is one approach to an infinite realm where God *might be*. There is one door that opens into a holy of holies. The true path is through personality. The search must *begin* in our own bosom: Who am I? What do I live by? What does personality involve? How am I related to my fellows and to nature? What does my sense of worth imply? What do I mean by goodness? Can I draw any finite circle about "myself"? Do I have any dealings with "a Beyond"? These are questions which take us into regions where microscope and telescope do not avail, but the full answer to them would bring us to *that which is.*

From *Social Law in the Spiritual World*,
pp. 30–37; 43–44.

THE direction of the quest for God has in our times turned emphatically from outside in space to the realm of the spirit within man. This change of direction is not a sudden and complete revolution in thought, for there have always been some persons who have had the conviction that God is to be found within rather than without, that He is here rather than in some remote realm. In all periods of man's intensive travail for truth there have been some seekers who have had at least a dim surmise that we have our dealings with a pervasive and deeply interfused Spirit rather than with an absentee Being. All the major religions of the world have borne some testimony, however feeble, to the fact and the presence of an indwelling and resident Life, with whom we are kin and who comes into communion with man's spirit. The Stoic movement often gave a crude and confused account of the indwelling *Pneuma*, or *Logos*, the Soul of the world, but the movement succeeded in carrying to all Western lands a confession of faith in an omnipresent Spirit, a faith which is nobly expressed in the 139th Psalm, "If I take the wings of the morning and dwell in the uttermost parts of the sea; even there shall thy hand lead me, and thy right hand shall hold me."

But the doctrine of the Spirit was raised by St. Paul to an entirely new level and to a new intensity, and it was, again, taken up by St. John and carried by him to its loftiest ancient expression. There is, no doubt, a Stoic influence apparent in both of these apostolic interpreters, but it was almost certainly an unconscious influence and that strand of Stoic thought is so completely outweighed by a mighty personal experience of spiritual energies that the interpretation becomes at once unique and original.

The famous words from St. Paul's sermon on the Areopagus: "In God we live and move and are," have a distinct Stoic quality and they are followed almost immediately by a quotation from a Stoic poet, but the moment we turn to the great passages in the Epistles that speak of the Work of the Spirit, the Life of the Spirit, the Power of the Spirit, we quickly discover that we have left Stoic levels of thought far behind. Who else would have dared say: "In Him we are builded together into a holy temple for a habitation of God through the Spirit" (Eph. ii:21). St. John's outlook is at many points quite different from St. Paul's and the former writer expresses his faith in a unique form, though they have much in common. It is not an exaggeration to say that the Johannine conception of the Spirit of Truth is one of the most wonderful interpretations that anyone has proclaimed anywhere at any time, for it rises to the clear and positive insight that God Himself is essentially Spirit, and that all true worship must be *real and spiritual*—"in Spirit and in Truth."

But in spite of this exalted teaching at the headwaters of the Christian stream, the prevailing tendency in the history of Western Christianity has been in the direction of a distinctly transcendent conception of God. Wherever the influence of Aristotle was effective on Christian thought it was quite natural for God to be conceived of as remote and absentee, and the Jewish thought of God as Creator working from the outside also pointed in the same direction. A combination of powerful movements of thought during the first three centuries sharply emphasized the dualistic aspects of the universe. It became the fashion to think of an undivine world here below and a far-away God beyond the seven circles who could effect His purposes for this lower realm only by miraculous interposition and interruption of the natural order of things. The great controlling systems of Christian thought were formed and built around that basic idea.

And yet there were all the way down the line of historical Christianity frequent outbursts of pentecostal faith and fervor. Something like the experience that occurred in the upper room fifty days after the Crucifixion has swept more than once over the lives of smaller or larger groups of believers, and whenever the experience occurred it gave the groups assurance that God was here as Spirit and not a remote Sovereign in the sky. St. Paul's personal testimony, and St. John's spiritual interpretation, have been quick and powerful influences in all centuries, however dark and medieval, and Pentecosts have been repeated with fresh outbursts of enthusiasm and kindled fire. A mystical writer in the twelfth century announced the beginning of the *eternal Gospel,* by which he meant the good news that God is Spirit and works as Spirit directly on men's lives, and not alone through ecclesiastical channels.

The modern emphasis on the immanence of God is therefore not something new and revolutionary. What has happened is that this view is no longer a rare exception, or an occasional sporadic outbreak of fervid experience. There has come through a fusion of many lines of thought a well-ordered interpretation of the universe that is essentially *immanentist.* That does not mean that God is swallowed up and lost in the vast congeries of things. It does not imply that He is a mighty Pan, or the Allness of the All. It does not blur His reality or thin it away to a mere energy or driving power or blind urge, for Mind, or Spirit, by its essential nature is transcendent as well as immanent. Whenever spirit appears, even in the finite form of our own personal minds, it always outreaches and goes beyond its given expression and embodiment. We always transcend ourselves. We always live beyond our margins. We leap beyond anything that *is*—the here and now—and we are by the necessity of our being concerned with a more yet that ought to be. A God who is immanent, if He is to be thought of as Spirit, is just as certainly transcendent.

A God who is the foundational Life of our lives must be the eternal guarantor of all that can be or that ought to be as well as of all that is. He must be both within us and beyond us, within the world and beyond it, in the midst of time and yet beyond it. . . .

We need to learn how to think of God as a resident presence coöperating vitally with us and in us here and now as an Emmanuel God, and at the same time we need just as urgently to see how our human lives can and do open out into a Beyond within ourselves. Almost every person who has attained to a mature spiritual life has had experiences which convinced him, at least in high moments, that he was *more than himself*. Help comes from somewhere and enables us to do what we had always thought could not be done. We find somewhere power to stand the universe when its waterspouts are let loose and even when they have gone over us. We discover strength from beyond our own stock of resources in the midst of our crises.

We do not know how far our own margins of being reach. We cannot completely map the full area that properly belongs to us. No one can with certainty draw the boundary between himself and the beyond himself, any more than we can tell where the tidal river ends and the ocean begins, but we unmistakably feel on occasions that tides from beyond our own margins sweep into us and refresh us. . . .

The monumental evidence of God is, I believe, the fact of spiritual personality through which divine traits of character are revealed. Stars and mountains and ordered processes of nature reveal law and mathematics and beauty, but they reveal and can reveal no traits of character, no qualities of personality, no warmth and intimacy of heart and mind. If we are ever to be convinced that self-giving love is a reality of God's nature, we shall be convinced by seeing this love break through some human organ of His Spirit. The supreme revelation of the ages was not in the thunder and fire of Sinai, but in the life of a Person who was born of a woman, who increased in wisdom and stature, who was tempted as we are, who struggled and suffered, who battled for truth, who gave His life out of love for the rest of us, and who felt through it all that He was the organ of the Life and Love of God. Here on the highest level that has been reached since the race began, God as Spirit has broken through into visibility and has shown His true nature in life and action. But it is an unending revelation. Christianity, in the best sense of the word, is eternity revealed in time,

> The silence of eternity
> Interpreted by love.

As the sap flows through the branches of the vine and vitalizes the whole organism so that it bursts into the beauty and glory of foliage and blossom and finally into fruit, so through the lives of men and women, inwardly responsive and joyously receptive, the life of God as Spirit flows, carrying vitality, awakening love, creating passion for goodness, kindling the fervor of consecration and producing that living body, that organism of the Spirit, that "blessed community," which continues through the centuries the revelation of God as love and tenderness and eternal goodness.

From *Pathways to the Reality of God*,
pp. 193–197; 199; 217–218.

→»)«←

As worship, taken in its highest sense and widest scope, is man's loftiest undertaking, we cannot too often return to the perennial questions: What is worship? Why do we worship? How do we best perform this supreme human function? Worship is too great an experience to be defined in any sharp or rigid or exclusive fashion. The history of religion through the ages reveals the fact that there have been multitudinous ways of worshiping God, all of them yielding real returns of life and joy and power to large groups of men. At its best and truest, however, worship seems to me to be *direct, vital, joyous, personal experience and practice of the presence of God.*

The very fact that such a mighty experience as this is possible means that there is some inner meeting place between the soul and God; in other words, that the divine and human, God and man, are not wholly sundered. In an earlier time God was conceived as remote and transcendent. He dwelt in the citadel of the sky, was worshiped with ascending incense and communicated His will to beings beneath through celestial messengers or by mysterious oracles. We have now more ground than ever before for conceiving God as transcendent; that is, as above and beyond any revelation of Himself, and as more than any finite experience can apprehend. But at the same time, our experience and our ever-growing knowledge of the outer and inner universe confirm our faith that God is also immanent, a real presence, a spiritual reality, immediately to be felt and known, a vital, life-giving environment of the soul. He is a Being who can pour His life and energy into human souls, even as the sun can flood the world with light and resident forces, or as the sea can send its refreshing tides into all the bays and inlets of the coast, or as the atmosphere can pour its life-giving supplies into the fountains of the blood in the meeting place of the lungs; or, better still, as the mother fuses her spirit into the spirit of her responsive child, and lays her mind on him until he believes in her belief.

It will be impossible for some of us ever to lose our faith in, our certainty of, this vital presence which overarches our inner lives as surely as the sky does our outer lives. The more we know of the great unveiling of God in Christ, the more we see that He is a Being who can be thus revealed in a personal life that is parallel in will with Him and perfectly responsive in heart and mind to the spiritual presence. We can use as our own the inscription on the wall of the ancient temple in Egypt. On one of the walls a priest of the old religion had written for his divinity: "I am He who was and is and ever shall be, and my veil hath no man lifted." On the opposite wall, some one who had found his way into the later, richer faith, wrote this inscription: "Veil after veil have we lifted and ever the Face is more wonderful!"

It must be held, I think, as Emerson so well puts it, that there is "no bar or wall in the soul" separating God and man. We lie open on one side of our nature to God, who is the Oversoul of our souls, the Overmind of our minds, the Overperson of our personal selves. There are deeps in our consciousness which no private plumb line of our own can sound; there are heights in our moral conscience which no ladder of our human intelligence can scale; there are spiritual hungers, longings, yearnings, passions, which find no explanation in terms of our physical inheritance or of our outside world. We touch upon the coasts of a deeper universe, not yet explored or mapped, but no less real and certain than this one in which our mortal senses are at home. We cannot explain our normal selves or account for the best things we know—or even for our condemnation of our poorer, lower self—without an appeal to and acknowledgment of a divine Guest and Companion who is the real presence of our central being. How shall we best come into conscious fellowship with God and turn this environing presence into a positive source of inner power, and of energy for the practical tasks and duties of daily life?

From *The Inner Life*,
pp. 97–101.

-»><«-

THE essential characteristic of the mystical experience is the attainment of personal conviction by an individual that the human spirit and the divine Spirit have met, have found each other, and are in mutual and reciprocal correspondence as spirit with Spirit. In short, mystical devotion means direct first-hand fellowship with God, and the deepened life-results which emerge.

We all begin life by simply living, not by following a program or a theory or a system. The roots of life are too deep for diagnosis. They escape our analysis. We follow the push of a life-impulse. There is a vital urge which carries us forward. The little lips of the baby feel the mother's breast and the right action follows. Correspondence with environment is life's main miracle. There is a fit of inner and outer, like that of hand and glove. But from the first the approach is deep, hidden, uncogitated, mystical. The outer world presents its stimulus, sometimes as gentle as the vibrations of light, or the touch of a soft finger, and the response comes from within with infallible skill and with an untaught wisdom which may as well as not be called a "mystical" correspondence. So, too, with the birth of religion. There is here once more a within and a without, a tiny finite being and a Beyond, a spiritual center and a vaster environment, and they feel and find one another as the retina does light, or as the electrode finds its polar mate. It begins, as life does, not with a scheme or a theory, but with living and being and responding. In short, both life and religion are rooted in mystical experience, mystical process.

There are, of course, all degrees of intensity and of attainment, as is true of any supreme human undertaking. As this purpose to find God for one's life aim is man's highest undertaking, it would naturally be expected to run through a wide gamut. It may begin, as in St. Augustine's case, with the discovery that our hearts are restless and that only one Reality in the universe will still that restlessness. It may appear as an exalted aspiration for personal contact with God as in the cry of the Psalmist: "As the hart panteth after the water brooks, so panteth my soul after Thee, O God. My soul thirsteth for God, for the living God." It may be the victorious flight of the soul from all earthly nests of ease and from all its secular perchings on things that perish to find the One Eternal Reality for which it was made. Or it may be the quiet discovery that one does not need to go somewhere, with chariots, or ships, or feet, or wings, since God is more truly like our spirits than like anything else in the universe, not remote, or absentee, close as breathing, the normal environment of the soul, and therefore a real Presence to be found and known and loved, as the swimmer finds the ocean. And this attitude of faith may rise, as it does with me in my best and sanest moments, to a joyous consciousness of acquaintance, fellowship and love. Sometimes it is a flash of sudden insight, sometimes it is a quiet assurance, sometimes it is an unspeakable joy in living, sometimes it is a dim awareness of a resource to live by and to draw upon for action.

It brings a sense of "at homeness" in this strange world. Nobody ever said this better than did that great mystic who wrote "the blessing of Moses" in Deuteronomy: "The eternal God is our home and underneath us are the everlasting arms." It is the consciousness of "Belonging," of being "no longer strangers and sojourners," as St. Paul discovered, "but fellow-citizens with the saints in the household of God . . . builded together into a temple for the habitation of God in the Spirit." Margaret Prescott Montague in her remarkable little book, *Twenty Minutes of Reality,* describes the experience as "beholding life for the first time in all its young intoxication of loveliness, in its unspeakable joy, beauty and importance."

The true secret seems to be found in the closing of chasms and cleavages. The divided will, the divided mind, the divided heart, become fused into a unity. The antithetic parts of the self, which were in a state of "civil war," become one harmonious whole. The entire inner being ceases its usual cross-road dilemmas and goes in *one* direction, straight forward. But even more important than this healing of inward breaches in the soul is the discovery of the conjunctness of God and man in a union of love and fellowship above all divisions. The divided life, the sundered self, the isolated ego, cannot be at peace. It cannot be "saved" in any true sense, while it is away from home in a far country on the other side of a wide canyon of separation from God. Nobody ever saw that truth more clearly than St. Paul did. *"Saw* it" is the right word, for what men usually call his "theology," "his system," was first of all an experience in life. He vividly saw and felt. To read forensic theological theories into Paul's throbbing letters is to miss the main artery by which he lived.

His doctrine of salvation is the outgrowth of his own personal experience of a mystic union through Christ, a union which does away with the "middle wall of partition" and brings together in an at-onement of reconciliation the two that were before separated by a chasm. "It is no longer I (the separate ego)," he says in one of his most striking autobiographical passages, "that live, but Christ liveth in me (by a mystical union), and the life I now live in the flesh I live in faith, the faith which is in the Son of God who loved me and gave himself for me" (Gal. 2:20). Here in this marvelous experience of union through love, one finds himself in the sphere of life, not in the realm of logical theory.

From *The Trail of Life in the Middle Years,*
pp. 192–197.

-»»«‹-

With all the heartaches and agonies that come with our finite limitations in space and time we have loads to bear which no practical philanthropist, be he never so wise, can lighten. There are moments when nothing will do for us except the assurance that God is with us as we tread the wine press. Anyone who can help in any degree to increase that assurance has served his age as truly as though he had invented a new engine or created a new type of turbine. There is, however, much more involved than that. Attitudes of faith are among the greatest of all known forces. Let a person's inner being be fortified with a faith in God and all his creative powers are quickened, his marching strength is heightened and his grip on everyday things is immensely increased. It is as though he had tapped a hidden reservoir of power. There are, on the other hand, "downs-and-outs" who still have large enough bank accounts, but who have simply lost their inner resources. The world would quickly become "another world" for them if they only knew how to open an invisible door that shuts them in. . . .

I am not interested in any of the ways of building Babel-towers in the hope of reaching up·to God, whether the towers are of brick and mortar, or whether they are of logic or of layers of Scripture texts, or of blocks from ancient creeds, or of sequences from causal proofs. All those man-built towers presuppose a remote and hidden God. The seeker, the tower-builder, on that supposition, must painfully rear his structure from below up by sheer human effort, with no sign of help, no evidence of coöperation from above. That kind of God could never be found, and such a quest would always end in confusion both of heart and of tongues.

Our entire hope of success in this search rests on the assurance that the one who is sought is also Himself the Seeker. If we are eager to find Him, even more so is He to find us and to bring us into the holy family, the blessed community of life and fellowship.

"Grace" is no hollow word of the theologians. It is not something manifested solely in a rare sacrament, or grudgingly dispensed by ordained men. It is a cosmic largess. We have been recipients all the way up from the cradle. Presentations have poured in on us from all the lovers and sufferers of the ages back to the beginning of smiles and tears. We have had the most priceless gifts bestowed for nothing at all. Love was here ahead of us with outstretched arms when we arrived and we came by birth into the richest of dowries. Every region we range over with our eyes is crammed with beauty unpaid for. Heroes and martyrs have been brave and faithful for our sake. The blood-red line of sacrifice, which has colored all the centuries behind us, comes with its redemptive power straight to our doors.

God is not an abstract reality, an absolute Alone, at the far end of Bethel-ladders and Babel-towers. He is central in the stream of Life and Love and Truth and Beauty. The Cross on Calvary is not a solitary instance of self-giving Love. It has always been at the Heart of the time-process, for Grace is perennial and contemporary with the uncoiling of the first nebula. The reason we can hope to find God is that He is here, engaged all the time in finding us. Every pulse of love is a tendril that draws in His direction. Every verification of truth links the finite mind up into a Foundational Mind that undergirds us. Every deed of good will points toward a consummate Goodness which fulfills all our tiny adventures of faith. We can find Him because in Him we live and move and have our being.

From *Pathways to the Reality of God*,
pp. IX–XII.

–>>)<<–

THERE is only one way that a God of supreme significance for our lives could reveal His character to beings like us. The universe in the structure of its ordered framework is no doubt some kind of a revelation. The harmony, symmetry and beauty which break in on us through the things around us take us closer to the nature of the World within the world we see. But power, order, beauty are not enough to satisfy beings of our type. What we have been calling "the Heart of things" is still lacking. It could not come to light except where love and sympathy and gentleness and traits of endurance and self-giving find expression. There cannot be such a manifestation until there is an adequate personal organ of revelation. The most sensitive interpreters of such values of life find in Christ a revelation like that. They feel satisfied that in this Person of Galilee and Judea we see what the Heart of God is like.

It will always be possible, no doubt, for objectors to say that there is no way to pass over from the subjective experiences which Christ felt and from the deeds He did and the things He suffered to the objective reality of God. No, nor is it possible to convince a thorough-going subjectivist of the validity of any kind of objectivity, even the objectivity of the external world which science describes or which the lover of beauty interprets. It ought, however, to satisfy most earnest and sincere minds that here in Christ the universe had produced a Person who made the supremacy of love vivid and vocal and victorious, a Person whom multitudes of men and women have felt to be good enough and noble enough to express the highest human ideal of God's nature. And the fact remains that Christ carries at least this indubitable testimony to objectivity that there must be something like Him at the heart of the eternal nature of things since the eternal nature of things has produced Him here in our world.

The fact that God can be revealed in a personal life carries momentous implications. It means that the divine and the human are not so far sundered as had been persistently supposed. It means that human nature can become an organ for the Life of God since it has been such an organ. It means that God is nearer to us than we supposed; more truly an Emmanuel God than we had been wont to believe. It may well be that God is all along endeavoring to break through and reveal His presence and character, the only difficulty being that He finds such poor, self-filled instruments for any true revelation to break through.

From *A Preface to Christian Faith in a New Age*,
pp. 126–128.

» II «

How Does God Reveal Himself?

II

A FEW days ago Helen Keller came to our Quaker meeting and sat with us in silence, a silence the depth and quiet of which in her experience must surpass anything we normal persons know. No outer sound ever breaks into her inner world. No disturbing visible happenings ever call her attention away from a concentrated hush. In the course of the meeting, which was the first one she had ever sat in, she rose and spoke most impressively, so impressively in fact, that many of us who were present felt our hearts profoundly moved and we found our eyes growing wet with spontaneous tears. Her message was very natural and simple. She told of her joy at being in a Quaker meeting, of the freshness and reality of the experience of worship. Then she spoke of the immense satisfaction she had felt over the position which Friends had taken during the war and over their work of relief in the long period of agony which followed the war. The thing which touched her most was the interpretation of love and brotherhood, the new way of life and the reconciling spirit. With extraordinary effect, but with uttermost simplicity, she referred to her own life as an illustration. Once there was a little girl, she said, who was shut up in utter darkness and unbroken silence with no real life, no world, no hope, no future. Then someone came, who with patience and tenderness, brought her into contact with the world out there beyond her, interpreted it to her, and opened in her undreamed-of capacities of intercourse with that new world of life and thought. Even with closed eyes she learned how to look out on a world full of beauty, hope and possibility. So you, she continued, have had the privilege of helping men and women and children to discover a richer life and a deeper love and sympathy than they knew before. They have found through you a world before unknown. You have shot through their darkness with an unexpected light.

I have given her message from memory and more or less in my own words, but I have faithfully expressed her central thought, and whether it applies accurately to our work of love and relief or not, it is a happy, suggestive thought for the interpretation of the true Christian life. The service which Miss Sullivan (now Mrs. Macy) rendered for this blind-deaf child as a vital organ of interpretation we, as disciples and friends of Christ, ought to render to those about us who have not yet been able to break through the walls of darkness behind which they are trying to live. We have always held as Friends, and I hope we always shall hold, that divine light reaches the human soul by a direct inner way—"the soul's east window of divine surprise"—but most persons need both sources of help, the inner and the outer touch. A great many persons never grasp and understand the inner flashes and intimations until some human helper brings a living personal interpretation which gives a sudden meaning to what was happening within. It is through such souls that God gives the supplemental light, somewhat as Ananias was able to do for Saul: "Brother Saul, the Lord, even Jesus, who appeared unto thee in the way has sent me unto thee that thou mightest receive thy sight and be filled with the Spirit." Here we have a striking case of direct approach and of added human assistance. The energies and forces of the physical world are not *applied* in terms of work and service until an instrument is found which acts as a coordinator or transmitter to them. The forces were there all the time but they did not work effectively until the instrument of human invention brought them into operation just where they were needed. Water boiled through all the centuries but its steam vanished unused until a curious engine was devised to coordinate and transmit its unsuspected power. Electricity forked and zigzagged across the sky and crashed in terrorizing thunder for long ages before the dynamo let it come through in harmless and constructive ways of service. There were wireless vibrations and radio-activities before the coherer and the coil fitted them to human ears and made them intelligible signs and significant messages.

So, too, love and sympathy, kindness and generosity passed from soul to soul and made a little earthly heaven in the world of men before Christ made it plain through His life that love is a revelation of God and that gentleness is divine. We have unfortunately been very slow to see that God must have an instrument—an organ is perhaps a better word—for the revelation of His love and tenderness, just as His physical energies must have their coordinator and transmitter. Love in the abstract means nothing. It is as impossible as *Alice in Wonderland's* cat, grinning without any face. If love is ever to reach and move and transform anyone with its wonderful impalpable power it must be a real love expressed in a real life. It can no more be transmitted impersonally than the human contacts which interpreted the world to Helen Keller could have come without anybody's finger-tips. A world might have been devised, no doubt, in which all truth, all wisdom, all experience, could have been flashed telepathically, or by immediate contact, from the mind of God to the mind of man; only we are not in that kind of world. *Here* we need one another and, strangest fact of all, God

Himself needs us. We are fellow-laborers with Him. He brings His Kingdom through us; He builds His spiritual world with our aid. The world—the spiritual world—moves forward not on an escalator but on altar stairs where each one of us makes his sacrificial contribution to the mighty task for which Christ lived and died.

St. Paul knew this truth and he testified to it in the bold words: "I fill up what is behind of the sufferings of Christ." But we have been inclined to adopt a theory of salvation which left that great principle out of sight. We have underrated the human factor and so have often missed the full glory of our fellowship with Christ, a glory deeply touched and tinged with suffering as all true glory is. It is desperately easy to be stupid, easy to argue and contend over empty husks and shells. When I shake myself awake and find that I have been doing that, I am always humbled and made heartily ashamed, for the one really big business in this world or in any world is the business of being a coordinator, a transmitter, of the love of God, the love of God revealed in a man like us.

From *The Friend,* London, Vol. 65 (1925),
pp. 29–30.

-»)«-

IF we sprinkle iron filings over a sheet of paper and move a magnet beneath the paper, the filings will become *active* and will combine and re-combine in a great variety of groupings and re-groupings. A beholder who knows nothing of the magnet underneath will gaze upon the whole affair with a sense of awe and mystery, though he will feel all the time that there must be some explanation of the action and that some hidden power behind is operating as the cause of the groupings and re-groupings of the iron particles. Something certainly that we do not *see* is revealing its presence and its power.

Our everyday experience is full of another series of activities even more mysterious than these movements of the iron. Whenever we open our eyes we see objects and colours confronting us and located in spaces far and near. What brings the object to us? What operates to produce the contact? How does that far-away thing hit our organ of vision? This was to the ancient philosopher a most difficult problem—a real mystery. He made many guesses at a solution, but no guess which he could make satisfied his judgment. Our answer is that an invisible and intangible substance which we call ether— luminiferous ether—fills all space, even the space occupied by visible objects, and that this ether which is capable of amazing vibrations, billions of times a second, is set vibrating at different velocities by different objects. These vibrations bombard the minute rods and cones of the retina at the back of the eye, and presto, we see now one color and now another, now one object and now another. This ether would forever have remained unknown to us had not this marvelous structure of the retina given it a chance to break through and reveal itself. In many other ways, too, this ether breaks through into revelation. It is responsible apparently for all the immensely varied phenomena of electricity, probably, too, of cohesion and gravitation. Here again, the revelation remained inadequate and without clear interpretation until we succeeded in constructing proper instruments and devices for it to break through into active operation. The dynamo and the other electrical mechanisms which we have invented do not make or create electricity. They merely let it come through, showing itself now as light, now as heat, now again as motive-power. But always it was *there* before, unnoted, merely potential, and yet a vast surrounding ocean of energy there behind, ready to break into active operation when the medium was at hand for it.

Life is another of those strange mysteries that cannot be explained until we realize that *something more than we see* is breaking through matter and revealing itself. The living thing is letting through some greater power than itself, something there beyond and behind, which is needed to account for what we see moving and acting with intention and purpose. Matter of itself is no explanation of life. The same elemental stuff is very different until it becomes the instrument of something not itself which organizes it, pushes it upward and onward and reveals itself through it. Something has at length come into view which is more than *force* and *mechanism*. Here is intelligent purpose and forward-looking activity and something capable of variation, novelty and surprise.

And when living substance has reached a certain stage of organization, something higher still begins to break through—consciousness appears, and on its higher levels consciousness begins to reveal truth and moral goodness. It is useless to try to explain consciousness—especially truth-bearing consciousness—as a function of the brain, for it cannot be done. That way of explanation no more explains mind than the Ptolemaic theory explains the movements of the heavenly bodies. Once more, something breaks through and reveals itself, as surely as light breaks through a prism and reveals itself in a band of spectral colours. This consciousness of ours is not merely *awareness*, not only intelligent response; it lays hold of and apprehends, i.e., reveals, truth and goodness. What I think, when I really *think,* is not just my private "opinion," or "guess," or "seeming"; it turns out to have something universal and absolute about it; my multiplication table is everybody's multiplication table. It is true for me and for beyond me. And what is true of my mathematics is also true of other features of my thinking. When I properly organize my experience through rightly formed concepts, I express aspects that are real and true for everybody—I attain to something which can be called *truth*. The same way in the field of conduct, I can discover not only what is subjectively right, but I can go farther and embody *principles* which are right not only for me but for every man. Something more than a petty, tiny, private consciousness is expressing itself through my personality. I am the organ of something more than myself.

Perhaps more wonderful still is the way in which beauty breaks through. It breaks through not only at a few highly organized points, it breaks through almost everywhere. Even the minutest things reveal it as well as do the sublimest things, like the stars. Whatever one sees through the microscope, a bit of mould, for example, is charged with beauty. Everything from a dew-drop to Mount Shasta is the bearer of beauty. And yet beauty has no function, no utility. Its value is intrinsic, not extrinsic. It is its own excuse for being. It greases no wheels, it bakes no puddings. It is a gift of sheer grace, a gratuitous largesse. It must imply behind things a Spirit that enjoys beauty for its own sake and that floods the world everywhere with it. Wherever it can break through, it does break through, and our joy in it shows that we are in some sense kindred to the giver and revealer of it.

Something higher and greater still breaks through and reveals a deeper Reality than any that we see and touch. *Love* comes through—not every-where like beauty, but only where rare organization has prepared an organ for it. Some aspects of love appear very widely, are at least as universal as truth and moral goodness. But love in its full glory, love in its height of unselfishness and with its passion of self-giving, is a rare manifestation. One Person—the Galilean—has been a perfect revealing organ of it. In His life it broke through with the same perfect naturalness as the beam of light breaks through the prisms of water-drops and reveals the rainbow. Love that understands, sympathizes, endures, inspires, recreates and transforms, broke through and revealed itself so impressively that those who see it and feel it are convinced of this, that here at last the real nature of God has come through to us and stands revealed. And St. Paul, who was absolutely convinced of this, went still farther. He held, with a faith buttressed in experience, that this same Christ, who had made this demonstration of love, became after His resurrection an invisible presence, a Life-giving Spirit who could work and act as a resident power within receptive, responsive human spirits, and could transform them into a likeness to Himself and continue His revelation of love wherever He should find such organs of revelation. If that, or something like it, is true, it is a very great truth. It was that that good old William Dell meant when he said: "The believer is the only book in which God himself writes His New Testament."

From *The Friend*, London, vol. 60 (1920), pp. 25–26.

->⟩)⟨⟨-

A GREAT deal of water has gone under the bridge since Emerson wrote that beautiful poetic essay, *The Over-Soul,* which stirred my youth to great enthusiasm. I am living and writing in the fourth decade of the twentieth century, not in the early nineteenth—and certainly not in the third century, though I am always greatly indebted to Plotinus.

If we are to suggest an Over-World that is cogent today, it must have its ground and basis in the implications and intimations of our actual experience. It must tally with these minds of ours and with the whole of Nature with which we are organic. It must not be shot out of an airgun for the satisfaction of the shooter, or for the delight of the spectators. It is fairly obvious now, I think, that no adequate explanation of the things which matter most to us, the realities by which we live, is forthcoming by the method of exact description of observed phenomena, or by the method of explanation in terms of antecedent causation. Antecedent causation, if taken with rigor, involves an infinite regress, a "bad infinite"—a cause behind each cause, with no *real* cause ever in sight; and exact description, if taken seriously, involves ever-increasing analysis, with more and more minute residual elements, which at last offer no explanation of the extraordinary principles of concatenation and mathematical and logical order. Then, too, there are all the time mind-experiences, mind-realities, and mind-values, which do not submit to methods of description, or to causal explanation. You know them only by having them, and you can explain them only in terms of themselves.

So long as one stays on the level of elemental vibrations, or of any type of described external facts, one could never predict an Over-World of Mind. It is only when we begin to deal with the actual facts of mind-experience, with its given realities and implications, that we find the clue, the guiding thread, to ultimate and real explanations of what we have on our hands, and on our hearts. No discoveries about the nature of matter throw any light on the nature of mental activity, or upon the unique unity of the life of the mind. Professor Montague is right when he says that those who know least about matter think most of it, while those who know most of it think least of it, as an all-sufficient explanation. I am not a matter-despiser—matter is a friend rather than an enemy. It is an indispensable feature of this double world system to which we belong. My main contention is that the approach to our supremely important ultimates must be through the mind-path rather than through the matter-highway, though, if we are wise, we shall not pry them apart and deal with either sundered half of the total whole.

Let me now proceed to gather up the implications which point to what William James called "our Mother Sea" or, again in James' words, "the More" that is "conterminous and continuous" with ourselves and operative in the universe, and which I prefer to call the "Over-World," revealed first of all as a Beyond within us.

We are already participating in this Over-World when we are immersed in the experience of the intrinsic values of Beauty, or of moral Goodness which ought to be, or of Truth which is eternally, inevitably true, or of Love for Love's sake. These are all typical realities which come into view only when there is a cooperating mind of what I have called the spirit-type. Only an interpretative mind, endowed with imagination and supplied with creative forms of judgment and appreciation, can create and enjoy Beauty, or have the conviction of Ought, or experience the necessary character of Truth, or love with a Love that suffers long, never lets go, is not provoked, endures and abides when everything else is "done away."

Not only do these supreme realities involve a peculiar type of mind on the subjective side; they equally involve a peculiar kind of world on the objective side. The Nature that presents the occasions for Beauty, Goodness, Truth, and Love is a Nature no longer exactly describable and explainable as a congeries of atoms and molecules and vibrations. It is a Nature deeply interfused with Spirit—Coherence, Order, Concatenation, Law, Logic, Mathematics, Significance, and Meaning. It is a sacramental universe through which Deep calleth unto Deep and significant realities of the impalpable and intangible sort "break in" on us and answer to our deepest being. We reach through the veil of what we call matter and are in a higher World which is kin to our minds and to which, as great amphibians, we really belong. In fact we lie open-windowed to it and partake of it. This Over-World of Beauty, Goodness, Truth, and Love is as truly and obviously beyond the welter and storms of the processes of matter and the basic stuff of the universe as our minds are above and beyond the swirl of the brain paths which somehow correlate with minds and appear to be the occasion for thought.

A great many persons in the history of our race have found themselves in direct communion with this Over-World of Spirit, have felt resources of life flood into themselves, have been invaded with life from beyond the margins of themselves. Among those who have had such experiences are some of the sanest, some of the wisest and best-balanced persons who have ever lived.

They have been as sure of the reality of their experience of a divine Other as ever they were of the hills and fields and rivers of their native habitat.

It is obvious that a second-hand account of such an event makes a much paler impression on the hearer of it than does a first-hand experience of the event itself. We know only too well how often we have been bored by the description of remote scenes that some traveler labors to present to us by a wordy picture, and the more he elaborates the less we care for the faraway scenery and circumstances of his travel. Somewhat so, readers of mystical experiences are quickly surfeited and soon cry "Hold, enough!" But I have been studying the mystics of history and the contemporary ones all my life— studying them with microscopical care and critical insight—and I am convinced that, after the necessary reduction and elimination, there is a remarkable nuclear residue of reality left on our hands. The original mystical experience feels like a thrust from beyond. Something breaks in on the soul like the tides from the Ocean beyond the ocean where we bathe. Thoreau writes in his *Journal:* "With all your science, can you tell me how and whence it is that light comes into the soul?"

The great religions of the race, and peculiarly the religion of the Hebrew prophets and the religion which took its rise in the Headwaters of the vast Christian stream, are fundamentally grounded in experiences that came to great spiritual geniuses. They have been among the foremost builders of the structure of human civilization. Most of our art and music and architecture and poetry has stemmed out of this source of life. I know the error and superstition and blunder and habit-drag that have gone along with this stream through the ages. But always at the source and always at the times of renewal and renascence there have been pillar personalities who have felt themselves in first-hand contact not with material realities, or with new economic facts, or with the discovery of larger food supplies, but with this Over-World of Spirit. And thereby they have been able to heighten life at its inner source and to raise the level of life itself.

What we have on our hands, as we consider our universe, is not an endlessly rhythmic and homogeneous and repetitive system, every stage of which is predictable from the nature of the system itself—"not exactly a bus, but a tram." Our real universe, quite the contrary, is an evolving world order, marked all the way up by unpredictable mutations, with unexpected emergents which inaugurated new epochs and changed the line of march of the entire process. And, on the whole, strangest of all, the process has been forward and upward. There have been "blackout" epochs, backslips and reversed eddies; but the moment one takes a long-sighted view, and a long-run estimate, there has plainly enough been an evolution and not a devolution. *We* are here and not the dinosaurs; and, in spite of a temporary "blackout" period which depresses us just now, there is no sign of the exhaustion of the process or of the stock of driving energies. There are good grounds for the prediction that the process is intelligible, is significant, and that the universe is going on, and is going somewhere, and means something.

So long as we are satisfied to confine our attention to exact description of what is, and to study of antecedent causes, the dramatic features of the universe will necessarily escape us, and we shall get no intimation of an Intelligence operative throughout the unfolding drama. But when we approach the cosmic process and the history of man's life on the planet as a vast drama with its multiform scenes and acts, on the whole suggesting a significant *dénouement*, we shall once more see good grounds for concluding that there is an Over-World operating as an influencing feature of the entire world-drama. And it is just possible—to claim no more—that the intelligible goal of the whole mighty movement is work *a fronte* toward the unseen end, as ideals do in our individual lives. We cannot consider the universe to be intelligible unless we can discover that it is *significant,* and it is not significant unless it is in some sense a spiritual drama. Professor Wilbur Urban, of Yale University, has well said that "a world in which there was no finality in the sense of an increasing purpose, no finality in the sense of an imperishable goal, would be an *intolerable* world, and to this extent wholly unintelligible."

We could not live, we could not even bear it without grinning, if we knew that the whole affair was an appalling Sisyphus episode of rolling a meaningless rock up hill, only to see it turn and roll down again to the stupid starting point—a dull repeatable operation with no meaning or purpose anywhere apparent. When the cosmic process does *seem* like that, and when life *looks* like a futile dance of ephemeral gnats, it is because we fail to deal with the *whole world* and are gazing at a little broken arc of it, as one might judge of the Parthenon by the badly broken torso of a single carving of Phidias.

If we are to think of the Universe as *intelligible,* as a significant drama, there must not only be evolving gains in the process, as there have been, but there must be also intimations of a fifth act to the drama, as the manifest destiny of it, which means an intelligible goal for those of us who are an important part of the drama.

From *Spirit in Man,*
pp. 54–63.

-»»«««-

It is a precarious undertaking to endeavor to show that History is a revelation of God and that there are glimpses of an Eternal Gospel in it. History has been a revelation of a great many things that are far removed from all our notions of the divine. Some periods of History have seemed in their exhibition of evil to be close to the satanic side of life. If we set out to find God in cosmic processes, or in the subliminal life of man, or in the unfolding course of History, we must begin by admitting that in all these spheres of exploration there is so much which "shrieks against" any such optimistic hope that our success is bound to be tempered and restrained. The only claim we can justifiably make is the presence of an eternal element in the temporal processes of History and that claim cannot be demonstrated. It is *not* absurd to have an invincible surmise that History "participates" in a time-transcending Reality. It is a well-grounded faith. Goals get expressed and realized, which are not the mere resultant of *a tergo* forces. "Creation" is not confined to an *ab initio* event, breaking in from outside but is "going on" from within the stream, as a resident operating power of direction. The eternal interpenetrates the temporal as a leaven does the flour.

All forms of monism and pantheism crack on the gigantic boulder of the fact of unmistakable *evil* in our world. They all make God, the One and Only, responsible for all the wrongs and miseries of the universe, or, if not, they resort to the dubious expedient of reducing what we call evil, and everything else that is temporal, to illusion, to maya, to mortal mind, to cinematograph "show." On that basis there could be no real revelation, for whatever got "revealed" would turn out in the end to be dust and ashes, or the shadow of a shadow. If God is to be the most precious hid Treasure for which a man would gladly give all his possessions, if He is the Pearl of infinite price, He cannot be just one thing among the many things, nor can He be thought of as a fusion of the Allness of the All.

In Plato's world there was the absolutely Real *and* something else which he called "the other," or, to translate his contraction into English, " 'Tother" —Reality and " 'Tother." There is unmistakably something about our visible and temporal universe that is not God. This strange " 'Tother" clings to it, dogs it, and makes it less than perfect. And thus if we are to find God in any of our fields of exploration we must expect also to find much that is not like Him, and it will call for nice discrimination to recognize the divine in the midst of what happens to be evidently undivine.

There have been all sorts of devices for explaining, or trying to explain, the presence of evil in what is assumed to be a God-made world. It was the malign influence of a fallen heavenly being, or it was the demonic work of spiritual hosts of wickedness in the upper world spheres, or it was a shattering "fall" which infected the whole creation with an evil slant or tendency. From somewhere the "grit" got injected into the machinery. The Gnostics inclined to the view that the world was really the creative work of a bungling "aeon," a subordinate being, a carpenter-creator, whom they called the "demiurge." He was only a second-rate workman. He did the best he could with the poor "stuff" he had to work with.

The difficulty with all these explanations is that they involve the defeat of God. It would seem that some power not Himself "spoiled" His high purpose and frustrated His will. Why did He allow the spoiler to spoil? Why did He permit such interference, unless in some way it furthered His plan and purpose? We must either admit that God is not all-powerful and can be defeated, or that there is some high and undefeated purpose expressing itself through this mixed and tangled web of things we call our world. I am distinctly for this latter alternative. I do not believe the plan is spoiled or frustrated. I think rather that the plan is being slowly revealed through a world that is being made, but made with difficulty and with pain, with groanings and agonies.... We are bound to raise the question: Do Science and History give any indication of human progress? It is no doubt an untoward time for the consideration of such a profound and baffling question. Many of the scholars who recently took part in the Harvard Tercentenary celebration, and those who spoke at the last meeting of the British Association for the Advancement of Science (1936), have emphasized the gravity of the effect of the strain of modern civilization both on human health and on mental development. We have discovered pituitary glands and thyroids, with all their potency over human destiny, and we can see before our eyes the malign possibilities of dictators who, like ancient Procrustes, are able to drill and regiment humanity to the shape and pattern which they wish to impose, but making man on the whole shorter rather than longer. Optimistic hopes have had a chilling frost and rainbow dreams have met with shattering disaster. To talk about progress now is like expressing fears of a flood during a period of drought and dust storms in the area where these distressing conditions are prevalent. What a time to discuss the prospect of progress when thoughtful persons are wondering whether civilization can be "saved" from débâcle! Dean Inge tells of a preacher, dealing with Joshua's miracle, who began: "My brethren, there are three kinds of motion—the progressive, the retrogressive and the one mentioned in my test, the standstill." The choice at the moment seems to many persons to be between the last two types!

In any case, there can be no return to the glowing expectations of the Victorian Era, or the earlier dreams of Rousseau. Those expectations have all gone down in a common wreck. It is difficult now for us even to imagine the enthusiams which once surged among men over Fourier's "phalansteries," which were to renovate the world, or over Saint-Simon's proclamation of "the golden age in front of us," or over Auguste Compte's "Law of the Three Stages," his cult of Humanity and his dream of a Utopia on earth. How could anybody have thrilled over these cheap human paradises which would bore most of us to death if we were in them!

Hegel's *a priori* philosophy of progress, through his Triads of History, has had a powerful influence on the modern world, but it is a very dead theory today, with almost none to do it reverence. It was in the main a mental reconstruction, spun out of a fertile brain, and imposed upon History rather than a sound induction drawn from the actual course of History itself. . . .

But nothing on the Continent could quite parallel the glow of expectation which captivated minds in England with the dawn of the doctrine of evolution. As usual Darwin was cautious and modest, though confident of unbroken progress, but Herbert Spencer became the apostle of progress, both to Christians and "Gentiles." He had been an evolutionist even before the appearance of Darwin's *Origin of Species,* and under the influence of Compte he had already taken a highly optimistic attitude toward man's future on the planet. But as his evolutionary philosophy expanded, his expectations of progress expanded with it. He came to believe that "the ultimate development of the ideal man is logically certain," and that "the purpose of creation is to produce the greatest amount of happiness" for the human race. "Always toward perfection is the mighty movement," he wrote, "toward a complete development and a more unmixed good; subordinating in its universality all petty irregularities and fallings back, as the curvature of the earth subordinates mountains and valleys. *Even in evils the student learns to recognize only a struggling beneficence."* (Italics mine.)

For Spencer, evolution was a vast cosmic escalator, always running, and always taking its precious freight in an upward direction. All that was needed was patience. What was most desired was bound to come in the end to those who could wait—or to their descendants. The escalator was running and was carrying everything forward to a higher goal. . . .

The change which has come over the modern world from the thin optimisms of two generations ago, to a state of doubt or even of relative pessimism, has been due, first of all, to the bankruptcy of ideals during the actual collapse of civilization, which overwhelmed the world from 1914 to 1918, and the years of the aftermath of the war, and in the second place to a much profounder grasp of the meaning and the limitations of evolution. Great disasters, like the Peloponnesian War, the Fall of the Roman Empire, the Thirty Years War, the Reign of Terror, as an immediate effect, cast a blight on the human spirit and topple down the imaginative cities in the sky which the mind of man is prone to build. The exhaustion which comes from such titanic efforts, and in this instance the unmistakable fact of defeat of hopes and ideals instead of victory, tend to produce a group inferiority complex which may amount almost to a disease. That inferiority complex about human nature is very widespread in the world of today and helps to explain the loss of faith in progress. . . .

There can be no question or doubt, on the part of those who know the facts, that life on this planet *has evolved* and has progressed upward from feeble beginnings. Up to a certain level the cosmic escalator has plainly been running. But on the higher levels of life, after self-conscious spirit has emerged, when free, autonomous selves are present, progress is no longer *inevitable*. It is not now the result of an escalator coming up from below. It depends on us, and persons like us, whether we go on to further goals or not. The possibilities are in us, there is no compulsion. We can sag down to the level of animal life, or we can climb an inward Jacob's Ladder and become rightly fashioned spirits, kindled by a flame from above. We are very strange amphibians of a new and higher order. We have the possibility of becoming superbiological. We may belong to two worlds and, made as we are, we shall never be satisfied merely with a lengthened period of survival, or with greater efficiency of our physical organs. But if we are to realize the higher possibilities open to us, we are bound to discover a new type of *provision of advance* in us. We shall not recover our faith in human progress until we enlarge the range of correspondence with the whole of our environment.

That essential type of "provision of advance" for moral and spiritual beings like us can be nothing less than some sort of correspondence with a deeper environment than that which appears to be adequate for a biological being. Shakespeare in *Macbeth* called the visible world, "this bank and shoal of time," which implies that it is environed by a deeper World of Eternal Reality —the World of Spirit—from which great birth moments may emerge. That "deeper World" which enswathes "the bank and shoal of time" must be *real* if anything in the universe is real. The visible fragment, the temporal "shoal," taken by itself, cut off and isolated from its mother life and source, cannot be made intelligible. We are bound to presuppose More in order to deal successfully with what we have on our hands. Sir James Jeans has said: "The universe begins to look more like a great thought than like a great machine. Mind no longer appears as an accidental intruder into the realm of matter; we ought rather to hail it as the creator and governor." I leave it to others who know much more than I do about the process of physical evolution, to discuss the question whether the momentous "mutations," which by their emergence have successively raised the level of life in the long process, may not well be traced to the *Creative influence* of some such deeper Environment. And I confine myself here to the issues involved in spiritual progress.

I think we must give up expecting Utopias and terrestrial Paradises either by evolutionary physical processes or by man-made social and economic panaceas and contrivances. And we must once for all discard theories of progress which assume that all past generations, and present ones too, are only means and instruments for the promotion of that final and fortunate epoch of bliss and perfection of "the crowning race" at the end of the series— "the far off divine event" at the long last lap.

The same trouble infects all apocalyptic conceptions of History. If one assumes, as apocalyptists do, that the entire historical procession of generations has been only a miserabilism, only a series of steady failures, and that future generations are to stagger along on the same tragic road until the divine relief expedition from the sky comes to bring the sorry business to an end and to inaugurate another kind of world, then there is no dramatic significance to History. It is an unnecessary loop that might much better not have been painfully traveled over by the tramping feet of so many frustrated generations, who were always "going on," but not going for any significant purpose or to any goal of human value. I am convinced that we have not formed the right theory of History until we see History itself as a spiritual drama, moving toward a significant dénouement and at the same time a process which has meaning and value as it goes on. A Hyde Park orator said: "I am speaking now with all 'istry vivid to my reckerlection." As far as I can claim to have "all history vivid to my recollection," I see it as a significant process. It has been well said that humanity has up till now always shown "a deathless capacity for resurgence." It has turned sunsets to sunrises.

If we are to talk intelligently about progress, it must be inherently based and grounded, it must be in process now, and it must be rooted in the deeps of Eternity, in creative Mind, which is to say, in the true spiritual Environment of man's mind. As there can be no genuine science without the presupposition of the intelligibility of the world, so, too, there can be no sure ground for the progress of the world without the presupposition that Mind is operative in the historical process of events. In short, we cannot properly talk about human progression unless we have a sound doctrine of divine-human interaction and a reasonable faith that every generation has a possibility of communion with the creative Spirit who broods over humanity, as well as over the face of the waters at the dawn of creation. Any working theory of progress must carry along with it some degree of faith in an "Eternal Gospel."

From *The Eternal Gospel,*
pp. 63–66; 69–80.

→»«←

PANTHEISM as a way of thinking is a hopeless muddle. So, too, is a thin rationalistic "naturalism." One might equally well call a circus a meeting for worship or a communion service, as to call the totality of the all "God." No, there are many things that ought not to be as they are. There are situations which at temporal moments are recalcitrant and defective and which must be put down and be conquered before there can be final triumph of aim and goal. The universe is no doubt malleable toward ends that are "good" but it is not essentially *bound* to produce the good, any more than a block of Pentelic marble is bound to be a glorious part of the Parthenon frieze, until some Phidias sees the possibilities in it and makes it take shape and significance. There have been many wise persons in the course of history who have believed the world to be the work of a malevolent being and to have a diabolical kink in it, and there is fully as much to justify this Manichaean conclusion as there is to warrant the soft optimism of Leibnitz that it is the best possible world. There are pitiful tragedies in the world process against which all our finer sentiments revolt and cry aloud. But on the whole, and in the long run, we may believe that the universe in its wholeness is a satisfactory "basis and framework" for the spiritual adventure which seems to be going on in it. The visible universe may very well be a sphere and starting point for building a moral order. It is because we find signs of this moral order in process of creation that we are confident that God is here at work and is slowly revealing the dawning good. ...

Liver and spleen and kidneys in our bodies are coherent with heartbeats and blood stream that feed the central life where we are working out our ideals and purposes, but the central aim could never be discovered if one confined his sphere of operation alone to kidney, spleen and liver. There is much in a drama, or in a musical creation which, if taken in isolation, throws very little light on the central dramatic purpose of the author or on the *motif* of the musical piece. Nevertheless the mind of the author has touched these lesser and subordinate parts and they add *something* to the total movement which would be missed if this scene were omitted or if this musical note were absent. So, too, it may well be with the cosmic drama. Its larger meaning is easily missed if we focus attention on isolated aspects or on separated parts of the whole, and it is not strange if it often *seems* as though no drama were underway at all so long as we are occupied only with the stage-setting of the main dramatic event.

Our main problem at this point is the task of discovering what is "the central spiritual adventure" in the universe, assuming that there is one, and what kind of a God is revealed through it and betokened by it. It seems to me that we are bound to turn for our answer to those highest peaks of intimation and revelation, where the meaning and value of things most clearly come in sight, and where *the surmise of a more yet* is most apparent. For that discovery we must take careful account of the fundamental significance of personality and its extraordinary implications. It is probable that the so-called "spiritual adventure" on our planet, which is revealed through personality, is at present only incipient, only at the starting stage, but even so it reveals lines of direction and we may catch a glimpse of the plan and the design. This sounds "anthropomorphic," no doubt. It compels us to foreshorten the perspective and to stain the white radiance of eternity with the many-colored dome of our finite life. Even so, religion is no more anthropomorphic than science is. The whole fabric of science is built upon the faith that we can trust the forms and categories of our human minds, that our mathematics fits the entire structure of the universe and that the organon of our logic works not only here but in Orion and the Pleiades as well.

If we refuse to take this path of anthropomorphism, we foredoom ourselves to a worse alternative, which is agnosticism and nescience and a universe devoid of intelligibility. The only way to truth that lies open to us at all is the way through our own minds. If we cannot find a clue here in our own human reason, we can find it nowhere. We shall never find any ways of proving the reality of God or of discovering His character except through the processes and the interpretations of nature, of life and of mind; and in any case no religion can help us much unless it meets us where we live and think and love and suffer and triumph over difficulties. "The word is nigh *thee,* even in thy mouth and thy heart." With deep penetration Hans Denck said in the sixteenth century: "The Kingdom of God is in your hearts and he who searches for God outside himself will never find Him. Apart from God no one can either seek or find God, for he who seeks God already in very truth has Him." . . .

It will be countered in reply, no doubt, that the obvious trouble with this approach is that we are thus forced to start with a *finite* process, and consequently we can never hope to get across the chasm to an infinite reality. My answer is that there is no such chasm to cross. Man is from the start a *finite-infinite* being, and not a "mere" finite one. Partaking, as he does, of Reason he cannot stop his quest and pursuit of truth at any finite point, for *finite truth* is a contradiction of terms. If a thing is true at all it is infinitely true, though these terms "finite" and "infinite" have genuine application only in the realm of space and mathematics. They do not correspond to spiritual realities nor do they tally with the dominant issues which attach to the realm of Spirit. A wiser term for what is meant by "finite-infinite" is *transcendence in immanence.* "Transcendence in immanence" appears wherever self-consciousness appears. Every aspect of our deeper life is embedded in more life than we are aware of. Every thought we think is a fragmentary aspect of a personal life and purpose that sweeps beyond it. It is what it is because of its place in the total life-system which overspans it with wider scope. Descartes was right when he insisted that we are conscious of finiteness only because we forever contrast it with an infinite that underlies all our thinking.

Man's moral adventure is something that, from its inherent nature, could not have a finite terminus. Every act of goodness which we perform bears witness to an ideal operating in us and that has no definable limits. To set up a finite goal at which moral adventure must come to a full stop is to make the inauguration of the adventure impossible. We cannot start toward a moral achievement unless we feel that it leads on into something *significant*. How often shall I forgive my brother? What are the boundaries of truth-telling? When shall I have attained a moral goal that will satisfy all the possibilities of my personal nature? There is no such goal. There is no such stopping place. There is no finality to this path on which we have set our feet. "Man partly is, but wholly hopes to be." His sunsets all involve sunrises. We are *moral* just because there is an unattained "more yet" in our very being. At the same time every right deed is intrinsically a perfect deed. *The goal is in the process.* The reward is bound up with the life. The victory of faith is the faith itself. The crown of life consists in living that kind of life.

> What if we still ride on, we two,
> With life forever old, yet new,
> Changed not in kind but in degree,
> *The instant made eternity.*

The revised version of the Bible makes the Book of Ecclesiastes say: "God hath set eternity in our hearts." It is probable that this strange book did not say that in the original. But the writer might very well have said it if he had only thought of it. The Book of Proverbs does in fact say that "the spirit of man is a candle of the Lord," which means that a kindled finite soul is a flame of the Eternal. It is every bit as true as the saying I used to hear frequently in Quaker Meeting when I was a boy: "Here we are doomed to live forever in a vale of mutability!" They are both true sayings. Here where we live, in a space-time world, the perfect can be revealed only in process. The eternal *lives* and is expressed only in unending mutability. The infinite is both in and beyond the finite. The unseen is immanent in the seen. The "more yet" hovers on the edge of every attainment. The horizon that bounds our achievements widens out as the sky line does at sea with the progress of the ship. What ought to be is always running ahead of what is. The heavenly vision of a beyond will not let us rest in the good of here and now. One can as easily catch up with the horse he is driving from the buggy-seat as one can overtake the flying goal of his moral passion. To be a moral person at all is to be *self-transcendent*, which means "finite-infinite." No one can appreciate music who does not rise above the seriatim notes and enjoy them together in a time-transcending now, which is a gentle breaking in of eternity into our time-world.

From *Pathways to the Reality of God,*
pp. 57–64.

-»)«(-

NOTHING is more certain than that some persons at some moments in their lives are carried beyond the usual level of their range of thought and reasoning, and arrive at flashes of truth and insights into the meaning of life and the nature of God, which seem to the recipient like spontaneous gifts of wisdom from above. Sometimes these "flashes" and "insights" come like sudden meteors that leave only a brief train of fading light behind, and sometimes they are linked up, in favored persons, with a great creative literary gift, which enables the inspired writer to put them into permanent form for the use of multitudes of others who are thus able to climb to a similar height through the medium of the literary creation or the artistic form.

When anyone is enabled to rise above himself and to produce some form of creative expression that, for successive generations, lifts men to higher levels of truth, wisdom and life than they could otherwise have attained, that may well be called "inspiration." There are many degrees of it and those instances of it which are worthy to be called "revelations" are the creations that know no limits of date or regional space, but that continue age after age and in all lands to speak to men as though out of eternity.

As there is obviously a human factor present in the revealer, so, too, there is bound to be a corresponding human element in the reader and interpreter of the inspired message. It does not drop in capsule fashion into a receptacle type of mind. Apprehension and appreciation of truth can occur only through the stock of ideas and imagination-material which the reader possesses. In a land like Japan, for instance, where no one ever sees a sheep or a shepherd, the beautiful imagery of the Good Shepherd will fail to produce the effect which is sure to be produced in a country where sheep are daily led to pasture.

Revelation literature stands or falls with the power of its appeal to the minds of men age after age. The test which Coleridge applied to the Bible in his remarkable little book, *Confessions of an Inquiring Spirit*, nearly a hundred years ago remains as vital a principle as ever. His test of its power is the way it searches the deeps of his inmost being and *finds him*. "The words of the Bible," he said, "find me at greater depths of my being than any other book does." And then he goes on to conclude: "Whatever *finds me* brings with it an irresistible evidence of having proceeded from the Holy Spirit."

The basis of Coleridge's position rests upon his underlying axiom that there is a divine root in man—a spiritual center answering to a higher spiritual Center in the universe. Deep calleth unto Deep and these spiritual deeps find one another as two corresponding electrodes do.

There are without question types of literature which work almost like a spell on the minds of men. The reader of such literature is held by a power which he cannot analyze nor fathom. It conveys a sense of reality. It seems to have come out of a depth of life in which the reader himself is also rooted. It finds him because in some real way it is kindred to his own nature. . . .

"A poem," Shelley declared in his *Defense of Poetry*, "is the very image of life expressed in its eternal truth." It is life interpenetrated with a diviner nature, or, in Shelley's own words, a way of redeeming "from decay the visitations of the divinity in man."

This power to transmute, remold, refashion as with an angel's wand, create and interfuse an eternal aspect, is what we mean by "inspiration." Something wells up from the obscure deeps within the soul, or surges in from "that mystic ocean whose rim no foot has trod." It comes as surprise, a divine splendor, an *élan vital,* or *élan mystique,* but always with the release of creative energy—

A flash that has revealed
The invisible world.

From time immemorial the poet and the prophet have always felt that the source of light and of creative energy was beyond themselves. They have given the impression of a visitation—a divine kindling spark has lighted up, with new colors, all the material that had been laboriously accumulated, or, to change the figure, some touch from beyond had in a moment fertilized with life what until then lay dead or dormant. All the supreme creations of genius point away to a higher source of inspiration. They open with a reverent "hail" to the divine muse, and the heavenly stimulus, that first gave them the creative impulse. Sometimes, no doubt, the inscription to the muse is formal and conventional, but where the inspiration is greatest and most genuine the finger of the poet points upward with perfect naturalness. The most important effect of the "inspiration" is a superordinary unification of all the inner faculties and powers of the being. Everything that has been gathered by the experiences of a lifetime seems to lie at hand for use as though they were "presented" by a magic valet. A sorting and shifting of the material is done without effort for the hand of the workman as though he had a retinue of invisible helpers. "Fecundity" is once more the right word. The frantic strain and effort which characterize second-class work vanish and the "creator" produces his masterpiece in an atmosphere of serenity and peace....

> Out of the heart of Nature rolled
> The burdens of the Bible old;
> Up from the burning core below
> The canticles of love and woe.

These lines of Emerson fit perfectly into the conception of inspiration which I have been here developing. This "burning core below," of which the poet speaks, is that deep ground-swell surge, the energies of which we have found operating wherever immortal creative literature is being produced. Sometimes "the ground swell" comes up from the submerged life of the individual and seems to reveal hardly more than the accumulated experiences of that particular person, but sometimes, on the other hand, it seems to be immersed in a larger Life of the Spirit, and to become in a mysterious way the organ of that Life. It seems most likely that the spirit in us is close within reach of the Spirit who is Truth and Life. The heart of Nature—the eternal Nature of things—seems to roll through the person who is inspired and to find a voice and utterance:

> The silence of eternity
> Interpreted by Love.

> From *Pathways to the Reality of God,*
> pp. 149–151; 159–161; 163–164.

->>><<<-

No other book that has ever been written has received such a searching examination, such minute and painstaking research, at the hands of an army of trained experts as has happened during the last three generations to the Scriptures of the Old and New Testaments. That the whole perspective has been altered by this historical research there can now be no doubt. For those who are familiar with the results of this extensive examination the great Book is bound to be seen in a new light and it can no longer be read in an attitude of Bibliolatry. The theory of its verbal infallibility is of course gone. The idea that it is a divinely "dictated" Book is untenable. That the book is an unbroken unity, all the parts of it on the same moral and spiritual level, is no longer a possible view. There are many types of literary style in it, and the different books which compose it all have their peculiar setting of historical background and of contemporary ideas and hopes and expectations. It is a library of books, not a single book. It is the chosen and selected spiritual literature of a remarkable people, covering more than a thousand years of history and of spiritual development.

It is, however, definitely the world's greatest literature of revelation. There is a *uniqueness* about this Book which research has only heightened, and it will still be read with awe and wonder, as the sifted spiritual literature of the ages. It contains almost every type of literature—epic, lyric, dramatic, historic, romantic, prophetic, apocalyptic, synoptic, epistolary, exhortative. It has furnished models and suggestive material for hosts of writers. It is woven into the seamless structure of the world's greatest poetry, and, what is even more important, it has gone into the moral and spiritual fiber of countless lives. It is bound to recover its place of influence in the race, and to be once more *the* Book of the family, the Church, and the educator. But that will happen only if it is seen and read in the new light that has been flooded upon it, and if it is interpreted so as no longer to be an *ipse dixit* out of line and harmony with the established truths of science and the known facts of history. Scientists and historical scholars will not read it, if it must be assumed to be an infallible record of scientific facts and historical happenings. When truth has once been established beyond a peradventure by exact methods of research it cannot be annulled by what was written in a period before any one of the laws of the universe was discovered. What is known in one field of truth cannot successfully go on being contradicted in another field of truth.

What is now perfectly obvious to the trained reader is the fact that there is an impressive human factor apparent in every book in the great collection, even in the greatest and most divine one. Each book bears the characteristic marks of its period. The prevailing conceptions of the age creep in throughout and get a hearing. Again and again the writers draw upon ideas and views that were current in Assyria, Babylonia, Egypt, Persia, Greece, and the Hellenic world. What we have is a growing, expanding revelation, indicating all the time the intellectual, moral and spiritual level of the time, but in every instance the writer proves to be a spiritual genius, touched with inspiration, so that even the most primitive sections—and there are primitive sections—are charged with insight and vision. They are never negligible by a person who is eager for spiritual guidance, and for the highest ideals by which earlier races lived. . . .

I have a profound faith that this literature of the ages, which has been passing through an eclipse in this scientific period, will come back into full sunlight splendor, as readers with highly trained minds come to see it for what it really is rather than viewing it in terms of a traditional theory. It contains the best story material by which the minds of children have ever been trained, and it is the greatest literature of revelation that has come out of the far past of the race.

From *A Call to What Is Vital,*
pp. 47–49; 63.

-->><<--

THE supreme evidence that the universe is fundamentally spiritual is found in the revelation of personal life where it has appeared at its highest and best in history, that is in Jesus Christ. In Him we have a master manifestation of that creative upward tendency of life, a surprising mutation, which in a unique way brought into history an unpredictable inrush of life's higher forces. The central fact which concerns us here is that He is the revealing organ of a new and higher order of life. We cannot appropriate the gospel by reducing it to a doctrine, nor by crystallizing it into an institution, nor by postponing its prophecies of moral achievement to some remote world beyond the stars. We can appropriate it only when we realize that this Christ is a revelation here in time and mutability of the eternal nature and character of that conscious personal Spirit that environs all life and that steers the entire system of things, and that He has come to bring us all into an abundant life like His own. Here in Him the love-principle which was heralded all through the long, slow process has come into full sight and into full operation as the way of life. He shows us the meaning and possibility of genuine spiritual life. He makes us sure that His kind of life is divine, and that in His face we are seeing the heart and mind and will of God. Here at least is one place in our mysterious world where love breaks through—the love that will not let go, the love that suffers long and is kind. He makes the eternal Father's love visible and vocal in a life near enough to our own to move us with its appeal and enough beyond us to be forever our spiritual goal. We have here revealed a divine-human life which we can even now in some measure live and in which we can find our peace and joy, and through which we can so enter into relation with God that life becomes a radiant thing, as it was with Him, and death becomes, as with Him, a way of going to the Father.

From *The Inner Life*,
pp. 178–181.

->>><<<-

A MAJOR question to be raised at this point is the question whether the coming of Christ can be thought of as a historical event or not. Does Christ belong to History, or is He "beyond History"? Is His coming a watershed in History, or does He stand entirely apart from History? Does He come in a wholly perpendicular direction, as a celestial visitant from another realm, entering our world from beyond, breaking in on it from another sphere, and then leaving it again when the brief span of His work on earth was finished? Both views have been held and still are held today.

If one begins with the assumption that human nature is spiritually sterile and in dualistic fashion wholly sundered from God, and the historical process is wholly horizontal and devoid of correspondence with an eternal environment, then the only conceivable way for Christ, or any revealer of the Eternal, to come to our world as a divine event, as a revelation of God, would be for Him to come perpendicularly from beyond the time-world, to remain apart while here, and to have no historical correlation with the normal currents of life and History before and after. This view that Christ was a stupendous injection into the world from beyond, uncorrelated with History, and without being contaminated by contact with life here below, leads very easily on into "docetism" which was serious heresy in the early Church. Those who were determined to maintain that Christ was absolutely divine and wholly other than man went to the extreme position of insisting that Christ's earthly birth and temptation and suffering and death were only "seemings," "presentations of ideas made visible and vocal to men's minds." He never actually shared in the common experiences of human life, and He never really entered this stream of human events. His coming was an instance of "misplaced concreteness."

To set Christ out of relation with human life and with History, to put Him in unique isolation, either ends in some form of "docetism," or at best turns Him into a mysterious being who moves so far above the life we know and share that He does not bring a real redemptive power to bear on us. Everything ends for us in unreality. This extreme type of interpretation has almost invariably resulted in producing a violent swing of the pendulum off to the other extreme, and there emerges an emphasis on the purely human aspect of Christ. The difficulty throughout has been due to a misreading of human life. If man were wholly separated from God, depraved in nature, and spiritually sterile, there could be no real incarnation in such a being as that. And in following the shifts and make-shifts to which theological interpreters have resorted, one can see through it all that the *impasse* is made by a false and unsound theory of man.

If, as I am convinced is the case, man is essentially related to God, created in His image, and never sundered from the deeper world of Spirit; if the time-stream itself is imbedded in the deeps of Eternity and expresses reality "splashed out" into succession, and if History as a living movement is under the guiding, steering hand of a Pilot, who in spite of the zig-zags, goes forward toward a goal, then it would not be utterly impossible to think of Christ as revealing the full significance of Life and History and as a revelation of the direction in which man ought to move. Then the *preparatio evangelica,* the slow stages of preparation for the event, would all be significant and full of real meaning, which otherwise they lack. . . . I know as well as anybody does how sinful man is, what a poor, pitiable thing he can be. But I insist that that is not the whole story. There is some unlost likeness in man to which God can appeal, and we somehow feel that "Christ is ours," and "we belong." Men's faith, their spiritual outlook, their interpretation of the significance of Life, have always been important factors in the shaping of History. In other words, the spiritual element has been all the way along a determining feature of the historical process.

I find an Eternal Gospel of the Spirit dimly breaking through the time-stream in many ways. I think of man in all his devious wanderings in far countries as a possible child of God, who is never too remote to hear authentic tidings of Home and Father, and who has actually progressed in the long upward journey. Christ is what we should expect at some stage of History. . . .

At the head-waters of the stream of Christianity we come upon a Person who exhibited in matchless degree the divine possibilities of our kind of life and who was in a most exalted sense a revealing center of that deeper Divine Life that is within the reach of us all. In Him both "worlds" were together in unity. He "participated" in Eternity. He revealed divine Grace as no else has done. He was a genuinely historical Person, living connected with the past and with the future. But no account of him in terms of pedigree, or background, or of country, or national traits, or of social-group influences, or of nurture, or *Zeitgeist,* will ever "explain" him. He is unique. He transcends all the known frontiers and boundaries. He shares in many of the ideas and in the outlooks and expectations of the time. But he is always far beyond them. One can see the lines of the influence of the past in much that he said and did. The prophets and the apocalyptists left their stamp on him. But he was always on ahead of their highest point. The gates of the future always stood open before him. If he winnows and gathers up the seed-thought of the past, he just as certainly anticipates the spiritual discoveries of unborn generations. It fills one with awe and wonder to see how his truth and wisdom and spiritual insight outstrip the stock of the ages behind him and move on ahead of the foremost files of after generations. He brought and continues to bring a new quality of life into humanity.

His *life*, his spirit, his personality, is incomparably greater than anything he said, or did, or taught. One is always aware that there is more where his words "come from." *He* is there all the time above and beyond his utterances. It was a remarkable stroke of insight that led St. John to declare that he was the *truth*. Truth as it is used here is not a logical judgment, or a spoken message, or a transmitted idea; it is something that a person can be. It is a *life* that corresponds with an ideal, a pattern, an architectural plan. A person has come at last who can be the way, the truth and the life. . . .

What Christ brought to light in the unfolding of the Eternal Gospel is the Face, the personal aspect, the revelation of the Heart, the Love, the Grace, the Character-Nature of God. We *see* Him at last. We know now what He is like. We are confined no longer to abstract attributes, such as "infinite," "omniscient," "omnipotent" and "absolute." We come closer into the Heart of things and find that the highest and most exalted Being is our Father, who had all along been seeking us while we were feeling our way to Him.

From *The Eternal Gospel,*
pp. 88–101.

>>><<<

"THE testimony of history" is not complete until Christ is seen to be an inherent part of it. So long as Christ was thought of as a mysterious, supernatural visitant from another world to this one, so long as His humanity and the temporal events of His life were treated as unreal in order to enhance His divinity, as was done during the Middle Ages, the interpreter of His nature and His mission dwelt mainly upon His miraculous birth and resurrection, and showed little interest in the significance of His life as revealed in and through the historical process. There can, however, now be little doubt that the historical method of viewing and apprehending Him yields the greatest spiritual results and values.

The whole level of life is at once raised and the entire meaning of history is immensely heightened when it is recognized that we have not treated either adequately until we have seen that life as we know it must include Christ and that He is a living part of what we call history. His place in history, however, is not found by studying the short span of years that He lived in Galilee and Judea, but it includes as well the whole process of transformation which His life and spirit have wrought through the centuries. History would be quite another matter if He were eliminated from its story. We do not fully know Him until we discover what He has done in and through the unfolding course of history. The abstract way of approach to His nature must yield place to the concrete way. By the former method the interpreter proceeded by endeavoring to eliminate the human factor and the historical element and to think of Him as a Being above and beyond the conditions that attach to this life-process. The climax of that speculative type of interpretation was reached in the sublime and awe-inspiring conception of Him as "the second Person of the Trinity." But the trouble with this method of speculation was that it ended with a mere assertion and left Christ still uninterpreted, at least in any way that made it possible to fit Him into the sphere of life as we know it. He moved in such a remote and abstract realm, so foreign to our human plane, that His real place among men was quickly taken by the nearer and more human Virgin Mary, or by the triumphant and yet tender saints of the Church.

We have at last begun to recover Christ as a real Person who lived and taught and loved and suffered and was victorious over temptation and misunderstanding and desertion and defeat and death. We are learning to know Him in the concrete setting of a definite historical period and through the events and deeds and words of a specific epoch and a well-known body of literature, and in the light of what He has done during nineteen hundred years of history. The excessively scientific historian has tended to reduce His authentic deeds and His verifiable sayings to a very small compass. He is, by this process, "leveled down" and "explained" in terms of antecedent conditions, and as a result, we get a foreshortened and diminished Christ— once more reduced to an abstraction—who supplies us with no explanation of the part He had in the building, the growth and expansion of the historic Church.

On the other hand, there have been in recent times some great instances of historical interpretation of His life and mission that have made Him stand forth as the most dynamic and creative Figure in human history....

The thing we need primarily is an enlarged capacity of appreciation of the range and quality of His personality. We need once more to *see* Him. The question mark has been used in this generation somewhat to excess. Problems of origin and attempted explanation of the miraculous element have bulked so large that they have often obscured the real Life. The interrogation point has been written all over the documents that transmit the facts to us. And we have blurred His whole life with this fog of questions. We have been so absorbed in the work of criticism that we have too often lacked the power to read the Gospels as great literature of inspiration. We need to come freshly to this Life, to try to see Him with eyes of love and wonder, as we have learned to see St. Francis of Assisi, and to substitute the exclamation point for the overused question mark. . . .

Christ must be accepted as the kind of Person who could arouse the kind of faith and wonder that He did arouse and who could do what He has done to inspire and revitalize lives through the centuries of history—and *that* the Christ of the cold, thin rationalism could never have done, nor, I am bound to add, could the purely "theologized" Christ have done it either. . . .

If we are to suppose, as I am compelled to do, that the universe in its loftiest aspects shows "a spiritual adventure" already in process, we shall find the clearest evidences of such an adventure in the revelation of love which breaks through the life and death of Christ. It must be borne in mind that He is not a visitant or a stranger here in the world. "He came unto His own." "He knew what was in man." He fulfilled the divine idea of man. He revealed the "Adam" that was meant to be. He is the type at last fully expressed, the adventure brought to its successful goal. He inaugurates the new humanity. We have not seen what the universe could do, until we see Him. We have not read the whole story of history until we have fitted Him into the historical process. It is not until we turn to this highest revealing-place that we are able to get a clear sight of the deepest, the eternal, nature of things.

Atoms can reveal mathematics. Flowers and stars and mountains and sunsets can reveal beauty. The biological order can reveal life in its ascending series. Historical events can present a dramatic story that expresses and vindicates a moral order. But it is only through a concrete person who is divine enough to show love and grace in consummate degree, and human enough to be identified with us, that we can be assured of love at the heart of things. Christ is the coming of God in and through the process of history—God revealed to us in the persuasive terms of personal life and loving will.

From *Pathways to the Reality of God,*
pp. 120–123; 128; 143–144.

» III «

What Is Man?

III

Was there ever such a short-story character sketch as this one of the prodigal son! No realism of details, no elaboration of his sins, and yet the immortal picture is burned forever into our imagination. The *débâcle* of his life is as clear and vivid as words can portray the ruin. Yet the phrase which arrests us most as we read the compact narrative of his undoing is not the one which tells about "riotous living," or the reckless squandering of his patrimony, or his hunger for swine husks, or his unshod feet and the loss of his tunic; it is rather the one which says that when he was at the bottom of his fortune "he came to himself."

He had not been himself, then, before. He was not finding himself in the life of riotous indulgence. That did not turn out after all to be the life for which he was meant. He missed himself more than he missed his lost shoes and tunic. That raises a nice question which is worth an answer: When is a person his real self? When can he properly say, "At last I have found myself; I am what I want to be?" Robert Louis Stevenson has given us in Dr. Jekyll and Mr. Hyde a fine parable of the actual double self in us all, a higher and a lower self under our one hat. But I ask, which is the real me? Is it Jekyll or is it Hyde? Is it the best that we can be or is it this worse thing which we just now are?

Most answers to the question would be, I think, that the real self is the ideal self of which in moments of rare visibility we sometimes catch glimpses.

> All I could never be,
> All, men ignored in me,
> This, I was worth to God, whose wheel
> The pitcher shaped.

"Dig deep enough into any man," St. Augustine said, "and you will find something divine." We supposed he believed in total depravity, and he does in theory believe in it; but when it is a matter of actual experience, he announces this deep fact which fits perfectly with his other great utterance: "Thou, O God, hast made us for thyself, and we are restless [dissatisfied] until we find ourselves in thee."

Too long we have assumed that Adam, the failure, is the type of our lives, that he is the normal man, that to err is human, and that one touch, that is, blight, of nature makes all men kin. What Christ has revealed to us is the fact that we always have higher and diviner possibilities in us. He, the overcomer, and not Adam, is the true type, the normal person, giving us at last the pattern of life which is life indeed.

Which is the real self, then? Surely this higher possible self, this one which we discover in our best moments. The Greeks always held that sin was "missing the mark"—that is what the Greek word for sin means— failure to arrive at, to reach, the real end toward which life aims. Sin is defeat. It is loss of the trail. It is undoing. The sinner has not found himself, he has not come to himself. He has missed the real me. He cannot say, "I am." ...

Democracy was in an earlier period only a political aim; it has now become a deep religious issue. It must be discussed not only in caucuses and conventions, but in churches as well. For a century and a quarter "democracy" has been a great human battle word, and battle words never have very exact definitions. It has all the time been charged with explosive forces, and it has produced a kind of magic spell on men's minds during this long transitional period. But the word democracy has, throughout this time, remained fluid and ill-defined—sometimes expressing the loftiest aspirations and sometimes serving the coarse demagogue in his pursuit of selfish ends.

The goal or aim of the early struggle after democracy was the overthrow of human inequalities. Men were thought of in terms of individual units, and the units were declared to be intrinsically equal. The contention was made that they all had, or ought to have, the same rights and privileges. This equality-note has, too, dominated the social and economic struggles of the last seventy-five years. The focus has been centered upon rights and privileges. Men have been thought of, all along, as individual units, and the goal has been conceived in political and economic terms. Democracy is still supposed, in many quarters, to be an organization of society in which the units have equal political rights. Much of the talk concerning democracy is still in terms of privileges. It is a striving to secure opportunities and chances. The aim is the attainment of a social order in which guarantee is given to every individual that he shall have his full economic and political rights.

I would not, in the least, belittle the importance of these claims, or underestimate the human gains which have been made thus far in the direction of greater equality and larger freedom. But these achievements, however valuable, are not enough. They can only form the base from which to start the drive for a more genuine and adequate type of democracy. At its best this scheme of "equality" is abstract and superficial. Nobody will ever be satisfied with an achievement of flat equality. Persons can never be reduced to homogeneous units. There are individual differences woven into the very fiber of human life, and no type of democracy can ever satisfy men like us until it gets beyond this artificial scheme and learns to deal with the problem in more adequate fashion.

A genuinely Christian democracy, such as the religious soul is after, cannot be conceived in economic terms, nor can it be content with social units of equality or sameness. We want a democracy that is vitally and spiritually conceived, which recognizes and safeguards the irreducible uniqueness of every member of the social whole. This means that we cannot deal with personal life in terms of external behavior. We cannot think of society as an aggregation of units possessing individual rights and privileges. We shall no longer be satisfied to regard persons as beings possessing utilitarian value or made for economic uses. We shall forever transcend the instrumental idea. We shall begin rather with the inalienable fact of spiritual worth as the central feature of the personal life. This would mean that every person, however humble or limited in scope or range, has divine possibilities to be realized; is not a "thing" to be used and exploited, but a spiritual creation to be expanded until its true nature is revealed. The democracy I want will treat every human person as a unique, sacred, and indispensable member of a spiritual whole, a whole which remains imperfect if even one of its "little ones" is missing; and its fundamental axiom will be the liberation and realization of the inner life which is potential in every member of the human race.

On the economic and equality level we never reach the true conception of personal life. Men are thought of as units having desires, needs, and wants to be satisfied. We are, on this basis, aiming to achieve a condition in which the desires, wants, and needs are well met, in which each individual contributes his share of supplies to the common stock of economic values, and receives in turn his equitable amount. I am dealing, on the other hand, with a way of life which begins and ends, not with a material value-concept at all, but rather with a central faith in the intrinsic worth and infinite spiritual possibilities of every person in the social organism—a democracy of spiritual agents.

It is true, no doubt, as Shylock said, that we all have "eyes, hands, organs, dimensions, senses, affections, passions," are "subject to diseases," and "warmed and cooled by summer and winter." "If you prick us we bleed, if you tickle us we laugh, if you poison us we die," and so on. We do surely have wants and needs. We must consider values. We must have food and clothes and houses. We must have some fair share of the earth and its privileges. But that is only the basement and foundation of real living, and we want a democracy that is supremely concerned with the development of personality and with the spiritual organization of society. We shall not make our estimates of persons on a basis of their uses, or on the ground of their behavior as animal beings; we shall live and work, if we are Christ's disciples, in the faith that man is essentially a spiritual being, in a world which is essentially spiritual, and that we are committed to the task of awakening a like faith in others and of helping realize an organic solidarity of persons who practice this faith. Our rule of life would be something like the following: to act everywhere and always as though we knew that we are members of a spiritual community, each one possessed of infinite worth, of irreducible uniqueness, and indispensable to the spiritual unity of the whole—a community that is being continually enlarged by the faith and action of those who now compose it, and so in some measure being formed by our human effort to achieve a divine ideal.

The most important service we can render our fellow men is to awaken in them a real faith in their own spiritual nature and in their own potential energies, and to set them to the task of building the ideal democracy in which personality is treated as sacred and held safe from violation, infringement, or exploitation and, more than that, in which we altogether respect the worth and the divine hopes inherent in our being as men.

From *Spiritual Energies in Daily Life,*
pp. 23–26; 86–91.

-»>«<-

For all practical purposes the contrast between a *person* and a *thing*— between a self and a not-self—is clear enough. The fundamental contrast is the possession of *self-consciousness* by the *person* and the absence of it in the *thing*. Nobody ever was a person without knowing it! The "marks" of personality are (1) power to forecast an end or purpose and to direct action toward it, (2) ability to remember past experiences and to make these memories determine present action, and (3) the power of selecting from among the multitude of objects presented to consciousness that which is of *worth* for the individual. But wherever we discover these "marks" we infer that there is self-consciousness, such as we have ourselves. If we found an individual who could forecast, and remember, and direct action and make selections, and who yet did not know that he knew and did not think that he thought, we should decline to call *him* a person. However important these outer marks or "signs" are, the essential characteristic is a unified self-consciousness.

Now do we know what self-consciousness is? Perfectly well—until we are asked. But a *description* of it is never forthcoming. There is nothing simpler by which we could describe it. It itself is ultimate (at least to us), elementary and unanalyzable. It is involved *in* every description we try to give, it is presupposed *in* every effort to grasp it; it must be used in every attempt to analyze it. In vain should we try to give any hint of its meaning to a creature which lacked it, and our descriptive phrases are exhausted when we have said, "You yourself know what it is, by having it." ...

How out of the mass of subjective states, "common sensations," as they are sometimes called, which mark the twilight period of consciousness, does clear self-consciousness arise? It never *would* arise apart from social influence. It would be as impossible to develop a personality without human society as it would be to convey sound in a vacuum, or to maintain life without atmosphere. The child, if we can imagine him living on without a human environment, would never get beyond his "organic self," his awareness of certain "warm and intimate" feelings which give him the sense of "at home-ness" in the body, and which probably most animals possess in some degree.

He becomes truly self-conscious because he is born an organic member in a social whole. Here he learns the contrast between "I" and "thou," "ego" and "alter," and between "self" and "not-self." Almost from the first, as though it were instinctive, the child reacts toward persons differently than toward anything else in his environment. In the second month of life he distinguishes the touch of his mother in the dark, and even earlier than that he has formed a peculiar way of behaving toward persons. But the most decided advance is made through imitation. There are few life-crises to compare in importance with the "budding" of imitation, which is well under way about the end of the first half-year. Slowly the facts are compelling us to admit that the range and scope of inheritance have been overemphasized. Much which was thought to be transmitted by heredity, we now know is *gained* by imitation both unconscious and conscious. The child is the most imitative being known to man, and this function of imitation is one of his most effective means for the mastery of the world, but its importance in the formation of selfhood has been frequently overlooked. From the beginning the child imitates *persons*. They are the fascinating objects whose movements fix his attention. The mother's smile makes him smile. The sad face and drooping lip are quickly imitated after the seventh month. The bodily actions which result from imitation give the child an experience which enables him in some degree to grasp the inner meaning of the persons before him. He imitates their deeds and in the process discovers a new and richer mental life, which furnishes material for interpreting farther the actions of other persons. In these responses to personal expressions there is to be found the nucleus of real emotions and no less surely the nucleus of volition. From now on, the child is not passive amid the play of forces in his environment. He learns to act by imitating actions, and through his actions he grows conscious of his powers. Thus through these early imitative processes there arises the first germ of conscious distinction between the *self* and the *other*, and there dawns also that sense of power on one's own act, which is, in fact, one of the main miracles of life.

A little later the child begins his slow mastery of human language, through which, as everybody knows, his mental life is unspeakably heightened and his personality defined. Here again imitation is the main function which makes this new achievement possible. The first words are all easy imitative sounds; then when the great secret is caught, progress becomes rapid; but from beginning to end, language is a social creation and could be attained only in society. Without it the gains of the past could never be inherited and without it very slender contributions could be made to the future, and that would mean that without it, conscious life would shrink into exceedingly narrow limits. The selfhood which we know could never be, without this achievement of self-utterance through social relationship. Every step of progress thus far in the path toward personality is made possible by the social environment, and it can be positively asserted that there can be self-consciousness only through social consciousness. . . .

Already it is clear enough that the "self" and the "other" are born together, that personal selfhood is organic with the society in which it is formed, but the moment we touch any of the spiritual qualities—even the simplest—which belong to personality it grows clearer still. You cannot sympathize without "another"—another whose inner life you can appreciate and with whom in some real sense you can share. Take away this power of contrasting a self and another with the power of identifying this self and its other, and you have removed all possibility of sympathy. In like manner every possibility of virtue would vanish. But so, too, would the so-called "egoistic tendencies" vanish. Pride and self-esteem and the rest of the list of egoisms go when the contrast of self and other is removed. If I have self-esteem it is because I read myself off as important in the eyes of others. There is no truth at all in any view which makes egoism more primitive or fundamental than altruism. They are born together and neither can claim the birthright, however much one may get the *blessing* over the other. Take away the *other* and there would never be an *ego*.

The point, then, which these facts out of the life of early childhood establish is this: there is no such thing as bare individuality, nor could society be the result of a "social contract." Individuality does not come first and society next as a product. Society is fundamental, and it is an essential condition for self-consciousness and personality. However contradictory it may sound, it is nevertheless a fact that there could be no self without many selves. Self-consciousness is a possible attainment only in a world where it already exists. *Personality at every stage involves interrelation.* An absolutely isolated self is as contradictory as an outside that has no inside. To be a person, then, means to be a conscious member in a social order. Every effort to discover the meaning of personality carries us straight over into the problems of the social life. . . .

But this social influence must not be pushed too far. It is not creative, and it can never *confer* personality. Only in society can personality be won, but it *must be won. The will to be* is something elemental, and until it asserts itself society can do absolutely nothing to make a person. We have found that the inner life first grows defined through a contrast between self and other. The little imitating subject soon discovers that there are activities and experiences beyond him. He finds himself trying for something not yet *his.* He "projects" something in his fellow which he has not in himself, but which he wants. He now gets the inner feeling of strain and effort which forms the nucleus of volition. In these dim processes the characteristic thing is the contrast between "self" and that which is not *yet* "self"—a central core of experience and a something more to be reached for. The final result of these complex actions and corresponding feelings is the power to contrast a present self with a past self and so, too, with a future self. We thus come into possession of that power which the great poets have made so much account of—the power "to look before and after."

A being who lacked this vision of a potential future self could never develop a personality. A feeling of contrast between this present and a possible future is the first requisite for advance. There must be presented to consciousness a better state of existence than has yet been realized. It must appeal to consciousness, furthermore, as a condition which would satisfy if it were put in the place of the actual present state. When we speak, then, of an ideal we never mean a merely possible future state, but a conceived future state which attracts—something inwardly dynamic. Ideals are not bloodless, ineffectual dreams or fancies which come and go and leave us where we were. Our real ideals are propulsive and directive. They go over into life, and make us what we become. All changes, so far as we know, below the realm of self-consciousness are changes which are caused by a force acting from behind—*a tergo,* i.e., a force which acts through a causal link. Thus the engine draws the train. The moon moves the tide. The wind blows down the tree. The forces of nature develop the plant. None of these things select or choose. They are caused from without. They are the effects of causes which can be described, and they are effects which can be accurately predicted.

When we pass over from causative action from behind to changes produced by ideals in front, we cross one of the widest chasms in the world. It is one of those facts which disproves the easy proverb, "Nature abhors breaks." It seems like a passage from one world-system to another world-system of a totally different sort. In one case the moving cause is an actual, existing situation antecedent to the effect; in the other, the moving cause is an unrealized ideal—something which as yet does not exist in the world of describable things at all. We act to realize something which has induced us to act before it existed in the world of things. The entire spiritual development of *persons* is of this *a fronte* type. Below man everything is moved by coercion. If things are moving toward a goal, they themselves know nothing about it, and it must either be accounted for as an accident or we must admit that from a deeper point of view all causation would be discovered to be toward a goal in front. In this case the end and goal would be present from the first as a directive force in the entire process of evolution.

However that may be—and let the man who soaks his evolutionary terms with purpose pause and reflect—it is certain that in a person the *ought* goes beyond the *is*, the vision of the potential makes the present actual unsatisfying and insufficient. It stands clear, of course, that no power on earth could force an ideal upon us, nor could the empirical, i.e., the describable world, give it to us, for from the nature of the case an ideal transcends everything that is realized. As soon as it is actual it ceases to be an ideal. But on the other hand, ideals are no more to be created out of nothing than a material world is. They are as truly *grounded* in reality as is the simplest actual fact, as the mountain peak is grounded in the common earth. The wish of the beggar produces no horse, the sigh of the old man for the days of his youth puts no vigor into the slow-moving blood, rather it tends to make him older. The directive and dynamic ideal must spring out of what is. It must not be less true, but more true, than any present fact.

We shall now see how the fact of an ideal takes us again into a social order. The ideal, which rules and sways and so develops a person, is never an individual creation; it has had its birth in society. Existing society always gives the direction to one's aims and it always forms the environment in which our true ideals take shape. As well might one try to build a bridge to the milky way as to try to get self-realization by ignoring the already accomplished stages of human endeavor and human striving.

Social customs, family traditions, established law, the ideals of art, literature and religion—all these are indispensable to the formation of a personal ideal. We begin to move out from a point which was once the highest goal of some earlier member of the race. The attainments of individuals and of society give body and filling to our purposes. It is in this rich and fertile seed field that our own ideal sprouts forth and we never get beyond the guidance and direction of what has already been attained. Let him be ever so creative or revolutionary a man must always bear the birth and nurture marks of his age, and the moment he cuts loose from the social whole, through which he has come to be what he is, he tries to fly in a vacuum. It is impossible to be a person without being in the broad sense a member of society, a citizen of a state, for it is through the organized life of the world that one comes to himself. It is among men that one learns what he can be. To withdraw into an isolated life to nourish one's noble dreams is to lose the one chance of finding a real ideal which will construct a life. We know nothing of any ideals which have not sprung out of the human struggles of the past. . . .

It has taken a thousand years to ripen the idea which we accept almost as instinctive. Whole ages have sifted out the literature by which we form our minds. The standards of taste and of right and wrong which we recognize have come through the testings of long centuries. Our institutions are the embodiment of the ideals of former generations, and they safeguard all our ethical ideals to-day. The home is one of man's supreme creations. It is the expression of human endeavor which began thousands of years before the earliest clay tablet was scratched. Without it modern morality and our modern ideals would be impossible. The state with its tremendous system of restraining evil action and of serving us in multiform ways is the outgrowth of the efforts of the entire race since man became a social being. It is no invention, no devised arrangement. It is the culmination of slowly developing ideals. But if we were not organic with this past and with the life of the world these slow gains would be nothing to us. Now they are the very blood of our life.

The Church or, as we should prefer to say, embodied religion in the world, has in the same way become an intimate part of the life we live. These great ideals of life which religion gives us have a racial history, and they come to us with a sanction greater than that of antiquity. We cannot trace them to any human source which is adequate to account for them. Into the atmosphere of religious ideals we are all born. The literature of revelation is put into our hands. The stories of saints and the victories of martyrs are in our nurseries and inspire us from the time thought begins. What we should be without this inheritance of the past, how we should fare if we cut away from the great religious ideals of the race, no one can dimly imagine. The school takes us and drills into us the accumulated gains of man in all the fields of research. The child first beginning to read learns many facts about nature which escaped the penetrating eye of Aristotle, and the boy reading his school astronomy or physiology laughs at the curious views of Plato. Through the school each generation is helped to master the labors of all its predecessors. We start from the heights which they have reached. In his search for truth in any field the seeker is interrelated with the entire past. He is a member of a whole, and without society he finds no truth whatever. There is, then, no self-realization for any individual who is only a bare individual. He can advance toward personality only by being an organic member of a whole.

From *Social Law in the Spiritual World*,
pp. 51–58; 69–73; 75–77.

➺➤✧✦➤

HISTORICALLY and psychologically speaking, religion has been one of the three supreme driving forces in the life of the human race. The quest for food, expanding into the acquisitive desire for possession; passionate interest in the opposite sex, which on its highest level we call "love"; and the adjustment, or joyous response, to supersensuous realities that are believed to be important for the fullness of life—these are the three supreme springs of activity, the three fundamental sources of anxiety and joy in the life of man as we know him here on the earth. The first two of these springs, or "urges" of life, are so obviously instinctive and "natural," so plainly biologically engendered, that they hardly seem to demand any elaborate philosophical interpretation.

This third great *élan* of life, however, has always seemed mysterious. Here is something more than a biological trait; something more than a "natural" urge. Here somehow "the finger of God" seems to be implied. Here if anywhere is where "grace" breaks in. And yet the *function* of religion has frequently been questioned, its validity has been doubted and its origin and genesis have long been in debate. What makes man a religious being, is a question which in ages of enlightenment we are bound to ask, though the answer strangely lags. . . .

Rudolf Otto has put all contemporary religious students into his debt through his extremely important book, *Das Heilige*, which has been admirably translated into English under the title, *The Idea of the Holy*. Otto insists on the primacy of religion. He is convinced that it is utterly unique, *ausserordentlich, sui generis*. It cannot be analyzed into derivative elements, or reduced to anything else. It is not based on a postulate. It is not an *addendum* to human nature. It does not stand in dependence on something else. It does not rest for its right of being upon the sense of ought. It stands in its own sovereign right. It has its own sphere of inward compulsion and it is inexplicable in terms of anything but itself. It breaks into expression as a state of wonder mingled with awe and reverent fear. There is in the religious consciousness a mysterious sense of something more than is visible, a Presence deeply interfused, a *numinous Beyond*, which throws the beholder into a peculiar state of mind unlike any other known state. It is a strange fusion of joy and awe, of thrill and hush. Edmund Spenser coined the phrase, "my dear dread," to express his attitude of joy and at the same time of restraint in the presence of his wife. She was his "dear dread." That feeling of "dear dread," raised to a higher level, expresses this sense of the *numinous*. . . .

Browning's line, "The child feels God a moment," expresses exactly those sudden flashes of awe and wonder, that sense of "something more" above, beyond, within, which makes the unseen seem as real as the things that are seen and touched. There is on such occasions a flooding, overbrimming, palpitating burst of enlargement and joy, but, interfused with it, the awe which comes in the presence of a *mysterium tremendum,* a divine Other, a reality wholly unlike the well-known finite things of ordinary experience. . . .

But, once more, we are left here with only one aspect of religion brought into emphasis. This time it is the "non-rational" aspect which receives especial emphasis, and there *is* unmistakably a non-rationalizable aspect to religion. Religion is rightly declared to be unique, but in this account of it, it forever remains a mysterious experience in the presence of a Something tremendous but unknown; Something awe-inspiring but inexplicable. So far as we are here told anything explicit, it is in terms of *feelings* which stir our being. We are thrown into a moved state. We palpitate, we overbrim. But we *know* no more about the Object which moved us than we did before we were moved. It is and remains a *mysterium tremendum.* We have felt a Presence which disturbs us with joy and wonder. But it remains an unknown Beyond. It is wholly Other. It is not revealed or revealable. It does not raise our human life to a new intelligible significance, since we know no more about what is ultimately real than we did before. The numinous experience does not bring the whole of our life into play. It does not at once inform the mind, stir the emotional deeps in us and fortify the will, as religion in its fullness should do. . . .

Is there any reality within our sphere which transcends time and space, and which thus may be a gateway of approach to a World of supersensuous reality such as we demand for genuine religion? Yes, there is. The knowing self within us by whatever name it is called—mind, soul, self-as-knower,

I myself, or central personality—belongs to a different order from that of observed phenomena. Plato made the point very clear in his day, and his greatest disciples have enlarged upon it, that the mind, the soul, what he called the *nous* in us, which organizes the facts of experience, the *data* of experience, and interprets them by means of universal and permanent forms of thought cannot itself at the same time be *one of the facts to be experienced*. The *nous* in us must have had its origin in, and must belong to, a higher World Order, the World of *Nous*—Spirit. . . .

One of our most common blunders is that of treating the mind as though it were only a spectator. There is, however, in beings of our type no real mind that is merely a spectator-mind—no mind that merely "receives" and "observes" presented facts. Every mind which deserves that name unifies, organizes and *interprets* everything that is presented to it. There is, therefore, something presupposed in the nature of mind which did not come from outside nor arise out of change and process. Change and process are facts *for it*, not the ground of its being. "Time and space" which are the basis of change and process are forms of the mind through which it arranges its world of experience in place and in succession. Every attempt to derive space and time *from* experience tacitly already presupposes consciousness of space and time. The little child who asked, "Mummie, where's yesterday gone and what's tomorrow doing now?" already was feeling the necessity for a transcendental deduction of time. Whatever else, and whatever more, space and time may be, they *must* be original forms, or potential capacities, of the mind itself.

It is no less true that the necessity for causal relation between phenomena is never a perceived fact, but even if it were a perceived fact, no number of instances of the perception of a causal connection would enable us to leap to the conclusion that every event *must* have a cause. *Must*, wherever it emerges, goes beyond any possible experience of sense. The mind that organizes facts with the coercion of *must* has added something to the mere bare "facts" themselves.

There is, furthermore, a unity to the knowing mind, as I have already said, which no observed facts in the outside world can fully account for. There is nothing like it in the world of relativity, and there is nothing outside itself which can explain it. The kind of mind which is essential for what we mean by knowledge, by truth, the mind which imposes its universal and necessary forms upon all that it knows, has no counterpart anywhere in the world of process and relativity. It is a unique reality. It belongs to a different order.

This unique mind, which we have been considering, not only organizes the facts of experience under universal forms and imposes the aspect of *must* upon what is known, but it goes beyond everything which sense reports as given fact, and anticipates by imaginative forecast what is to be, but is not yet. The mind may by a flash of insight, by a stroke of genius, announce a law of nature which in its operation reaches far beyond all observed facts and which determines in advance of further perception whole vast areas of facts and events in regions not yet explored. Something similar is true in the realm of ideal goodness, and, again, in the realm of creative art. Ethical insight may enable a person to anticipate a form and type of goodness that never has actually been before, but now is made real in this actual world, through this man's creative ideal. So, too, the synoptic mind of an artist may produce a beautiful creation which transcends in unity and harmony any object that has previously existed in the world of things. . . .

What I am leading up to is the point that minds of this type—and we all possess some of this organizing and creative capacity—go beyond *what is*, surmise *the more yet*, transcend *the given*, have the inward power to see the invisible and to *live* in correspondence with a Beyond which is absolutely real. Beings of that scope and range are something more than "forked radishes with heads fantastically carved," or "unfeathered bipeds with broad flat tails." They partake of another order, another level of reality to that of the biological series. They are spiritual beings. They belong in a noumenal order and have correspondence with an Over-world, in spite of the fact that they have visible bodies with avoirdupois weight, that they consume food and often do foolish things.

Not only do these minds of ours expand life in ideal directions and go beyond what is, but at their best these ideals of ours correlate and correspond with some sort of objective reality. They advance truth. They set forward the march of goodness. Through coöperation with God they build a new stage of the Kingdom of God in the world. We are in that respect not dreamers; we are actual builders. We exercise a dominion over events. We carry the ball on toward the goal. Something not ourselves co-works with us, as the currents of the ocean co-work with the mariner who is traveling in their direction. Something more than our finite will pushes behind our effort. Something large and luminous backs our deeds. When we are on right lines of advance doors open before us. We find ourselves in coöperative union with a larger Mind and a wiser Will. We have sound reason to believe that what is highest in us is deepest in the nature of things. We become organs of a spiritual kingdom and stand in vital relation to an Eternal Mind and Heart and Will with whom we coöperate.

There is something in us and of us that did not originate in the world of matter, in the time-space order, in the phenomenal process. We are more than curious bits of the earth's crust, more than biological exhibits. We have a spiritual lineage. We may have collateral connections with flat-nosed baboons, but at the same time we are of direct noumenal origin. We belong to an Over-world of a high order. We carry in the form and structure of our inner selves the mark and badge of linkage and kinship with a realm which can best be called Eternal, since it is real in its own essential being and of the same Nature as God who is the centre of its life and of ours.

Men in all ages, ever since there were men, have felt this Beyond within themselves. They have traveled out beyond the frontiers of the seen, and have lived in mutual correspondence with the More that is akin to themselves. Saints and prophets and supreme revealers of the race have interpreted for the others vividly and vitally the splendor of their unique insights and contacts. But first, last and all the time, religion has lived and flourished because man in his inner deeps is in mutual and reciprocal correspondence with eternal reality, and is in some measure the organ of it. We are religious beings because we partake or may partake of this higher Nature and share by our inmost form of being in a realm that is *eternally real*. At one apex point within ourselves we break through the world of change and process and *belong* to another Order which may become our fatherland and home. Religion at its best is the discovery of home and fatherland.

From *The Testimony of the Soul,*
pp. 50–51; 55–59; 63–70.

→»)«←

NOBODY knows how the kindling flame of life and power leaps from one life to another. What is the magic quality in a person which instantly awakens faith? You listen to a hundred persons unmoved and unchanged: you hear a few quiet words from the man with the kindling torch and you suddenly discover what life means to you forever more, and you become forthwith another man—carrying perhaps your own torch.

I heard Phillips Brooks preach twice in my youth and I knew instantly that the man I had been waiting for had come. I knew almost nothing about him in advance—before I heard him. After I had heard him I felt the kindling power of his mind on my mind and a new faith was born in me in answer to the great faith that possessed him. I have always put him in the list of supremely great persons in our Western world, great by the sheer power of personality, and for me, at least, he stands as the greatest Christian preacher America has yet produced.

One of his favorite texts was: "The spirit of man is the candle of the Lord."

It is a remarkable phrase embedded in that book of practical wisdom and everyday common sense, the Book of Proverbs. This phrase is a spiritual fragment of human experience of a deeper level than most of the words of the Book in which it is found. It is like a piece of floating star-dust, caught and preserved in the amber of this Book of practical sayings. Only the profoundest of prophetic souls could have discovered this truth and have uttered it with such extraordinary simplicity.

It means that there is something in man's inmost being that can be kindled and struck into flame by God and as we feed the flame with our lives we can become revealing places for God, a flame of God's life. If it is true, as I believe it is, it is one of the greatest words that was ever spoken. It puts the basis of religion at the center of man's life where it belongs. Religion in this view is not an addendum to life, not something added on by a remedial scheme to a spiritually barren and bankrupt being. Religion is not a foreign bestowal; it is a divine spring and capacity which belongs to our being as men. Religion is just overbrimming, abounding life. *My cup runs over.*

The process of salvation is thus not away from normality; it is, rather, the attainment of complete normal spiritual health. Salvation, as Phillips Brooks used to declare it, *is health.* I quote his words: "The cool, calm vigor of the normal human life; the making of the man to be himself; the calling up out of the depth of his being and the filling with vitality of that self which is truly he—*that* is salvation."

The task of religion is not like that of laboriously endeavoring to teach an elephant to fly; it is rather the discovery of the potential capacities for flight in a being that was framed for the upper air. There is somewhere in one of Phillips Brooks' sermons a vivid description of the birth of a waterspout at sea, which I give in my own words. Far away in the distance the sailor sees a dark cloud hover over the sea. Suddenly the water becomes strangely disturbed and tremulous. The cloud comes down closer and the water rises to meet it. Suddenly cloud and sea join in one indivisible whirling movement and together sweep irresistibly onward. It is impossible to sunder cloud and sea or to say where cloud ends and sea begins. It is so with divinity and humanity, the above and the below. Or it is like the meeting-place of the river and the ocean. The river runs far out into the ocean and again, the tides of the ocean flood back into the river and no fixed line of division can be drawn.

This is a lofty type of Christian humanism, quite unlike the prevailing humanism of our time. It is possible to read human life at many different levels. We can read it up or we can read it down. We have been passing through a period of stark naturalism, and the humanism that has emerged from this naturalism is windowless above. It has no Pisgah heights, no "soul's east window of divine surprise."

The humanism of this text believes in man, not because he has leaped a tiny bit on ahead of the beasts from which he has sprung, but because something new and unique has come to birth, because eternity is set in his heart, because he is a being of love and wonder, because he is essentially self-transcendent, finite-infinite, because there is a beyond within him, because he is a potential child of God and may become a spiritual flame of the eternal light, "and it doth not yet appear what we shall be."

Aristotle said that the true nature of any being is what it can become. The true humanism must, on the same count, be read not in terms of origin and beginnings, but rather in terms of possibility and goal. We are the builders of the Kingdom of God, not merely self-satisfied denizens of a secular society. We must level up and not be disturbed too much by the down-levellers. . . .

Christ and not Adam is the head of the race. Christ is the new Adam, the new creation, the type and norm of a new humanity, the complete expression of what man in his potential spiritual nature implies and suggests. When the full nature of human possibility is revealed in a completely fulfilled life, it proves to be a perfect organ of the life and love and character of God. We have this possibility brought to fullness in one Life and there we see the light of the knowledge of the glory of God in the face of Jesus Christ.

In Christ we may say that we see what life in its full range of diviner possibilities really *means*. Here at the headwaters of our faith we find one Life in which divinity and humanity are unsundered, one Life which reveals equally the nature of God and the possibilities of man. We may say with an early Christian writer that the eternal Christ is forever being born anew in the hearts of those who believe, and just as certainly we may say that the spirit of man is continually proving to be "a candle of the Lord."

From *The Luminous Trail,*
pp. 147–151.

->>><<<-

It is obvious now that *thinking* is a very small part of our mental life. Important as thinking is, it would be very futile business if that were *all* we could do. Our main driving energies are deeper. They are mysterious *urges*—impulses, instincts, emotions, sentiments, loyalties, ideals, and many other inarticulate and indescribable forward pushes. "Thinking" is one of those forces, but who does not know what it means to have some unconquered "urge" sweep up from below and defeat his carefully thought-out purpose? There has been in our recent time a great cult of the unconscious, the submerged. It has been exploited somewhat as "oil" has been. The so-called "new psychologists" have bored their wells down into these underlying strata of the self. They have discovered many ways of tapping the unconscious and they believe they have worked a great revolution in the handling of the explosive driving-stuff within us.

I do not wish to underestimate the value of this pioneer work beneath the surface of the inner life. I only want here to insist that there still remains a vast mystery of darkness which most of the boring methods of the experiments have failed to light up. The emphasis has been laid upon the primitive driving forces that lie deep down in us, instinctive urges and blind fear complexes. The "new psychologists" have set going a new wave of sex passion and they have given the impression that a human being is in the main a cyclonic center of erotic forces. The first gush of force that spurts up when they bore down into the lower strata is a dark, primitive urge of passion, dangerously explosive but which civilization has tried to control and make to explode in minute forms and by harmless methods!

What they have not discovered, but what is still there to be discovered, is a wholly different kind of submerged energy. Here in the inner deeps of man, down below his luminous peaks and underlying all his thinking, are upward and forward urges which link him up with the eternal Spirit and which point beyond his imperfect present self to a nobler man who is to be, in the riper times which lie before us. We are at least as much allied with God as we are with the beast; and there is just as good interior evidence for bursts of divine life within us as there is for primitive explosive passions. The wind, the lightning and the earthquake—the titanic forces—are perhaps more obvious than the still small voice. The explorers, too, have been interested in these racial thrusts and they could turn their discoveries in this direction into quicker returns, but some day the balance will be restored, the deeps below these deeps will be found, and there in the darkness and quiet we shall come upon impressive and convincing proof of Him, who dwells both in the darkness and in the light.

From *The New Quest,*
pp. 31–33.

->>><<<-

WHEN we go back to the headwaters of our faith we do not find there a new theological creed. We do not meet there the establishment of a new ecclesiastical institution. We do not discover the formation of a new ritual system for all time. What we find at the headwaters of the mighty stream is a unique type of person. We date our calendar from His birth, and He more than anybody else that has ever lived has shaped the ideals of life in the western world, so far as we have ideals, and to the same extent He has formed for us our basic conceptions of the nature and character of God. Most of us think of God in terms of "the God and Father of Jesus Christ." One of his greatest early followers, a man who claimed that he had seen with his eyes, and heard with his ears, and his hands had touched this unique person, declared that "God is love," and that love originates from God. That is, I think, the heart and substance of the new revelation here at the head-waters. We shall need to consider later what we are to mean by love, for it is a word that needs a cleansing bath, but I want to stop first and consider the type of person we find when we go back to the beginnings, for after all this person Himself *is* the revelation. If we saw Him vividly and truly we should all believe in God. You cannot get love revealed in the *abstract*. One does not fall in love as a result of definitions. You are not swept with a contagion of love by hearing about the psychology of it. Love *exists* only where it is incarnated in a person, where it lives and moves and is expressed. Love, to be love, must be revealed in a person, who exhibits it, and awakens it, and *is* love.

There are always persons who are afraid of losing the *divinity* of Christ, but the much greater danger all down through the history of Christianity has been the tendency to lose His humanity. He has been thought of again and again as a foreign visitant from another realm, who never truly "belonged" here in our sphere. He was, according to this view, merely acting a human part on a human stage, but all the time He was a heavenly guest from yonder, of another world—not one of us in any true sense. That is not merely a "heresy" of past ages, it is a very common "heresy" now.

That was almost bound to be so, with the prevailing conception of human nature. Man—and I am sorry to say, woman, too—was thought of as a total ruin, sometimes majestic, but none the less a ruin. Human nature, from the cradle to the grave, was thought of as corrupt, fallen, and incapable of becoming an organ of spiritual reality, or of intrinsic goodness. There was, and is, in this type of thought, a sharp *dualism* between the divine and the human. The former belonged to the heavenly realm, which was believed to be above the sky, and the latter, the human, was of the earth, and only by a miracle could the two realms have any vital intercourse. There was nothing in common between them. The divine was up there; the human was down here, and never the twain could meet. The spiritual and the natural, the divine and the human, were forever sundered with a great gulf between. As long as that theory of human nature prevailed—and it still prevails with many persons—there could be no genuine incarnation of the divine conceived of without a stupendous miracle, of the type which would mean that Christ was not truly human.

But the unmistakable fact of the Gospels is that Christ always acted as though He were truly human; He always talked as though He were; He was tempted as though He were. He grew in stature and wisdom; He was hungry and tired as though He were human; He rejoiced and He wept with those that rejoiced and wept; He suffered real pain and He died a real death. He ate His food and nourished His body as other persons did. The persons who knew Him best never had any doubt about His humanity. I think we must admit and hold tenaciously to the fact that He was genuinely human. He could not understand us altogether if He were not. And that means, and it is a tremendous fact, that the divine can be revealed in and through the human, when the human is of a unique type, as it was in Christ—a "mutation" from the usual run of persons—for there is not the least ground for doubt that Christ was divine, that He was and is a revelation of God. The greatest single fact of history is the breaking in of the Life of God through this unique Life. Here at last the Love of God found complete expression.

St. John declares (XIII, 3) that Christ came from God and knew that He was going to God. I have no doubt about that. Here in that life God was unmistakably present. Every glimpse we get of Christ in our Gospels makes the point clear that He felt that in a unique sense He belonged to a divine order. He stemmed as truly from God as from man. The "auditions" which He heard on high occasions, "Thou art my beloved Son," only confirmed His own consciousness. "He who sent me" is used in the four Gospels forty-four times. If we are ever to see and know what God is like in nature and character, we see and know that likeness in this life. The underlying Christian faith that *God is Spirit* makes it easily possible to think of Christ as the revelation of God in life and history. There are not two worlds—a divine one far away, and an undivine one down here where we live. God is Spirit and dwells in His world. He has in all ages stirred men's hearts with love and desire. He has quickened aspiration and awakened ideals. He has, stage after stage, prepared the way for higher and holier living. He has been working in and through the unfolding events of history and at length in Christ He has found a perfect organ of revelation—the revealing of His life, His character and His will. All true religion is divine-human. Something of God comes into our world with every child that is born. There is here with the newborn child a divine spark, a light within, something potential, that raises the child out of the animal class, and introduces a unique spiritual element. Much has come no doubt from the two human parents, but something has come into time out of eternity with the newborn child. Christ had this God-man endowment in a perfect degree, and His life unfolded without the set-backs of sin to which our usual human nature is prone. The

Spirit element in Him triumphed, though not without struggle, over the body tendencies.

I maintain, therefore—and it seems to me tremendously important—that Christ is as truly a revelation of *man* as He is a revelation of God. We see at last in Him what man was meant to be. That means that in the light of His life we ought to reinterpret—as we usually have not done—the divine possibilities of the human nature we bear. We have seen God revealed in Christ. I wish now that we might learn to see the divine possibilities of *man* revealed in Christ. He was "a new Adam," as St. Paul puts it, with a stroke of genius—"the first born among many brethren" (Rom. VIII, 29). Nobody has ever said anything bolder than that. He was the first born of a new order of humanity, and nobody really and truly knows *man* until he has seen humanity reinterpreted in Christ. We have thought of man as a "ruin" and we have seen specimens of the race that plainly revealed the marks of ruin. But Christ is the first born of a new order of humanity. What we *see* in the everyday man makes us very solemn, but our hope is in the finished product that is forecast in this new type. I agree with Bishop Barnes of Birmingham that "man is rising, slowly with many set-backs; a great future stretches before him. He is an unfinished product, slowly growing to full stature, for he is born for eternity."

From *A Call to What Is Vital,*
pp. 105–110.

❯❯❯ IV ❮❮❮

How Explain Conscience?

IV

THE most august thing in us is that creative center of our being, that autonomous citadel of personality, where we form for ourselves ideals of beauty, of truth, and of goodness by which we live. This power to extend life in ideal fashion is the elemental moral fact of personal life. These ideals which shape our life are manifestly things which cannot be "found" anywhere in our world of sense experience. They are not on land or sea. We live, and, when the call for it comes, we joyously *die* for things which our eyes have never seen in this world of molecular currents, for things which are not here in the world of space, but which are not on that account any less *real*. We create, by some higher drive of spirit, visions of *a world that ought to be* and these visions make us forever dissatisfied with *the world that is,* and it is through these visions that we reshape and reconstruct the world which is being made. The elemental spiritual core in us, which we call conscience, can have come from nowhere but from a deeper spiritual universe with which we have relations. It cannot be traced to any physical origin. It cannot be reduced to any biological function. It cannot be explained in utilitarian terms. It is an august and authoritative loyalty of soul to a Good that transcends all goods and which will not allow us to substitute prudence for intrinsic goodness. This inner imperative overarches our moral life, and it rationally presupposes a spiritual universe with which we are allied.

From *The Inner Life,*
pp. 150–151.

–»»«««–

Must is one of the easiest verbs in the English language to conjugate. It is gloriously defective, with its one mood and one tense. But if ever a word weighed a ton it is this same little defective verb. We meet it at all ages and on all levels of life, and it holds us like a tested line of trench.

We very early discover that all mathematical facts not only are what they are but that they *must* be so. When we have once learned the multiplication table, we come to realize that it is good not only for the local latitude and

73

longitude where we happen to live, but it holds for all lands and for all possible worlds. When we once find that the shortest distance between two points is a straight line we instantly see that it must be so everywhere and that if angels wish to take the shortest way home, they must fly in straight lines. When we prove that the sum of the angles in a triangle is equal to two right angles, we see that it must always and everywhere be so—even in a triangle with its apex at Arcturus and its base across the earth's orbit around the sun. All our sciences write *must* into all their laws, for a law is not a law until it carries *must* into all the facts with which it deals. And yet no person ever sees this fact of "must be so" with his eyes nor can he find it with any one of his senses. The only thing we can find with our senses is what actually happens, what is there now. We can never perceive what *must* happen. Senses can deal only with facts, only with *is,* not with *must be. Must* belongs in a deeper, invisible world where mind works and not eyes. For ages men wondered what held the earth up in space. They always looked for some visible support. It was a giant like Atlas who held it on his back, or it was a huge tortoise, or it was an elephant standing on another elephant, with elephants all the way down! But it turns out that nothing visible or tangible is there. The discoverers of the North and South poles found no real "poles" that ran into grooves on which the earth spun round. There was nothing to see. The cable which holds the earth in space and swings it on its mighty annual curve is invisible to all eyes and yet it holds irresistibly, for the *must* of a universal law is woven into it, and the mind can find it though the eyes cannot.

There is another, and a higher, kind of *must* which holds men as that force of gravitation holds worlds. It was one of the most august events of modern history when a man in the light of his own conscience challenged the councils and traditions of the Church, refused to alter the truth which his soul saw, and boldly declared, "Here I stand, I cannot do otherwise." This is a strange thing, this inner "must," this adamantine "I cannot do otherwise." It reveals a new kind of gravitation toward a new kind of center, and it implies the existence of another sort of invisible universe in which we live. It often carries a person straight against his wishes, into hard conflict with his inclinations, and it may take him up to that perilous edge where life itself is put at hazard.

> Though love repine and reason chafe,
> I heard a voice *without reply;*
> 'Tis man's perdition to be safe
> When for the truth he ought to die.

Some persons do not feel this irresistible pull as powerfully as others do, but probably nobody, who can be called a person, altogether escapes it. A little boy, in the first stages of collision between instinct and duty, said naïvely to his mother: "I've got something inside me I can't do what I want to with!" This is exactly the truth about it. It holds, it says must, like the other invisible realities that build the universe.

Different individuals feel this inner pull in different ways. They read off their call to duty in different terms. Their *must* confronts them in unique fashion, but whenever it comes and however it comes, it is august and moving. We no doubt mix some of our cruder self in it and perhaps we color it with the hue of our human habits, but at its truest and its best, it is the most glorious thing in our structure and it closely allies us to a Higher than ourselves.

> So nigh is grandeur to our dust,
>   So near is God to man,
> When duty whispers low, "Thou must,"
>   The youth replies, "I can."

From *The World Within,*
pp. 71–75.

-»>«<-

I PROPOSE to deal, all too briefly, with that strange, inevitable, irrepressible "something inside us" which, with a voice of authority, rules over our instincts and propensities. Whatever else it may be, it is something "we cannot do what we want to with." Its very owner and possessor cannot suppress it, cannot evade it, cannot brush it aside, cannot bribe it, cannot eliminate it. *It is not an instinct,* for an instinct is a specific way of reacting to a specific external situation, while *conscience is capable of the same endless variations of response that mark our appreciation of beauty;* and it has no fixed set of reactions, determined by some mechanism in the physical structure. It is not a "special sense," for a sense must have a definite "end-organ" in the body, which is aroused by a specific stimulus and provided with a specific brain center in the cerebral cortex.

Conscience has been thought of as "an oracle in the breast," and therefore as something alien to ourselves as finite persons. But, on the other hand, it obviously tallies with the rest of our experience. It is not something apart or independent or unattached. It is embedded in our actual, concrete life. It harmonizes and is consistent with our everyday human experience. It does not stand aloof above our life, as the rainbow stands above the onward flood of water at Niagara; it is rather a binding, organizing principle which makes life stable and coherent. It attaches to the original capacity of self-consciousness, the capacity to create ideals, to look before and after, to outspan and overarch its own states and processes, and to review and judge, value and revise its own operations. Conscience is not an affair of some isolated part of us, the function of some fragment of our being. It appears rather to belong to our entire self and to underlie all the activities that are essential to personality. It is the whole integral self, becoming awake and active whenever the deepest issues of life are put in jeopardy or are at stake. It is the affirmation of our innermost character, the arousal in us of those ideal values which constitute our proper self. We move along unconcerned and unconscious until our central aspirations are threatened, or until the innermost ideals of our soul are challenged, or until the end or aim that forms the submerged ground-swell of our life is exposed to danger. Until the crisis came, we may have lived almost unaware of these deep-lying currents of our being. We could not have answered perhaps easily, quickly and without halting, if some one had challenged us with the query, what do you want? what does life mean? what, after all, is your aim? It had not been thought through or explicitly envisaged. But now a situation emerges which calls for decision and action, and suddenly we see revealed the fact that our choice between the alternatives will settle irrevocably the kind of person we are to be. That inarticulate ideal which all our previous life had been weaving, now becomes alive and vocal. The ayes and noes are called for, and we vote to express and at the same time to guard and preserve what constitutes the permanent trend of our character as a person. *That which we are*, the whole of ourself, asserts itself and stands for its sacred rights of being. Conscience is thus the inner man's recognition of what is essential for the preservation and development of that which constitutes his real life. Not to have it would mean not to have consciousness of onward direction, or of any values to preserve, or of any worth to life, or of any integrity to maintain. Whatever we may finally conclude about the nature of conscience we shall not be able to detach it from the soul's central ideal. It is at least the revelation of the kind of person we propose to be....

It does not seem possible for any extension of our scientific knowledge to reduce conscience to a naturalistic explanation. Its power over us cannot be explained on the ground that it aids survival. The distinction of right and wrong does not rest in the ultimate analysis upon prudence, foresight, or any consideration of utilitarian results, in fact upon any extraneous or self-advantageous considerations. It cannot be reduced to a fine calculation of results. It cannot be traced to an emotion, or to an instinct, which aided survival, or to a racial habit or custom. We do not catch the secret of conscience by any study of the slow results of restraint or the fear of punishment, here or hereafter. The difficulty about the whole situation is that fear of consequences is not morality—it is fear of consequences!

It proves to be impossible to explain the higher, the essential features of conscience by a reference either to biological history or to the influence of social environment. We have in the sublime obligation of duty a fact of the most momentous significance. It attaches not to an accident of biological survival. It is rooted in the fundamental nature of self-consciousness. It is bound up with the unique fact that man is *man* and not animal. It has the same standing and the same sure ground of validity that *truth* has in the sphere of knowledge. When we speak of truth we always mean something wholly different from "opinion." Truth rises above the variations of sense reports and the accidents and contingent happenings. It voices something as universal, permanent, unalterable, irreversible, eternal, and absolute. It gives us contingent items of experience, but here at length they are organized through a universal, rational principle which abides and holds firm through all the welter of change and variation. Its basis, the basis of truth, is not to be found somewhere outside in the stream of events, it is to be found inside, *in the nature of the mind that knows.*

Archbishop Temple has finely expressed this fundamental distinction which belongs to our nature as rational spiritual beings. He says: "However far our doubts may go, they cannot root up from within us, without our own consent (nor, I would add, even with it), the power which claims to guide our lives with supreme authority. They cannot obliterate from within us the sense of right and wrong, *and of everlasting difference between them.* They cannot silence, unless we join in silencing, the voice that bids us believe that, in spite of all that can be said, seen, or felt, the law of right is the eternal foundation on which all things are built. By this a man may yet live if he has nothing else to live by, and God will assuredly give him more in His own good time."

The central meaning of *ought,* and the categorical distinction of right and wrong, cannot be stated in terms of anything else, or identified with any other content of consciousness but themselves. We have here come upon something *sui generis,* like the appreciation of beauty, or the truth of mathematics. One either has the trait or does not have it, but if a man is not elementally susceptible to the meaning of *ought,* he cannot be taught morality—any more than he could be taught mathematics, if he had no perception of the special distinction of "up and down," or "out and in." It is quite likely—in fact it is only too obvious—that there are men and women who are almost neutral when confronted with moral issues. They are not so much immoral as unmoral. They hardly know what one means when one talks of categorical imperatives and the overwhelming sense of ought or ought not. They have not been there. They see as those do who have no eyes. Plotinus has well said: "As it is not for those to speak of the beauties of the material world who have never seen them or known them—men born blind, for instance—so must those be silent about the beauty of noble conduct and knowledge who have never cared for such things; nor may those tell of the splendor of virtue who have never known the face of justice and temperance, beautiful beyond the beauty of the morning and evening star."

Every analysis of conscience reveals an element in it which cannot be explained by anything else, any more than the taste of sugar, or the smell of a rose, or the perception of redness can be explained in terms of anything else. There is an elemental aspect which could not be derived or acquired. The categorical distinction of right and wrong which conscience voices may possibly aid survival but in any case it does not get its lofty place in human life on the ground of its survival value. Its origin in us appears to be due to the fundamental fact that a person is an ideal-forming being. He always extends his world in ideal directions. A person is never confined to the world of "things as they are." He is never limited to objects that are given in experience. He always transcends and sees beyond the facts and items which his senses present. This creative, idealizing tendency is one of the most unique and original traits in us, one of the deepest facts of personality as well as one of the most mysterious. Our driving forces are to be found in our instincts and emotions, but our ideals are our directive powers. They organize the instincts and emotions; they raise and transform them so that they are no longer instincts in the blind and primitive sense. They cease also now to be mainly egoistic and self-seeking, and yet their energy and effectiveness are greatly heightened as they come to be expanded and transformed through ideals.

Our moral grandeur springs from this capacity of ours to live beyond and to outrun anything which the world of experience gives us, and with this idealizing capacity—the power to look before and after—is linked an inevitable sense of obligation to act in conformity with what the soul sees *ought* to be. It is a normal feature of personality to live not only in reference to considerations of prudence and foresight, but also to live in reference to an ideal spectator, to do right even when the world is not looking on or viewing the deed. We assert by an irresistible compulsion the incomparable worth of our personal ideals, and the moral insights which attach to them. We build on ahead of experience and fashion the inner world that ought to be, and this vision makes us dissatisfied with anything that comes short of our ideal good. Some persons no doubt possess this power of transcending the actual more strongly than do others. The reference to an ideal spectator is weak in some and powerful in others. The appeal from what is here and now to that which ought to be does not operate alike in all bosoms.

Plato, with his symbol of Gyges' ring, has expressed the view that the "many" do right because they fear consequences. This ring enabled the possessor of it to become invisible at will. He could always escape notice, and could therefore pursue his pleasures and achieve his ends without being observed or caught. Could anybody be found who might own this extraordinary ring with perfect moral safety? Are there persons who would take no advantages of the privileges of its magic? Plato knows at least one such person. He has drawn the portrait of a moral genius whose supreme prayer was for inward beauty, and who took his hard course of action, not out of fear of any kind of consequences but in order to conform with a heavenly pattern in his soul.

It is probably true that conscience rises to its august height only in persons who may be called spiritual geniuses. We do not estimate the significance of music by the performance on the Indian tom-tom. We find it revealed in Mozart or some other outstanding creator. We do not judge the scope of art by the Maori carvings on a walrus' tusk. We see it at its full glory in the Sistine Madonna or in Michel Angelo's Moses. So, too, we shall never apprehend the nature of conscience if we study it only as an anthropological emotion. We see what it means and we discover its full implications in persons of marked moral profundity.

There is an underived ethical core in us, or at least in some of us, which gives us a fixity of soul for that which ought to be. This elemental basis of our conscience cannot be traced to any physical origin, it cannot be reduced to a biological function, it cannot be explained in utilitarian terms. It attaches to our deepest spiritual being—our inalienable tendency to form ideals and to feel the imperative call of what ought to be. Its development can be traced; its origin cannot be traced. The elemental distinction of right and wrong is presupposed in every appreciation of moral quality, just as every judgment of beauty presupposes an appreciation of beauty. The structural distinction of right and wrong is an endowment of reason which cannot be identified with anything else or traced to any "naturalistic" origin. It is that basic foundation of the soul which the mystics called "synteresis," or junction of the soul with God. It is what Kant calls the categorical imperative, or the soul's fundamental assertion of a distinction between right and wrong. It is so essential to a rational being that in denying it you tacitly affirm it, and when it appeared the race first began to be human—man emerged, "Adam" was born!

Every little creature in the myriad hosts of life's immense output is different in some respect from every other. Every tiny being that gets born has some slight mark of uniqueness. This fact—a fact which we do not explain—is what makes life a varying affair. Every germ in "the enormous fecundity of nature" has its own irreducible peculiarity. Somewhere, sometime, in the great stream there came a being that was unique in this, that he did not live merely by fact and act for the sake of consequences, but he felt the moral worth of certain acts and could recognize an "ought." *He judged his conduct by an ideal which outran his deed.* There have been many crises in the history of evolution—moments when something qualitatively new appeared, and of which no exhaustive psychological explanation can be given. *Mutations* are not only unpredictable, but they are inexplicable in terms of environment. The birth of self-consciousness is one of these crises. The appreciation of beauty is another. The birth of religion, the soul's consciousness of a great Companion, is another. The appearance of conscience, the distinction of moral right and wrong—is another. It is as original and irreducible as the consciousness of up and down or of before and after. In a word, it is as underived from anything else as the perception of time and space is.

All knowledge of concrete times and spaces implies a susceptibility to time and space already in the capacity of the mind that perceives. Without an underived distinction of "before and after" I could never learn about times, and without the capacity for "within" and "without," and "up" and "down," I could never get an idea of particular spaces. The idea of space is presupposed in all experiences of spaces. The mind of a rational being comes already equipped with these essential conditions of knowledge—these capacities for experience—which are filled with content by actual experience. So, too, a person must be susceptible to the meaning of "ought" before ever he can learn from experience what is right and wrong in a given concrete situation. The capacity for duty is, thus, native and original, a condition of all moral appreciation; our judgment upon the particular definite things that are right and wrong is always colored by experience; that is to say, the formation of our actual standards, the creation of our concrete conscience, is an immense social process, as I shall endeavour to show. If this view is correct, we discover why conscience is so imperative. It is an irreducible fact of reason itself, using reason in the broad sense which has become familiar since Kant. It cannot be eliminated or destroyed without abolishing rationality itself. It is bound up with the very nature of reason, as is our absolute certainty of mathematical truth, or as is the inevitable idea that an effect must have a cause. Deny it, ignore it, disobey it, transgress it; it still confronts one as unsuppressed and absolute as ever. . . .

Each person thus forms his own moral ideal—the ground swell of his own inward voice of what is right for him in the social environment into which he is born. He is, from his earliest days, a member of the society already moralized, a fellow citizen of a state in which morality is more or less objectified and made visible. He must form his own moral ideals by means of the moral attainments of the race, and these ideals will always have the mark and brand of a temporal epoch, and there will always be a local coloring upon them. But he may, as has been said, and in fact he should, transcend the common level of his time, and push the moral goal beyond any previous attainments, though it must be along lines already potential; and his ideal, his attainments, must be tried out in the siftings and testings of social history.

Conscience, as we have seen, in its loftiest stage, is no longer negative. It affirms a unique personal life. It has a positive aspect; it is the knowledge of a higher will than that of our momentary, isolated self. *It is the voice of our ideal self, our complete self, our real self, laying its call upon the will.* This voice, this call, comes up out of the deep, for the ideal which a man has and by which he shapes his life is, as I have said, subconscious rather than explicit and thought out. But it is not something foreign to the man himself, it is not something external to him, it is not some one particular instinct among other instincts. It is the complete self voicing its ideals and exerting its sway over passion and impulse and momentary self and courses of action which fall below our vision. It forms itself slowly under education and environment as the character forms, and it is unique and august because it is the deepest self rising into consciousness and asserting itself. It is the true self vocal.

If this is a sound view, we see that the moral standard is always being made—never final. It shows, too, why we do not all have the same conscience. There will always be the personal element present, for each man's ideal has formed under particular circumstances, has aspects that are unique, and has been slowly shaped by experience. But conscience is more than subjective opinion or individual caprice. A person's conscience to be sound must have imbibed the spirit of the social group, past and present, living and dead, in which it was formed; and if in any particular it is unique or peculiar it should be by transcending the realized morality of the group on lines already forecast by past experience.

Though we cannot make the immense assertion that conscience is absolutely infallible and a precise guide under any and every circumstance of life, it is nevertheless the surest moral authority within our reach—a voice to be implicitly obeyed in the crisis of an action. It is our highest guide. No command on earth can take precedence of it. Nothing more autonomous or more worthy of obedience can be discovered. But, even so, *it must not be allowed to crystallize or to become a static, habitual moral form.* The Pharisee, the inquisitor and the bigot are appalling illustrations of the dangers that beset the arrested, conformed conscience, even when it is honest. It needs constant re-examination and revision. The influences which re-make and re-vitalize it must have no terminus. *There must always be adjustments to new light, a healthy, living response to fresh truth, and a continual transformation of conscience in relation to the growing revelation of God.* It must be under the watchful guardianship of the awakened and enlightened spirit. Conscience is, thus, like the mariner's chronometer. While he is in port he tests it out by all the expedients known to the science of the clock maker. He perceives and realizes that it is subject to slight variations. But when he is at sea he implicitly trusts it, reckons it as reliable as the movements of Orion or Arcturus, and sails his ship by its pronouncements. . . .

The last place of refuge amid the confusion of the world is this inner citadel of the soul. We owe almost everything to the larger society of which we are an organic part—almost everything, but there is one thing we can never surrender, barter, or disobey at the command of any social authority whatever, *the august voice within us.*

From *The Nature and Authority of Conscience,*
pp. 12–15; 22–27; 44–55; 70–73; 74–75.

⹁⹁⹁ V ⹁⹁⹁

What Is Vital Religion?

V

Iᴛ is a good sign of spiritual progress that our generation has become deeply, genuinely interested in the interior aspect of religion. We do not feel as certain as Christian thinkers in other epochs have felt that we can expound the entire nature of God and man and the cosmos from texts of Scripture. We are not optimistic in our expectations that we can explore all regions of the universe with our logic and bridge all the dizzy chasms of speculation with syllogisms. We modestly tend to return home and to explore our own inner domain. We are eager to discover the primary facts of our interior life and to follow out the clues and implications of our own indubitable experience. The laboratory method has carried us so far in other fields and has enabled us to speak with such coercive authority that we are naturally ambitious to apply a kindred method to religious life, and to find some central truths of the soul which can stand all probings and all tests, and which carry a similar conviction to that which the demonstration of experiment carries. We cannot perhaps expect to travel very far yet in the religious field with the slower, surer method of experiment and experience. We shall hardly be able to match with our method of experience those daring feats of logic which marked the great epochs of theology, but we may nevertheless accomplish a few simple and essential things which logic seemed always to miss.

The foundation fact for this experimental way is the fact of an immediate inward revelation of God within the sphere of personal experience. The person himself undergoing this experience feels as though the Fountain of Life itself had somehow burst into the rivulet of his own consciousness and was flooding him with the elemental energies of a world more real than the one we see. This experience, which those who have it call "the experience of finding God," is extraordinarily dynamic. It is attended by a release of energy, by the opening out of new dimensions of life, by a greatly heightened élan of joy, by the discovery of unusual power to endure hardship and suffering, by an increase of insight and wisdom and by a sudden increment of love and grace. There is of course no way to appreciate the full value of an experience like that *except to have it*. Like the *feel* of one's own hat on his head, or like the rapture of seeing the Grand Canyon, it cannot be completely translated into the categories of description or turned into the coinage of communicable thought. As flowers can give poets thoughts that do lie too deep for tears, so, too, there are events within our own souls that cannot be put into the *patois* of any human speech. And yet if these inner events are real and transforming we should certainly be able to speak intelligently about them as in all ages men have succeeded in speaking of love and beauty and other similar realities which exist only for appreciative spirits. The New Testament which is the supreme source for many other aspects of Christianity is also the richest source of material for the study of this first-hand religion; this religion of the experience of God; this religion which is concerned with the formation of the inner life. But the religion of the New Testament is too rich and many-sided to be reduced to one single type. It is profoundly inward and mystical, but it is at the same time out-reaching and social. It brings enlarged vision and it stirs the deepest emotions, but it also moves the will to action. It calls all the aspects of personality into full function and it is the spiritual activity of the whole life of a whole man.

From *The World Within,*
pp. 143–146.

-»)«(«-

RELIGION is an experience which no definition exhausts. One writer with expert knowledge of anthropology tells us what it is, and we know as we read his account that, however true it may be as far as it goes, it yet leaves untouched much undiscovered territory. We turn next to the trained psychologist, who leads us "down the labyrinthine ways of our own mind" and tells us why the human race has always been seeking God and worshiping Him. We are thankful for his Ariadne thread which guides us within the maze, but we feel convinced that there are doors which he has not opened— "doors to which he had no key." The theologian, with great assurance and without "ifs and buts," offers us the answer to all mysteries and the solution of all problems, but when we have gone "up the hill all the way to the very top" with him, we find it a "homesick peak"—*Heimwehfluh*—and we still wonder over the real meaning of religion.

We are evidently dealing here with something like that drinking horn which the Norse God Thor tried to drain. He failed to do it because the horn which he assayed to empty debouched into the endless ocean, and therefore to drain the horn meant drinking the ocean dry. To probe religion down to the bottom means knowing "what God and man is." Each one of us, in his own tongue and in terms of his own field of knowledge, gives his partial word, his tiny glimpse of insight. But the returns are never all in. There is always more to say. "Man is incurably religious," that fine scholar

Auguste Sabatier, said. Yes, he is. It is often wild and erratic religion which we find, no doubt, but the hunger and thirst of the human soul are an indubitable fact. In different forms of speech we can all say with St. Augustine of Hippo: "Thou hast touched me and I am on fire for thy peace."

In saying that religion is energy I am only seizing one aspect of this great experience of the human heart. It is, however, I believe, an essential aspect. A religion that makes no difference to a person's life, a religion that *does* nothing, a religion that is utterly devoid of power, may for all practical purposes be treated as though it did not exist. The great experts—those who know from the inside what religion is—always make much of its dynamic power, its energizing and propulsive power. *Power* is a word often on the lips of Jesus; never used, it should be said, in the sense of extrinsic authority or the right to command and govern, but always in reference to an intrinsic and interior moral and spiritual energy of life. The kingdom of God comes with power, not because the Messiah is supplied with ten legions of angels and can sweep the Roman eagles back to the frontiers of the Holy Land, but it "comes with power" because it is a divine and life-transforming energy, working in the moral and spiritual nature of man, as the expanding yeast works in the flour or as the forces of life push the seed into germination and on into the successive stages toward the maturity of the full-grown plant and grain.

The little fellowship of followers and witnesses who formed the nucleus of the new-born Church felt themselves "endued with power" on the day of Pentecost. Something new and dynamic entered the consciousness of the feeble band and left them no longer feeble. There was an inrushing, upwelling sense of invasion. They passed over from a visible Leader and Master to an invisible and inward Presence revealed to them as an unwonted energy. Ecstatic utterance, which seems to have followed, is not the all-important thing. The important thing is heightened moral quality, intensified fellowship, a fused and undying loyalty, an irresistible boldness in the face of danger and opposition, a fortification of spirit which nothing could break. This energy which came with their experience is what marks the event as an epoch.

St. Paul writes as though he were an expert in dynamics. "Dynamos," the Greek word for power, is one of his favorite words. He seems to have found out how to draw upon energies in the universe which nobody else had suspected were even there. It is a fundamental feature of his "Aegean gospel" that God is not self-contained but self-giving, that He circulates, as does the sun, as does the sea, and comes into us as an energy. This incoming energy he calls by many names: "The Spirit," "holy Spirit," "Christ," "the Spirit of Christ," "Christ in you," "God that worketh in us." Whatever his word or term is, he is always declaring, and he bases his testimony on experience, that God, as Christ reveals Him, is an active energy working with us and in us for the complete transformation of our fundamental nature and for a *new creation* in us.

All this perhaps sounds too grand and lofty, too remote and far away, to touch us with reality. We assume that it is for saints or apostles, but not for common everyday people like ourselves. Well, that is where we are wrong. The accounts which St. Paul gives of the energies of religion are not for his own sake, or for persons who are *bien né* and naturally saintly. They are for the rank and file of humans. In fact his Corinthian fellowship was raised by these energies out of the lowest stratum of society. The words which he uses to describe them are probably not over strong: "Be not deceived; neither fornicators, nor idolators, nor adulterers, nor effeminate, nor abusers of themselves with mankind, nor thieves, nor covetous, nor drunkards, nor revilers, nor extortioners shall inherit the kingdom of God. *And such were some of you:* but ye are washed, but ye are sanctified, but ye are justified in the name (i.e., the power) of the Lord Jesus and by the Spirit of our God."

It is to be noticed, further, that St. Paul does not confine his list of energies to those mighty spiritual forces which come down from above and work upon us from the outside. Much more often our attention is directed to energies which are potential within ourselves—even in the most ordinary of us—energies which work as silently as molecular forces or as the "capillary oozing of water," but which nevertheless are as reconstructive as the forces of springtime, following the winter's havoc. If the grace of God—the unlimited sacrificing love of God revealed in Christ—is for St. Paul the supreme spiritual energy of the universe, hardly less important is the simple human energy which meets that centrifugal energy and makes it operate within the sphere of the moral will. That dynamic energy, by which the man responds to God's upward pull and which makes all the difference, St. Paul calls faith.

We are so accustomed to the use of the word in a spurious sense that we are slow to apprehend the immense significance of this human energy which lies potentially within us. Unfortunately trained young folks and scientifically minded people are apt to shy away from the word and put themselves on the defensive, as though they were about to be asked to believe the impossible or the dubious or the unprovable. Faith in the sense in which St. Paul uses it does not mean *believing* something. It is a moral attitude and response of will to the character of God as He has been revealed in Christ. It is like the act which closes the electric circuit, which act at once releases power. The dynamic effect which follows the act is the best possible verification of the rationality of the act. So, too, faith as a moral response is no blind leap, no wild venture; it is an act which can be tested and verified by moral and spiritual effects, which are as real as the heat, light, and horse power of the dynamo. . . .

Faith in the sphere of religion works the greatest miracles of life that are ever worked. It makes the saint out of Magdalene, the heroic missionary and martyr out of Paul, the spiritual statesman of the ages out of Carthaginian Augustine, the illuminated leader of men out of Francis of Assisi, the maker of a new world epoch out of the nervously unstable monk Luther, the creator of a new type of spiritual society out of the untaught Leichestershire weaver, George Fox. Why do we not all experience the miracle and find *the rest of ourselves* through faith? The main trouble is that we live victims of limiting inhibitions. We hold intellectual theories which keep back or check the outflow of the energy of faith. We have a nice system of thought which accounts for everything and explains everything and which leaves no place for faith. We know too much. We say to ourselves that only the ignorant and uncultured are led by faith. And this same wise man, who is too proud to have faith, holds all his inhibitory theories on a basis of faith! Every one of them starts out on faith, gathers standing ground by faith, and becomes a controlling force through faith! . . .

I am told that when the great Hellgate bridge was being built over the East River in New York the engineers came upon an old derelict ship, lying imbedded in the river mud, just where one of the central piers of the bridge was to go down through to its bedrock foundation. No tug boat could be found that was able to start the derelict from its ancient bed in the ooze. It would not move, no matter what force was applied. Finally, with a sudden inspiration one of the workers hit upon this scheme. He took a large flat-boat, which had been used to bring stone down the river, and he chained it to the old sunken ship when the tide was low. Then he waited for the great tidal energies to do their work. Slowly the rising tide, with all the forces of the ocean behind it and the moon above it, came up under the flat-boat, raising it inch by inch. And as it came up, lifted by irresistible power, the derelict came up with it, until it was entirely out of the mud that had held it. Then the boat, with its subterranean load, was towed out to sea where the old waterlogged ship was unchained and allowed to drop forever out of sight and reach.

There are greater forces than those tidal energies waiting for us to use for our tasks. They have always been there. They are there now. But they do not *work*, they do not *operate*, until we lay hold of them and use them for our present purposes. We must be *co-workers with God*.

From *Spiritual Energies in Daily Life,*
pp. VII–XVII; XV–XVI.

Two great tendencies come into prominence in the entire course of religious history—the tendency, on the one hand, to regard religion as something permanent and unchanging, and on the other hand, the equally fundamental tendency to revivify and reshape religion through fresh and spontaneous experiences. It is natural that both tendencies should appear, for religion is both eternal and temporal—it is the child of permanence and change. No religion can live and be a power in this evolving world unless it changes and adjusts itself to its environment, and no religion can minister to the deepest needs of men unless it reveals permanent and time-transcending Realities.

Religion has many times lost its power because one of its two essential aspects has been ignored and the other aspect has been pushed to an absurd extreme. It will not do to forget or to overlook the advantages of habit, custom, and system—the storage of the gains of the race. The tendency to value what has worked well furthers order and stability, and keeps the future organic with the past. The conserving spirit, like an invisible mortar, binds the ages together and makes possible *one humanity*. It is the very basis of our social morality and the ground of all our corporate activities.

But, on the other hand, as soon as religion has closed up "the east window of divine surprise," and is turned into a mechanism of habit, custom, and system, it is killed. Religion thus grown formal and mechanical, though it may still have a disciplinary function in society, is no longer religion in the primary sense. The spring of joy which characterizes true religion has disappeared, the heightening, propulsive tone has vanished. It may linger on as a vestigial superstition, or a semi-automatic performance, but it is *live* religion only so long as it issues from the centre of personal consciousness and has the throb of personal experience in it.

The creative periods in religious progress have come when the crust of custom, the mechanism of habit, has been broken up by the impact of persons who were capable of fresh and original experiences, persons who have shifted the line of march and brought new energies into play, because they have gained new visions and new insights. The Church, it is true, has never in any period quite sunk to the level of tradition and the automatism of habit, for it has always had beneath its system of organization and dogma a current, more or less hidden and subterranean, of vital, inward, spiritual religion, dependent for its power of conviction, not on books, councils, hierarchies or creeds—not upon anything kept in cold storage—but on the soul's experiences of eternal Realities. But the main weakness of organized Christianity has been the tendency to settle into a "sacred" form and system.

Our generation has grown weary of ancient traditions and accumulated systems. We have discovered new worlds in all directions by following the sure path of experience, and we can never again settle down with a naïve and childlike trust in the house which the past has builded. Our first question in any field is, not What do the scribes and schoolmen say? not What is the unbroken tradition? but What are the facts? What data does experience furnish? This shifting of centre from "authority" to "experience" runs through all the pursuits of the human spirit in the modern world, and, as would be expected, religion has been profoundly affected by it. In religion as in other fields of inquiry, the questions of moment have come to be those which deal with life. We take slender interest in dogmatic constructions; we turn from these with impatience, and ask for the testimony of the soul, for the basis of religion in the nature of man as man. This profound tendency of the modern world has brought strongly into prominence a mystical type of religion, that is to say, a type of religion which is primarily grounded in experience, and with the tendency has come a corresponding interest in the mystics of the past.

Mysticism is a word which cannot properly be used without careful definition. To many readers it carries no clear and concrete meaning; to others it has an ominous significance and a forbidding sound, as though the safe and beaten track, which the defenders of the faith have builded, were being left for will-o'-the-wisps and wandering lights. I shall use the word mysticism to express the type of religion which puts the emphasis on immediate awareness of relation with God, on direct and intimate consciousness of the Divine Presence. It is religion in its most acute, intense, and living stage. . . .

Something of this sort is familiar to the sanest and most matter-of-fact person among us. There is a mystical aspect in our highest moral moments. We never rise to any high level of moral action without feeling that the "call" of duty comes from beyond our isolated self. There is an augustness in conscience which has made men in all ages name it the voice of God; but however it is named, everybody in these high moments of obedience has an experience which is essentially mystical—an experience which cannot be analysed and reduced to "explanation" in terms of anything else. . . .

There is likewise a mystical element in prayer whenever it rises to the level of real communion, or, as Lowell puts it, when, "stirred below the conscious self," the soul feels

"That perfect disenthralment which is God."

Everybody who prays knows the difference between saying words and phrases, uttering requests, proffering petitions, and *coming into vital communion with God*. There are moments of prayer when the soul feels itself face to face with ultimate Reality and in joyous fellowship with perfect Personality. This latter experience is as normal as the lower form of prayer is, but they are worlds apart in significance and value. It is because prayer does rise to the height of actual fellowship with a Divine Companion that men who accept the conclusions of modern science go on praying, undisturbed by the reign of law. They are not concerned about the superficial question, whether prayers are answered or not; for prayer is its own reward, is an end in itself and carries the person who truly prays into a joyous state which transcends explanation. . . .

There is, too, a mystical element of this normal type in any genuine *faith*. I am not speaking, of course, of a faith which consists in believing something on authority, for that is faith of a lower order. Faith in the primary sense is a way of corresponding with Realities which transcend sense-experience. It is an inward power by which the soul lives above the seen and temporal, and "overcomes" the world of the causal, mechanical order. It is a conviction, arising apparently from the very rationality of the spirit in us, that there is an inner, unseen, spiritual universe—an eternal moral order. It is the soul's vision of what *ought to be* and its confidence in the reality and permanence of that estimate of worth—"the assurance of things hoped for and the evidence of things not seen." It is no mere product of sense-experience, but it is the very pinnacle of rationality and as normal a function as our responses to ocular vision.

It is not an uncommon thing for persons who are entirely free from abnormality to have an experience in which the meaning, the significance, the worth, the richness of life, vastly transcends their concepts and descriptions—when life vastly overflows all that can be said about it. This experience is marked by the emergence of a sort of undifferentiated consciousness like that well known to us when we rise to a high appreciation of the beautiful in nature or art or music. At the highest moments of appreciation there comes, not a loss of consciousness, but the emergence of a new level of consciousness in which neither the *I* nor the *object* is focused in perception or thought. There is in these experiences an absence of self-consciousness, and an absence, too, of the consciousness of any concrete, finite object contemplated, a penetration into a region more real and all-inclusive than that of finite "things." . . .

In truth, at times, we are aware of a More than "ourselves" impinging on the skirts of our being. There is no time in our lives, of course, when we do not draw upon this wider consciousness which is the matrix in which our "ideas" and concepts are born. We are all aware how often we arrive at conclusions and actions without reasoning or thinking; how often we deal wisely with situations, without being able to trace the source of our wisdom. The supreme issues of life are settled for us, all the way up and down the scale, by unreasoned adjustments, by intents rather than contents of consciousness, by value-responses, which far overflow any knowledge explanation which we can give. It may, I think, be said that all great work, all work which has the touch of genius on it, comes from persons who in special degrees draw upon this matrix consciousness. Such persons feel often as though a Power not themselves were working through them; as though, without tension or effort, the creation at which they are working was "given" to them or "brought" to them. There are, I repeat, times when in extraordinary ways the dualistic character of ordinary thought is transcended and the soul comes into possession of itself as a whole, when all we have been, or are, or hope to be, becomes real; and not only so, but in these deeper reaches of experience some higher Power than ourselves *seems* to work with us and through us—a larger life, continuous with ourselves, seems to environ us. Our own consciousness appears to be only an effective centre in a vast spiritual environment which acts along with us. As Matthew Arnold has finely said:

> A bolt is shot back somewhere in our breast
> And a lost pulse of feeling stirs again.
>
> .   .   .
>
> And then he thinks he knows
> The hills where his life rose
> And the sea where it goes.

From *Studies in Mystical Religion*,
pp. XIII–XV; XVIII–XXII;
XXIII–XXIV.

ONE of the most unique things about our finite human life is surely the religious response which we make to unseen realities. It is just that attitude in us which would most completely puzzle the traditional visitor from Mars, assuming that the Martians are what the Gnostics used to call "hylic men," i.e., men without any spiritual traits whatever. It is always extremely difficult—in fact it seems impossible—to account for religion of a spiritual order when one starts with the assumption that men are sheer "hylic" beings, what the theologians used to call "mere men." That old eighteenth-century guess that religion owes its origin to the crafty work of rulers and priests, who invented it as a scheme and means of human control, is so completely exploded that no one with historical insight is likely to make that guess again.

Whether religion is a pathway to reality or not, there seems at least no question that its springs lie deep down in the elemental nature of human life itself. It is not something foisted off on man by clever manipulators. It is a response as native to his being as is his unpredictable response to beauty or to harmony. There may conceivably be "hylic men." I have seen dangerously close approaches to the "hylic." But it is more probable that where the religious attitude seems lacking the absence of it is due to the excessive cultivation of the theoretic or the practical side of life and to the starving out of potential spiritual aptitudes.

Whenever religion is found in its loftiest development, and in its richest types, it seems to be a vital correspondence with reality, and we may safely assume that worshipers have felt that way about it in all ages. It heightens the whole value of life and it seems like the most complete form of life-adjustment that man knows. The consciousness of objective reality is as great in moments of joyous worship or of intense mystical experience as it ever is when we are beholding beauty or enjoying harmony, and the reality aspect often rises to a height as great as in any form of sense-experience. The conviction that one is having direct dealings with realities beyond himself in his highest religious moments is frequently as clear and as compelling as is the conviction that something beyond the beholder is there when he is seeing a mountain. Religion has almost certainly lived and flourished not on the transmitted "deposits" of a dead past, but on the vivid testimony of the quick and vital souls of men who somehow have succeeded in achieving present correspondence with a Life greater than their own.

This unique response of religion to what is felt to be a real beyond, like all our other fundamental reactions, roots back into deep-lying instincts and emotions, though there is apparently no one original religious instinct. It is not a sound psychological fact that "fear has created the gods," as Lucretius thought, but fear and those kindred instinctive tendencies, awe and dread, mystery and reverence, together with wonder, curiosity and what Professor Otto calls a "numinous attitude" have always been underlying or embedded native springs of religion. But here, as in the case with loyalties and appreciations, the instinctive and emotional springs are gradually lifted up, transfused and recreated through the slow accumulation of ideas and ideals in the unfolding process of experience. It has seemed to some interpreters of religion that it is essentially intellectual—something due to man's rationalistic outlook. That view is almost certainly one-sided, but it is probably nearer the truth than is the attempt to base religion *wholly* on the instinctive or volitional side of human nature. Religion, when it comes to ripeness and complete development, gathers up all the essential aspects of man's nature, instincts, emotions, intellect and will. It is an immense unifying and integrative power and, like the highest loyalties of life, it holds like adamant and carries one forward to goals as though nothing else mattered.

Once more we must call attention especially to the fact that religious experience, peculiarly so where it is vital and first-hand, rolls up and accumulates, step by step, a central stock of spiritual insight and wisdom. Just as we gather our "apperceiving mass" for the interpretation of new sense data, and as we build up our expert wisdom in matters of aesthetic taste and judgment, so, too, we form within ourselves a spiritual core of life that is rich with the gathered wisdom of years of correspondence with God. Single flashes of insight may be illusory, sudden "inrushes" may be due to a temporary subjective state, a sporadic ecstasy may be a sign of some abnormal trait, but the slow sifting and testing processes of a life of correspondence with a wider and deeper environment than the physical one, gradually build up within the soul a pretty reliable body of expert wisdom which gives the mind of the religious man confidence that he is dealing with a More of reality kindred to and not utterly unlike his own essential nature— "a Beyond that is akin." A moral expert sees the eternal significance of his deed by an intuition as sure as the mathematician's flair for a curve that completes a given arc. A person who has had long experience in interpreting the lines of character in a life feels as sure of his insight as though he were plotting out the orbit of a planet. Somewhat so the great mystics feel the illumination of a conviction within their souls based on the experiences of a lifetime, that their little lives are rounded by an unseen world of the Spirit, as the tiny islands of the Pacific are environed by the waters of the sea.

From Pathways to the Reality of God,
pp. 186–190.

-»)«(-

CHRISTIANITY'S power to survive in this present world and to be a religion of life depends upon the capacity of its prophets and guides to understand the conditions, the needs and the spirit of this new time and to reinterpret the message of human salvation and the mission of the Church in the light of the accumulated truth of the centuries and in terms of the spirit and wisdom of the Galilean Founder of this stream of life. Christianity has many times met epochs of new culture, periods of ferment and mutation, and has, through the absorption and mastery of the fresh tributary stream been able to enrich its own life and to reshape its interpretation and its mission. Can it once more prove to be equal to the situation that has emerged? Can it become enriched through the achievements of the coöperative minds of the present age and can it lead the way to a new spiritual adventure? That is the vital question we shall endeavor to answer.

If there are no basic spiritual realities to be discovered, if life is by the very nature of things bound to be a sheer biological process, with no legitimate upper story to complete it, we must, of course, face the facts and make the best we can of our one-story compartment of life. The severely honest modern person abominates hypocrisy and sham more than most things, and he has a deep-seated dread of fancy-built additions to the realistic world. He will not save his own face, nor will he even save civilization, by imaginative supplements to the universe as it actually is. If religion is ever to be his personal comfort, and if it is to be accepted as a creative power toward a better civilization, we must find realities that are as stable as mountains for the foundations of the spiritual structure.

There will always be some persons who are content to satisfy their hopes and drown their fears with iridescent dreams, and there will be a comfortable residue who will accept unquestionably ancient faiths just because they are ancient. But a stage of the maturing of the human mind has now been reached when henceforth a large and ever-increasing proportion of enlightened people will insist that religious truth, if it is to be truth for them, must not rest upon a less secure foundation than is adequate for any other kind of truth. The days are over, almost certainly forever over, when easy-going, jog-trot, "good-enough" faiths will hold the allegiance of the mature and solid section of our communities. The challenge is as clear as a bell. The house, as of old, must be set in order. We must face the issues of the religious life with the same honesty and the same severity of truth that we show when we deal with the nature of atoms and the processes of the stars.

The new age cannot *live* on naturalism or on secularism. Life becomes sterile and futile without the depth and power which come from participation in eternal realities. But this new age cannot any more successfully *live* on religious faiths that are out of harmony with known truth, or that hang loose in the air, cut apart from the fundamental intellectual culture of the age. The hour has struck for the serious business of rediscovering the foundations, and of interpenetrating all life and thought with the truths and realities of a victorious religious faith.

From *A Preface to Christian Faith in a New Age,*
pp. 40–42.

->》《《-

IT is interesting to see what a supremely great and many-sided soul like St. Paul has to say of the inwardness and interior depth of religion. That he was a man of action is plain enough to be seen and nobody can easily miss his clarion call to arm *cap-a-pie* for the positive, moral battles of life. He was ethical in the noblest sense of the word, but there was an inner core of religious experience in him which is as unique and wonderful as is his athletic ethical purpose or his imperial spirit of moral conquest.

There was for him no kind of "doing" which could ever be a substitute for the spiritual health of the soul. Nobody has ever lived who has been more deeply concerned than was St. Paul over the primary problem of life: How can my soul be saved? To be "saved" for him, however, does not mean to be rescued from dire torment or from the consequences which follow sin and dog the sinner. No transaction in another world can accomplish salvation for him; no mere change from debit to credit side in the heavenly ledgers can make him a saved man. To be saved for St. Paul is to become a new kind of a person, with a new inner nature, a new dimension of life, a new joy and triumph of soul. There is a certain inner *feeling* here which systematic theology can no more convey than a botanical description of a flower can convey what the poet feels in the presence of the flower itself. There is no lack of books and articles which spread before us St. Paul's doctrines and which tell us his theory—his *gnosis*—of the plan of salvation. The trouble with all these external accounts is that they clank like hollow armor. They are like sounding brass and clanging cymbals. We miss the *real thing* that matters—the inner throbbing heart of the living experience.

What he is always trying to tell us is that a new "nature" has been formed within him, a new spirit has come to birth in his inmost self. Once he was weak, now he is strong. Once he was permanently defeated, now he is "led in a continual triumph." Once he was at the mercy of the forces of blind instinct and habit which dragged him whither he would not, now he feels free from the dominion of sin and its inherent peril to the soul. Once, with all his pride of pharisaism, he was an alien to the commonwealth of God, now he is a fellow citizen with all the inward sense of loyalty that makes citizenship real.

He traces the immense transformation to his personal discovery of a mighty forgiving love, where he had least expected to find it, in the heart of God— "We are more than conquerors through Him that loved us"; "The life I now live, I live by faith in the Son of God who loved me and gave Himself for me." *Faith,* wherever St. Paul uses it to express the central human fact of the religious life, is a word of tremendous inward depth. It is bathed and saturated with personal experience, and it proves to be a constructive life-principle of the first importance. Faith *works;* it is something by which one lives: "The life I now live, I live by faith."

But the full measure—the length and breadth, depth and height—of his new inner world does not come full into view until one sees how through faith and love this man has come into conscious relation with the Spirit of God inwardly revealed to him, and operative as a resident presence in his own spirit. No forensic account of salvation can reach this central feature of real salvation, which now appears as new inward life and power. St. Paul takes religion out of the sphere of logic into the primary region of life. There are ways of living upon the Life of God as direct and verifiable as is the correspondence between the plant and its natural environment. To *live*, in the full spiritual meaning of this word as St. Paul uses it, is to be immersed in the living currents of the circulating Life of God.

From *The Inner Life*,
pp. 84–88.

->>><<<-

WE must somehow recover our power to see essential realities vividly. It demands new eyes—what the Bible calls *vision*. Our optical structure, with its marvelous retinal system of rods and cones, and its adjustable lens, is well fitted for the perception of colors and shapes of objects, for dealing with "the visible choir of heaven and the furniture of earth." We have immensely enlarged its scope, both upward and downward, by the invention of telescopes and microscopes. These inventions have enabled us to discover objects that were never dreamed of in ancient astronomy and physics. Here were "new eyes" that could see in heaven and on earth objects which old unaided eyes were forever bound to miss. Nobody knew that the planet Jupiter had moons until Galileo's telescope found them. Nobody suspected the inside mysteries of plant and flower until the microscope made them common properties, which are familiar to school boys and school girls now.

But there are realities of a different order which no increase of the microscope or telescope will ever reveal, which rods and cones and lenses are not made to deal with. "We look," St. Paul said, "not at things that are seen with the eyes, but at things that are not seen, for seeable things are temporal but things which eyes cannot see are eternal." It is for *that* that "new eyes" are needed.

This great passage of St. Paul is of course an instance of oriental overemphasis. He is so impressed with the importance of seeing invisible realities that he tells us not to look at the things that are seen. But we should probably never find the invisibles if we wholly neglected the visible world. We are more apt to find the invisible Reals by *looking through* the visibles, as the medium. We should never have discovered the laws of the universe if we had neglected to observe the objects through which the laws are revealed. What St. Paul would say if he were here now would be something like this: "You belong to two worlds; do not miss the invisible one while you are busy with the visible one. Cultivate your *vision*, learn to see the realities which your eyes miss. Look through the world that is seen and discover the realities which it suggests and implies."

This other kind of perception, with "the new eyes," turns out to be an essential feature of life. It is not a luxury; it is a necessity. "Where *vision* fails the people perish." Again and again the experts in the domain of life tell us that it is persons who endure as seeing the invisibles that build the permanent civilizations of the world.

The "eyes" I am talking about, the eyes that see the invisibles, do not belong to a chosen few persons, the spiritually *élite*, they belong, potentially at least, to all of us who have minds. Intellect is never the whole of our type of reason. When Wordsworth said that "Imagination is Reason in its most exalted mood," he was using "imagination" as the capacity in us to *see* the realities by which we live. We all do it in our measure, but it is a capacity which can be cultivated, improved, expanded, as certainly as the capacity to see perspective is cultivated by the artist. Most of us see objects with "innocence of eye," without any attention to perspective, while the artist sees everything as he would draw it. . . .

We have been living for several generations now in the era of the interrogation point. We have written the question mark all over the earth and the sky, probing endlessly for causes and origins, pushing back the skirts of time and the canopies of space with our never-ceasing questions, What? Whence? Why? We have written this question mark over every holy book and every sacred place. We have invaded the inner deeps of the soul with our crooked, crabbed question mark and we have asked that interior dweller of ours to stand and deliver its mysteries.

We all recognize, of course, that the use of the question mark is one way to truth. We cannot dispense with it and we must not rail against it and call it, as Lowell did, "the devil's crook Episcopal." But the time has come, I am sure, to return to the way of wonder and to *see* with the eyes of joy and admiration, the eyes that see the invisibles. We should find our way more frequently to the discovery of God, if we cultivated more effectively our power to *see,* with reason in its most exalted mood, and learned how to make the response of joy and wonder. Nowhere else in literature is this type of creative vision at such a noble level as in the Bible, and nowhere is this feeling of surprise and wonder raised to such a lofty stage. . . .

When Holman Hunt told his artist friends eighty years ago that he was going to paint Christ, they pointed out the absurdity of the undertaking. "You can paint only what you can *see,*" they insisted, as the principle of their school of painting. "You will only waste your time trying to do the impossible." "But I am going to *see* Him," Hunt replied. "I will work by His side in the carpenter shop. I will walk with Him over the hills of Galilee. I will go with Him among the poor, the blind, the lame and the leprous. I will go to Gethsemane with Him. I will travel with Him to Calvary and climb the Cross with Him, until I *see* Him, and then I will paint Him." Those of us who have stood with moved hearts as we have looked at Holman Hunt's "Light of the World," knocking at the closed door, feel convinced that the great painter did live with Christ until he *saw* Him with eyes of joy and wonder. But it was not a dead Christ that he saw, but the living Christ trying to find entrance into the human heart.

To see the eternal in the midst of time, to feel and to enjoy the infinite here in the finite, is one of the greatest blessings life has to offer. Plato used to say that life comes to its full glory when some beautiful object, or some loved person, suddenly opens for us a window that gives a glimpse into eternal reality. It is no doubt a satisfaction to know causes and to understand and explain what before was mysterious, but even greater is the thrill when something breaks in on our souls that is exactly as it ought to be, which is what occurs with consummate beauty. It is a state beyond mere knowledge. We now both know and adore, because we *see*.

Gerritt Beneker, the American artist, who paints men and women engaged in the hardest and most dangerous types of labor, aims to express the nobility and the divine quality of sacrificial toil. He was once painting a man was was engaged in testing, for bridge-girders, the quality of a swab of molten steel that was swung out on a crane from a blast furnace. The man stood at his work almost naked in the fierce heat, covered with sweat and grime. As Beneker, with quick strokes of his brush, caught and interpreted the skillful tester of the modern steel, another laborer who came up and was looking on as the artist painted, called to his companions in labor: "I say, fellows, come up and see this. Here is the greatest painter that ever lived. He is painting God where nobody else can see Him." Some happier day perhaps we others will learn *to see with new eyes,* and be able to catch hints and intimations of the divine presence where few suspect it now. . . .

But how are we ever in this busy and material world going to realize all this? We must have new eyes—the eyes of our heart enlightened. That means that we must see essential realities vividly. We must have our imagination captured. Matthew Arnold said that conduct is three-fourths of life. But it isn't. Getting your imagination captured is almost the whole of life. The minute the eyes of your heart are enlightened, the minute your imagination gives you the picture of your path, your goal, your aim—it is as good as done. The way to become the architect of your fate, the captain of your soul, is to have your imagination captured.

We talk about the momentous will, but you tug at your will in vain until imagination dominates the scene, and at once you are on the way to your goal. There is no other way to spiritual victory except by having the eyes of the heart enlightened. That is the way you saddle and bridle and control your instincts and emotions. This happens to be the psychology not only of St. Paul and St. Augustine but of William James as well. "Consent to an idea's undivided presence at the focus of attention," our Harvard Psychologist declares, "and *action follows immediately*." That is what I meant by the capture of the imagination—the guiding idea for the will.

But we all know that there is something deeper than thinking or willing, a subsoil, an abysmal inner life, out of which ideas and ideals emerge like capes of cloud out of the invisible air. The master secret of life is to feed or to fertilize that inner depth-life by worship, by meditation, by great literature of reality. Thus the eyes of the heart are enlightened. Thus one may out of the shadow see:

> The high-heaven dawn of more than mortal day
> Strike on the Mount of Vision.

From *New Eyes for Invisibles*,
pp. 1–7; 12–14.

»» VI ««

Is Science Enough?

VI

WITH its effective technique, its methods of demonstration, its successes in verification and predictions, and its triumphs in the field of practical invention science has become a well-nigh universal educational discipline. It has scored an immense number of triumphs. It has changed the very basis of the explanation and interpretation of the world. It has pushed back the span of time and widened out the frontiers of space in quite revolutionary fashion. It has lengthened the reach of our hands and the dominion of our minds. It has profoundly altered the intellectual formulations of thinkers, and, no less, it has affected the habits and practices of all persons who engage in labor. Almost every student in institutions of higher learning comes under its spell. Its method carries conviction. Its power of demonstration satisfies the mind. Its directness, simplicity and mathematical accuracy impress all who are capable of understanding. The person who sets himself against the scientific method and the long results of research and demonstration is like a warrior going out with a bow and arrow to meet an army equipped with machine guns and armored tanks.

The expansion of the range and scope of life through scientific study is everywhere in evidence. The enlargement of man's control over natural forces and over many of the diseases and perils which threaten existence here on earth is also generally recognized. Science, taken in its largest sense, has, furthermore, made a genuine contribution to the spiritual life of man. It has banished many of the fears and terrors which obsessed primitive man. It has enabled us to feel more at home in the universe, which at least we partly understand. It has shown us how organic our life is with the whole of things. It has made it possible for us to read intelligently the great past of which we are inheritors. It has given us a deeper and truer conception of the spiritual revelation that has come through our Scriptures and the other creative books of the race. It has made us more aware of the forward "pull" of a future that is big with possibilities. The *idea* of an evolving world and of unfolding life has unmistakably had an awakening and kindling spiritual influence upon many minds. If there is a progressive tendency in operation, as science seems to indicate, if there is increasing coherence and integration, if there is an intelligible and dramatic order revealed in and through the process, then it is a natural inference, at least to the lay person, that an intelligent Mind is somehow present and that there is a spiritual Ground out of which the process has sprung.

This scientific temper has inevitably produced, by slow and almost unnoticed influences, a subtle change of outlook which has affected every aspect of human life. Even the non-scientific mind, however little it suspects it, is altered in its attitude and in its approach to all problems by the very atmosphere which scientific research has produced. Ancient and time-honored explanations of sacred events have weakened their hold on many minds as scientific explanations have permeated human thought. A preference for demonstrable methods of procedure has crept in, grown to be a habit of mind, and has become second nature with people generally. Views that have been transmitted by tradition, distinctly religious interpretations resting on faith, and "deposits" of thought from the uncritical past, are at once met by a powerful drift in an opposite direction. Whether one likes it or not, and whether one admits it or not, some such profound change has been silently taking place. . . .

To hosts of experts and to multitudes of young students, the scientific method has come to be thought of as the only way of approach to truth and reality that is worthy of respect. Not to be able to prove and demonstrate seems to such minds synonymous with complete failure to explain and to *know*. Soviet Russia has put the scientific method at the center of its creed. Every educational institution of higher rank in the mission field of the Orient has a large group of students who claim to do their thinking entirely on the intellectualist platform and who discount any alternative to scientific knowledge. They bracket their own national religions with Christianity as inheritances of "superstitions," and as having no place in the life of grownup men. It is, too, a basic conviction in the minds of a very large proportion of the young men and women who fill the colleges and universities of America that the key of the scientific method is the only one that can unlock the secrets of the universe.

This situation has brought a narrowing of the range of life and thought which amounts in its limitations to a real tragedy. The first limitation comes from an unnecessary narrowing of the scope and meaning of "knowledge." It seems strange that any person who has considered the full rich nature of human experience should conclude that only the method of explanation employed by exact science can reveal the truth of things. Some of the most marvelous *perceivers* of reality that have ever lived, the poets and the artists of the race, without reflectively understanding or explaining through causes and formulae, have come very close to the heart of things. We could hardly *live* without their type of knowledge. . . .

The exact quantitative scientific method of description and explanation cannot be applied to the entire sphere of reality. There are many aspects of this rich and complex world which cannot be exhaustively interpreted from an *outside* point of view. When such aspects are known only externally they are only partially comprehended. They are of such a nature that they are incapable of division and analysis and therefore they do not yield to exact description. The mind itself which *does* the describing and the explaining in every case cannot, for one thing, adequately be dealt with by a method of analysis and external description. There is always something more involved in the nature of mind than can be brought under any system of observation. There is something over and above the bare facts that get caught and presented. The supreme attitudes too of a personal mind such, for instance, as conviction of truth, or joy in beauty, or awe in the presence of sublimity, or dedication to goodness for its own sake, or the personal surrender of all selfish interests for the sake of exalted love, are realities of an order quite different from changes in the orbit of a planet or from any movement of masses of matter in space. Any life-forming *loyalty* is an instance of something real and something dynamic which can be known in its true meaning only from within. When science as a descriptive method of knowledge comes face to face with the facts of religious experience it is utterly incapable of dealing with the *essential* feature of it. It studies it from the outside as an observable phenomenon, but it misses just the interior attitude of the participant that makes all the difference.

Science can show that certain temporal interpretations of facts and events in religious history are immature and inadequate and need revision. It can demonstrate that events did not happen exactly as earlier interpreters *thought* they happened and that more factors were involved than were taken into account by primitive observers. No one need be disturbed over later revisions and reinterpretations of early human experience or of primitive man's observations of his world. Science can deal with the facts and events of the visible universe, down to infinitesimal magnitudes and out to cosmic worlds unbelievably remote. Its range in this field seems to have no limits. But it has nothing to say, and can have nothing to say, on the question of ultimate realities of an eternal order which are essential to a spiritual religion, nor, it must be added, can such a scientific method unaided give a completely intelligible explanation of the things which it reports and describes. It cannot deal with ultimate origins or goals. If there are other positive ways of approach to such realities, or if there are inescapable implications of a spiritual order no less real than the visible one, science has no right to close the door to it, and it has no dominion over it....

It requires but little serious reflection to discover that science has no magic key which can unlock all the realms of the universe, or to be convinced that science has no legitimate method by which it could deprive man, if it would, of the reality of the spiritual. If we ever lose our spiritual birthright and fall to a material and secular level it will not be due to the authoritative pronouncements of science. Science has not closed, and will never close the soul's east window of divine surprise. We are built for two kinds of worlds—one a space-time world and one a world of spiritual values —and we can be denizens of either world. We have senses or perception that link us up with the world which science describes, and we have just as certainly inlets of connection with a world of beauty, truth, goodness, and love that can be achieved and realized only by our own creative attitudes and activities. The mind is its own kingdom, and can find its own correspondences and relationships. A very little consideration will convince any thoughtful person of the reality of this kingdom of the mind. The taproot of religion is to be found in the nature of the human mind itself, and its true environment which is an order of realities that fits the deepest nature of man's mind.

From *A Preface to Christian Faith in a New Age*,
pp. 5–9; 47–50; 55–56.

->>><<<-

WHETHER we like it or not, science is going on making new discoveries about our world, organizing and explaining in fresh ways the facts of this vast frame of things, and its furniture, which we call the cosmos. Nobody with wisdom in his soul would want the research to slacken. Let us know all that can be known and verified. We cannot have too much knowledge if it is *genuine knowledge*. But every important new discovery and every fresh interpretation affect our outlook and the structure of thought and insight which ages of human experience have slowly fashioned. There is a story, probably a legend, of an oriental who had vowed never to destroy anything living, and who saw through a microscope a swarm of animalculae in the water he planned to drink. He met the crisis by breaking the microscope; then his mind was free to act in the accustomed way.

But the new discoveries, the new revelations, the new interpretations, the new formulations have piled up to such an extent that there is no relief in breaking microscopes or telescopes, or in burning copies of the latest returns. Our boys and girls are in the scientific laboratories, and they know the new facts and, however transforming they are, we are bound to face them and adjust our lives and our holiest aspirations somehow to conform with what is settled as truth. Religion, which is man's noblest attitude and response to what is highest and purest in the universe, cannot be preserved and maintained in some watertight compartment of the mind, unaffected by the total outlook on the facts and processes and interpretations of the world as a whole. If, therefore, religion in these times is to be *vital*—and if it is not vital it is negligible—it must maintain its reality, not apart from the intellectual currents of the times, but as something unmistakably real and in complete conformity with all that we know to be *true*.

Carlyle was very wise when he wrote the words: "A man's religion is the chief fact with regard to him. I do not mean here the church creed he recites. But the thing a man does practically *believe;* the thing a man does practically lay to heart, and know for certain, concerning his vital relations to this mysterious Universe, and his duty and destiny therein." A religion of that high order—and that is the kind I have got—must fit all the facts that are known. It must not be an untested affair, transmitted to us from the childhood ages of the race, when none of our present problems was known.

There can be, I think, no doubt in the mind of anyone who knows the facts that there has been a shrinkage of interest in religion on the part of those who make up the main body of the institutions of higher learning in our country, though this is by no means true of all of them. A large number of these institutions were founded and nurtured by intensely religious men to be the nurseries of faith and training places for religious leaders. They, as much as the *Mayflower,* were intended to be the bearers of a precious freight of faith for the coming times. In many instances that vision has miscarried and the institutions founded in high faith have become to a great extent secularized, with religion only a feeble if not negligible feature. "Secularized" means of course that the primary interest of life centers in the affairs and the concerns of the world of space and time and matter.

There can be no question, I think, that this shrinkage of religion on the part of both professors and students in institutions of higher learning is tragic both for the cause of education itself, and for the highest welfare of the nation. We are gradually ceasing to be a religious nation and our leaders of thought and action come to their tasks in many instances with no religious vision and with practically no concern for maintaining the faith of the founders of their institutions. I am convinced that no nation can long maintain its moral leadership in the world or can preserve a solid and creative civilization without a faith that transcends material and economic interests. The most important issue, therefore, now before us, is the recovery of this transcendent faith, and a genuine return to spiritual leadership. I repeat: There is nothing in our world today as important as the recovery of vital faith and spiritual leadership. We must recover what William Blake called "the end of a golden string."

This shrinkage of religion in institutions of higher learning is due in about equal measure to the immense expansion of science, and to the feebleness and failure of the interpreters of Christianity to square their message of faith with the known and proven facts of the universe as they have been discovered. . . .

Science can deal adequately only with what comes within the field of observation, with what can be described and explained in terms of antecedent causes, or at least in terms of absolutely accurate description, preferably in mathematical terminology. It speaks with very slight authority, and is outside its proper field, when it undertakes to deal with what we may rightly call *intrinsic values,* such as beauty, moral insight, *love* of the purest and highest order, consciousness of nonsensuous universals, mind that knows that it knows, i.e., self-conscious mind, and the amazing insight that the spirit within us frequently has direct intercourse with a pervasive spirit, that seems to us to be the ultimate and eternal reality of the universe, which is in fact the very heart of religion. There is, furthermore, an extraordinary body of literature of revelation, which has had a major transforming influence in fashioning the highest types of civilization that our world has so far known. This, too, belongs in the list of intrinsic values, the insights of which cannot be dealt with by the scientific method. Here is a whole range of life-imparting *values,* with which science is not at home and about which it speaks but haltingly.

Unfortunately scientists, though not usually those of the highest order, have in our time assumed that the scientific method is the only method of knowledge. They have quietly taken for granted that there is nothing in the universe which cannot be brought under their method of treatment, and they have consequently been giving their students a greatly reduced universe. The effect of the scientific method has been so extraordinarily successful in bringing order and explanation into what a short time ago was an unknown universe, full of mysterious gaps, that it becomes easy and natural to leap to the conclusion that the laboratory can furnish the final word, not only about "the choir of heaven and the furniture of earth," meaning the visible universe, but about what I have called ultimate realities and intrinsic values. The result has been that in the field of higher education the great moral and spiritual issues of life have been seriously neglected, and the realities of religion have become more or less dubious, because the focus of attention has been in other directions.

I am not blaming the scientists for not being preachers of religion and interpreters of moral ideals. What I am complaining of is the fact that the scientific method is so often assumed to be the only way of approach to reality, and that the whole field of intrinsic values is assumed to be either negligible, or capable of being dealt with under the same method as physical phenomena, which means being reduced to an *extrinsic* basis, and explained like other matters of fact.

If our institutions of higher learning should proceed to deal with the range of intrinsic values with the same seriousness of purpose and with the same depth of insight that have characterized scientific research in recent times we should at once have a new atmosphere in our institutions of learning, and it would soon be apparent in the life of the nation. We have rendered unto Caesar the things that are Caesar's, but we have not correspondingly brought up to the same level the whole side of human interests that have to do with shaping the inner life of man and the ideals by which complete life is fashioned. The intrinsic value side of life is very seriously neglected. A psychology of the physiological laboratory type has taken in most cases the place of the profound and searching study of the absolute uniqueness of mind in man, and the creative aspects of the human spirit. This ought to be, as it was with Plato and with Kant, the highest occupation and the supreme aim of the pursuit of truth. And along with this serious pursuit of truth, if we had it, would come all those aspirations of this unique spirit which I have been calling *intrinsic values*.

From *A Call to What Is Vital,*
pp. 1–4; 5–7.

-->>><<<-

We are familiar with two ways of dealing with the nature of things: (1) the method of observation and exact description from the outside, the spectator method, and (2) the method of vital experience—discovery of reality by living your way into the heart of things. The first way is "knowledge about" and the second way is "knowledge of acquaintance.". . . Mother love is something quite different from, worlds asunder from, a book about mother love, just as the botanist's flower in the crannied wall is utterly different from the poet's flower. There is no doubt a place for both of these approaches; only, one of them is apt to rise to such importance that it eclipses the other way of approach.

At the present time the first method has pretty much captured the field. It has steadily, since the time of Descartes and Newton, become more and more exact and mathematical, since perfectly exact description can be attained only in terms of mathematics. The conclusions of the scientific laboratories become more and more unescapable, but at the same time ever more abstract, universal and *remote* from our warm and throbbing concrete life, with its aspirations, its hopes and faiths, its sense of free creative action, remote, too, from confidence in the reality of the values of life, by which we live, in so far as we truly *live*.

The result of all this has been a widespread sense of frustration and inner defeat. The more one knows in terms of exact description, too often the less is the feel of the reality of the significance of life. The doors of life seem to shut to. The windows of the soul suffer "blackouts." There are no goal-posts for the thrilling game of life. The process of description, ruthlessly carried through, entails reduction and the stripping away of everything that will not submit to description and explanation. We end, therefore, with a reduced world, a reduced man, and greatly reduced hopes and aims and aspirations. We are like the centipede which was happy in its stride and in the manipulation of its many legs until it started reflecting about which leg came after which. This reduced her mind to such a pitch,

> She lay distracted in the ditch
> Considering how to run.

It is an apt parable of our present frustrations due to the endeavor to manage life by abstract "knowledge about," when one can live only through knowledge of acquaintance.

But the method of science (which of course in its proper area is a sound method) has been so successful that for many persons it has absorbed the whole field. Descartes and Hobbes and the scientist who swept the sky with his telescope and found no God—no realm of creative Spirit—and the recent physiologist who "swept" the brain with his microscope and found no mind, have won.

And *that*, I think, lies at the heart of our world tragedy. There is nothing to shake our consciousness with thoughts "beyond the reaches of our souls." If life has no ultimate scope, no intrinsic meaning, no free purpose; if only *things* matter, let us have a Leviathan, a Fuehrer, a totalitarian Director to manage our affairs and enable us to conjugate the verb to eat successfully. Many persons at the present time see no other practical solution in a world reduced to basic material elements, and one of the reactions has been an escape into an attitude of "unreason," but that is only another type of frustration.

The only solution of this *impasse* is certainly not to give up the scientific method, but to bring up in proper balance the true, rich, rounded appreciation of life itself, with its own sure springs and sources of direct experience. Here there comes into operation a world of infinite scope which "lends a *yonder* to all ends."...

As soon as we live our way into the heart of the realities we need for creative life, the sense of frustration is over and there is a hole in the sky and free water to swim in. Nobody in the thrill of action has any doubt about freedom. And nobody who has truly fallen in love has any doubt of the intrinsic value, the infinite value, of love. It is its own evidence, its own excuse for being.

> Is there nothing then but love, search we sky and earth?
> There is nothing out of love hath perpetual worth.

What is true of love is just as true of God and the world of spiritual realities. There come high moments when we find ourselves where we know we *belong,* when the Beyond is here and the Yonder is present. These eternal moments take the soul to the very heart of reality. Many times I have found my way home in the dark because my feet felt the road when my eyes could not see it. There is Something in us, deeper than hands or feet, that finds the way to the Central Reality, and when we arrive we know it.

From *The Radiant Life,*
pp. 28–32.

-»><«-

It can be taken as settled, I think, that we shall never prove the existence of God by a purely logical, speculative argument. These arguments, in the days before their thinness and hollowness grew apparent, comforted and buoyed up many souls and performed a valuable service. Even now they are not wholly devoid of meaning. But they awaken little more vital interest in us to-day than do the pieces of broken pottery brought from the mound that was formerly Jericho and where men once lived eagerly and intensely. The juggle with syllogisms leaves us with the same lack of conviction that we have when we see the Indian fakir throw his coil of rope into the air and then profess to climb up hand over hand on the rope, for all the time we know that there is no place in the sky where rope can catch to support itself—and the man. So, too, there is no way of getting more out of syllogism than you put into its premises. Like the Tower of Babel, it fails to reach all the way up.

We get immense results through the scientific method, but at the same time it entails a severe reduction of the rich complete universe as it really is discovered to be when we approach it in terms of actual life and of those interpretations of intrinsic value in which we are bound to clothe it. The aspects of reality which are of such a nature that they must be felt and appreciated in order to be known, are left out of account by a method whose sole aim or purpose is to describe and explain rather than to comprehend and interpret. "Describe" has in scientific language for better or for worse come to mean "describe in terms of mathematical formulae," and "explain" has come to mean "explain by antecedent causes,"˙a method which lands the explorer at last in a tight mechanistic system, and leaves him in a world in which this event and that event *appear* to be explained by another event but in which in the last resort nothing is either actually comprehended or luminously explained, for the *whole* is meaningless and incomprehensible —it clanks in orderly fashion but it satisfies nobody.

Any object that a rigid science deals with, from the most minute to the most sublime, would necessarily be a finite thing among other things—one object caused by another object, or objects—or at best the added sum of all the things there are, and that method certainly does not lead to what we mean by "God." The astronomer is quite justified in not expecting to find God through his telescope and the physicist is equally justified in not introducing God as part of his explanation of the movement of matter in space. The kind of God that science by its present method could give us would at best be in the nature of a "cause" that would at once need another cause of that cause to explain it. J. A. Thomson was right when he said: "We cannot by scientific searching find out God." Our hearts would never be satisfied nor our lives inspired or sustained by a God of that type—a *deus ex machina* God. One of the worst disasters to religion and, for that matter, to life itself, would be the elimination from it of all mystery and sublimity, all awe and wonder, and the fringe and halo of penumbral splendor. In the end all thin rationalizations rob life of meaning and spoil it at the heart of it.

It is at the same time true that the progress of science may greatly clarify our ideas about the kind of God we have a right to expect to find in the universe. It may at least give us negative clues and tests. It will help us to eliminate child-minded and primitive conceptions of God. It will disillusion us from the doll-stage of religion. We shall not any longer expect to find God on Mount Olympus or at the top of a Tower of Babel or as a Monarch in the sky. As we grow in scientific insight we shall increasingly discount superstition and magic. We shall be dissatisfied with the conception of a God who exhibits caprice and favoritism and we shall expect to find unvarying order, enduring wisdom and intelligent purpose in the God of our new faith. . . .

Our way of approach, however, to the central problem of the reality and nature of God must be, as I have implied, neither pure logical speculation, nor the mechanistic scientific method. Neither of these ways of approach would ever bring us to any of the intrinsic values by which we live our deepest and most essential life. Beauty and love and unselfish goodness lie just as much beyond the scope of syllogisms as God does. No one could have anticipated by any speculative argument or by "bare rationality" that moral goodness and beauty and love would one day overtop practical efficiency and introduce a new level of creation altogether.

Just as impossible is it, too, to arrive at the meaning and significance of beauty or love or goodness by methods of description or by causal explanations. No process of analysis, no piling up of descriptive accounts, no reversion to antecedent causes, brings us any nearer to what we *mean* by beauty, goodness or love. When we have succeeded in "explaining" love, when for example, we trace it to some utilitarian advantage, or when we discover that a person's goodness is a piece of fine calculation, we are no longer talking about either "love" or "goodness"; we are back once more on the well-known level of "causal explanations" and "utility values." And yet nothing is more real, nothing is more certain, nothing is more significant to us, than any one of these so-called intrinsic values; and even those persons who on rationalistic grounds deny their standing or validity nevertheless *act* in reference to them, find joy and happiness in them and, in their best moments, *live by them*. The world we actually *live in* is unreduced and includes far more than the total items in the scientific category.

Our best point of approach to the reality and nature of God is beyond question through this type of experience. It is essentially different both from the logical method and the scientific method. We need not insist and we do not insist that the method of appreciation, or life-valuation, is "absolutely" different from the method of scientific description, just as we do not claim that a fact and the appreciation of its value for life are utterly and completely sundered. It is true, however, that the procedure in describing and explaining a fact is quite unlike the situation when we enjoy an object, wonder at it, feel the meaning and significance of it, and raise the quality and level of our own personality and our social relations with our fellows through the appeal and the lifting power of it.

In the case of the value-experience there are evidences of objective reality similar to those of fact-experience. The universe is as truly *behind* the one as it is behind the other. Our values, our appreciations, our joys and our aspirations have been as important factors in our adjustment to the universe, in our learning how to live in it, as any biological structure which we possess has been. We should not be "men," and we should not be here at all, with these aspects gone. These aspects which make us men and which lift us above the level of fact-recording beings are thus not some capricious addendum or overplus which *we* supply to the otherwise sterile world of things. Our universe itself is built to the scale of values and is the home and habitat of beings that live that way. The main difference, however, between fact and values is that we can conceivably think of *facts* as having a kind of abstract and realistic existence; whereas it is impossible to think intelligently of intrinsic values—by which I mean beauty, love, goodness or truth—without thinking at the same time of their inward meaning to someone who cares, enjoys, lives in and appreciates the worth and worthiness of the object. Appreciation is not appreciation without a mind that appreciates and discovers meaning.

The universe in its unfolding processes from lower to higher, seems to be basis and framework for an immense spiritual adventure. For the religious attitude this adventure turns out to be the very heart and center of the whole creation. It is, no doubt, quite possible to be so busily occupied study-ing the framework, describing the mechanism of it, as to miss all the signs and suggestions which indicate that there is any "spiritual adventure" going on at the heart of things. But if we are to find God we must look for Him where there are indications of such a spiritual adventure.

From *Pathways to the Reality of God,*
pp. 50–56.

-->>)(<<-

THE Western mind turns naturally to what we are pleased to call practical conduct—life in action. When we talk about living a rich, full life we are apt to assess it in terms of service, of positive contribution, of deeds, of things accomplished, of spiritual output. Contemplation seems like a waste of time to the practical Occidental. He wants to be going somewhere, to be doing something. Western ethical systems do not usually lead up to con-templation of the eternal; they find the goal of life in the realization of a better social order and the formation of a truer personal life to fit the pro-posed new order. This latter way of life is generally called "realization" or "energism" and the contemplative way of life, set over against it, is called "mysticism." They are, however, by no means inconsistent ways of life and I shall undertake to show that contemplation is an essential part of practical, energetic action, in fact that the mystical experience contributes as almost nothing else does toward the task of building the truer personal life and the better social order. The greatest of the mystics have not been spiritual drones; they have been hundred-horse-power persons pouring into the world of time their unwonted additions of spiritual energy. But, at the same time, it is true the mystic does feel the experience of God to be a sufficient end in itself, precisely as the lover of beauty feels that the experience of beauty is itself sufficient without any supplementary thought of how it can be used for practical purposes. There are experiences in which the desire for action is relatively held in suspense. The experience yields an immediate satisfaction and seems for the moment an end in itself, detached from all problems of origin or consequence. Like the mountain experience of transfiguration, this mystic experience, too, seems to be a fitting occasion for building a permanent tabernacle, for banishing all thought of going somewhere or of doing something. A level of life has been reached which changes all values for a man and floods all life with power,

> That sets the undreamed of rapture at his hand
> And puts the cheap old joy in the scorned dust.

Mysticism, then, is one of those experiences which hold within themselves a sense of finality, of adequacy. They need no plus to make them satisfying. To break through the veils and wrappings of things and to discover God to be real, real as nothing else is real, *that* is an experience which needs no additions, nothing beyond itself. But nevertheless, as we shall see, the most remarkable thing about a mystical experience is the increased efficiency of life which it produces. The man who climbs Mount Everest will be satisfied at the peak with the achievement itself. There he is at last at the top of the world, rapt and ecstatic with the overpowering consciousness of the experience. But when he comes down he will ever after be "the man who first climbed Mount Everest," and it will give him unique influence and standing in the world which will count, though the desire to use the fruits of his climb may not, and certainly should not, remotely occur to him as he stands there on the back of the Himalayas.

An outbreak of mysticism is always a sign that the soul of man is uttering its vigorous protest against the encroachment of some organized system of life or thought which threatens to leave scant scope and area for its own free initiative and its spontaneous creative activity. It is a proclamation that the soul has certain inherent rights and capacities—a domain of its own which must be respected and held sacred. Sometimes mysticism has been a protest of man's spirit against the hardening crust of dogma, and like a hot lava surging up from within it has burst through the cooled strata of intellectual systems. Sometimes it has been a powerful revolt against a more or less rigid external ecclesiasticism and then the mystic has stood forth as the champion of the invisible Church which, like the Jerusalem above, is free and is the mother of us all.

For more than a generation now we have all been dimly aware of the steady encroachment of science upon the inner domain of the soul. Science has so often aided man's conquests and it has done so much to strengthen his hands and heighten his practical powers that he has frequently been oblivious of the slow winding of the coils that have been binding in and constricting his spirit. But when, like Samson, one awakes and shakes himself from his lull of slumber, he is surprised to see how far science has materialized and mechanized the universe, and what a tiny area of scope and free movement is left for the human soul.

Every precinct of man's inner domain has been invaded and every sanctuary of the soul has had some of its sacred vessels rifled and carried away. The Copernican theory swept the heavens clean and left no place there for God's dwelling or for the eternal home of the triumphant soul. The sky is not a fixed dome, it is only an illusory gateway to the cold stretches of infinite space. Going up into space does not mean getting any nearer to God or to the habitation of the saints. The Darwinian theory stretched out time as the Copernican had stretched out space. It left no assignable point in time where the finger of God, or the breath of the Divine Spirit, entered and operated, as the other theory had left no domain in space for God's presence. Both tended to obliterate in men's thoughts the line between natural and supernatural by expanding the former and eliminating the latter. Then the higher critic began to apply the scientific methods of historical study to the books of holy Scripture, putting the emphasis upon historical development and upon the play of a most important *human* factor. Finally, most ruthless of all the invading hosts of science, psychology comes with its exact descriptions and laboratory tests, and questions whether there is any spiritual agent within or behind the mental states and the describable behavior which make up this strange thing we call a man's life. We are told of multitudinous brain-paths and complex neural processes but we are given no spiritual entity. Is it any wonder that the man of settled scientific habits finds it difficult to discover any legitimate sphere for religion, or that the college youth is confused?

The way out of this "fix," however, is not to run amuck against science, to deny its verified facts and conclusions, to join in William J. Bryan's eloquent scream against "the old man with his bag of monkeys from the jungle," nor to turn with Sir Conan Doyle and others to the task of assembling a new set of superstitions. This is no way out. We can make no progress with religion until we learn to have respect and reverence for facts. The solid work of more than two centuries of splendidly equipped workers in science will not be swept away either by sallies of cheap humor or by the trance reports of mediums and the phenomena of haunted houses.

Only by discovering more in the realities of the universe than science has read there can we find hope of deliverance from the barrenness of our present world. We must learn to see that there are many realities which elude the scientific method, that science always reduces its world for purposes of description, and that we do not need so much to break with science as to supplement it. There are many great moments when what the poet calls "the heart" stands up and answers, *"I have felt."* Walt Whitman says in his vivid way:

When I heard the learn'd astronomer,
When the proofs, the figures, were ranged in columns before me,
When I was shown the charts and diagrams, to add, divide, and measure
      them,
When I sitting heard the astronomer where he lectured with much
      applause in the lecture-room,
How soon unaccountably I became tired and sick,
Till rising and gliding out I wander'd off by myself
In the mystical moist night-air, and from time to time,
Look'd up in perfect silence at the stars.

When I talk about mysticism I mean something fundamental to the normal essential nature of the soul. I mean a native capacity in us for intercourse and communion with God, who is not "up in the sky," but rather is the foundational Life and Spirit within us and by whom we live and are. Every experience which makes us sure of our own soul and its abysmal deeps, *ipso facto* makes us sure of God. For centuries and millenniums men have turned to the sky or raised their hands upward in their quest for God. The ancient posture and attitude will no doubt long persist and rightly so, for the upward look befits the act, but God cannot be our God unless He is Spirit, unless He is kindred to our souls, and if He is of that nature then we must find Him where we find ourselves—in the spiritual sphere, not in space. We must find Him knocking at the gates of our own dwelling and entering to share Himself with us there. This experience of the mystic—if it be not a futile "projection" of man's own subjective feelings—implies that the finite human spirit can, in the vast immensities of the universe find the living, loving, palpitating Spirit and can come into vital contact with infinite and eternal reality.

By far the larger number of mystics probably live and die without explicitly knowing that they are mystics. They are active conative mystics rather than cognitive. They practise the presence of God instead of arriving at a clear state of knowledge about it. They do not point to some moment when they could say with Penington, "I have met with my God." They quietly manifest in acts that energies not their own and incursions of power from beyond themselves are coming through them. Lord Rosebery's fine estimate of Oliver Cromwell expresses what I mean. He says of Cromwell: "He was a practical mystic, the most formidable and terrible of all combinations. A man who ... has inspiration and adds to it the energy of a mighty man of action; such a man as that lives in communion on a Sinai of his own." Christ's teaching was almost invariably an interpretation of some deed or act or work which he had performed. He began with action and ended with telling what it meant. He could well say, "The deeds which I do bear witness of me." This may well be called "practical mysticism," or as I have named it, "conative-mysticism"—mysticism of life and action. It is the greatest kind there is and its power in any given life is cumulative. It gathers momentum and force like a rolling snowball.

The mystical experience, which is far more common than the sceptically minded and the critics of mysticism realize, finds its most solid support not in ecstasy or miracle but in the verifying facts of our everyday life. Our simplest faith in the triumphant worth of normal goodness, our steady confidence that the truth we hold is universally true, our conviction that love is something more than a subjective thrill, our intimations that the beauty which we see here and now is only a glimpse of an infinite and eternal beauty—all these convictions are built upon the fact that there is a junction of our finite individual lives with one real foundational Spirit who is the ground and source of all the self-transcending values by which we live. Isolate us, insulate us, leave us as lonely oases in a sterile desert and we could not even have mirages of the good, the true, the lovely and the beautiful. Life would dry up and shrivel away. We are these strange eternity-haunted beings just because we are conjunct with God whom some of us at least discover walking with us in the cool of the day, as the fish feels the ocean or the bird feels the air. These experiences of inner fortification and joy help us immensely to bear the "heavy and weary weight of all this unintelligible world" and give us an unwonted buoyancy.

From Fundamental Ends of Life,
pp. 86–90; 96; 115–117.

->>)<(<-

WHEN we move up to higher levels and include in the survey of our universe the processes of life, the scope and range of self-consciousness, the intrinsic nature of beauty, the absolute value of truth, the infinite worth of the good will, the unfathomable aspects of personality and the reality of a type of love which transcends all utilitarian considerations, we are confronted with a nature of things totally unlike that which is presented to us in the best-constructed "naturalism."

Before we undertake to raise the question whether there are realities of a spiritual nature above and beyond ourselves in the universe, it may be best to consider the undeniable spiritual pathways revealed within ourselves. The strange fact confronts us first of all that we who are so seemingly finite, ask, and are bound to ask, ultimate questions. We find it impossible to regard ourselves as chance dust wreaths whirled up from below. We cannot consistently hold that we are bits of the earth's crust, or curious shapes of cooled star waste. We are haunted with intimations of the infinite and eternal. We live out beyond the bounded and the limited. We ponder on realities which by no stretch of imagination can be thought of as made of dust, even of star dust.

The most significant thing of all in our make-up perhaps is our inescapable faith in the reality of some sort of truth. The completest skepticism that can be imagined always presupposes faith that there is something that can be called truth. If I say in my darkest moments of despair, in my lowest approaches to a dust-wreath condition, "there is no truth," "all is mad error and insane confusion," even so, I have asserted a universal statement to which I attribute "truth." My mind has organized a body of facts, and has come to a positive conclusion. In making it, as is always the case with truth, I go far beyond anything that sense experience has reported, or ever could report. There is a downright and absolute aspect to all assertions that belong in the sphere of truth.

In this particular case, my statement is either true or false. Whether it is true or false will eventually be settled by an appeal from the mind in its narrower ranges of the moment to the mind in its more inclusive scope. All experience is an appeal to more experience. If the statement is true, we are then faced with this odd situation that "it is absolutely true that there is no such thing as truth." In the domain of logic and in the realm of truth the mind falls into self-contradiction when it denies its capacity to know and when it tries to take refuge in mere relativities. We cannot know *without knowing that we know.* In any case, all assertions of truth or of the impossibilities of truth carry universal implications and involve that strange aspect of logical necessity which we express by *it must be so.* That carries us far beyond anything a dust wreath could conjure out of its empty hat!

Materialists of all types and fashions in one breath banish everything spiritual from the universe and in the next breath claim that they know that they know. But knowledge with such ranges of universality and certainty could not possibly be got through sense-observation. There is no "sense" for *universality* nor is there a "sense" for *certainty!* There is no way that such knowledge could get stamped in on the brain. Knowledge involves vast coherent mental processes. First of all there is the organization of observed facts, then a comparison of them and a reflection upon them. The mind seizes upon universal implications and makes a judgment of logical necessity. That far-reaching work of interpretation by the mind carries with it the glowing refutation of the claims that are made for materialism. If *truth* is real the reality of something that is spiritual irresistibly follows.

From *A Preface to Christian Faith in a New Age,*
pp. 59–62.

->>><<<-

IT may conceivably be, as Napoleon asserted, that God is on the side of the heaviest battalions. Those of us who share the modern outlook will in any case not expect to see bullets deflected by divine intervention so that the "right cause" may win the battle over those who are fighting on the "evil side," nor shall we count on having the sun and moon and stars lined up in contributive fashion on our side so that the truth may prevail. What I am contending for is that in the long run of history ethical and spiritual ideals prove to be real factors and play an important role in shaping events and in opening doors for new forward movements for the race. Something besides the environment of rivers, seas, mountains, soil, weather and contiguous neighbors, and the fundamental capacity gained through inherited instincts has evidently operated in the march of the race forward. Not only have ideals *operated* in creative and dynamic fashion, but they have shown a cumulative power that has rolled up a marked increment of gain to the ethical and spiritual element in the world, even during the short span of the historical period.

I do not need to labor the point that ideals are decisive factors in shaping the course of events. Nothing is more obvious in the life of an individual person than the fact that his forecast and vision of unrealized good must always be taken into account in estimating his next step. He builds his life by successive advances in the aim of what he aspires to be and of the goal which he proposes to attain. What is true of an individual in this respect is no less true of a tribe, or a people, or a nation. The great moments in the history of people are the occasions when the entire group is unified, fused and swept forward by some great loyalty to an ideal purpose. The material assets, the economic status, the geographical situation, climate and food conditions, and psychological traits and disposition will always need to be considered, but the forecast of faith, of vision and of loyalty can and often does produce effects that are little short of miraculous.

Hosea Bigelow was no doubt right when he declared that "history *doos* get for'ard on a powder-cart." But it gets forward no less certainly on the ground swell of some great ideal purpose. Sometimes the ideal purpose makes use of the "powder-cart," and sometimes it uses less violent means, but in all instances of real achievement the gain will be found to have been due to the creative power of ideals. Very often, probably in most instances, the ideal was only dimly present to consciousness, as is true in the case of most individual decisions. It was in very truth a "ground swell," more or less submerged and involving more and carrying farther than any leader, or than the entire group together, saw or suspected at the time.

This situation raises the central question of the source and origin of ideals. If they can be reduced to the push and drive of instincts then, of course, there is no *breach* involved between the food-seeking animal and the advantage-seeking nation. We can "explain" the new and the higher in terms of the old and the lower. We shall continue on the biological level and we shall go on interpreting in terms of "struggle for existence" and "survival of the fittest." If one is content to deal with the problem after the manner and method of mechanistic science he will incline to the view that all so-called ethical and spiritual ideals have been built up out of primitive instincts and practical interests. He will set about to explain what we usually call the higher forms of life by antecedent causes and more elemental conditions, and he will seem to find in the higher forms only more complicated combinations of the elements that were already there on the earlier levels.

The trouble with this method is that at the end of our story we have no real explanation of the real facts. A moral value is not the sum total of a number of elemental instincts. The magisterial command of duty, for which one joyously surrenders physical life, is not made up of a complex of pre-human traits. It is something *new*, as uniquely *new* as beauty was when it first made its appeal to an appreciative mind. All attempts to reduce moral, i.e., intrinsic, goodness to pleasure, to calculation, or to any type of utilitarian inducements, have so far failed. They end in talking about something quite different in type and quality from the august thing which we really have on our hands.

As the taste of lemonade is not the taste of lemon plus the taste of sugar, but something wholly unique, so, only on a loftier scale, *love* in its highest ranges is not a sex-instinct, plus a gregarious impulse, plus a tender emotion; and moral goodness is not a subtle forecast of some remote gain, plus an instinctive surrender of present want in order to secure the far-off "good." It is different from any aggregate that ever was made, just as the felt beauty of a flower, or of the curl of a wave or of the swirl of a waterfall introduces something wholly different from masses of matter in motion. We know of no alchemy that can turn the water of prudence into the wine of spontaneous and uncalculating good will. We pass over from an act judged and estimated in terms of advantageous results to an inner court where conduct is valued in the light of fitness to conform to an ideal standard. Professor Pringle-Pattison is speaking soberly when he says: "The breach between ethical man and pre-human nature constitutes without exception the most important fact which the universe has to show."

What has happened is that we have passed over from a biological being acting from the push of inherited structural instinct to a being that can see and feel the intrinsic worth of a deed for its own sake. An ethical and spiritual being introduces a superfluous element, that is, something that goes beyond what is needed for survival purposes. Living becomes on this level *a fine art,* a thing of grace and beauty and joy. The loyalties and ideals that have been shaping factors in the destiny of nations and peoples have had to do with more than economic and physical advantages, though these tangible aspects are of course not to be ignored or belittled. The great national leaders of history have risen above the merely practical, the crassly advantageous for themselves and their people; they have been guided, at the highest moments, by a wisdom of what ought to be.

Instead of trying to explain the higher in terms of the lower we are on much surer ground when we read the feeble beginnings, the dim adumbrations, in the light of the completer goal that has been achieved. The meaning of the earlier conditions comes in sight only in the developed effects. The new cannot be juggled out of the old by processes of combinations or of additions. Life, when properly viewed, demonstrates the patent truth that real evolution is *creation.* We shall never understand evolution until we read it and interpret it in terms of the best and highest that it has brought into being.

It can be taken, I think, without further debate, that ethical ideals have introduced something new and creative into the stream of biological progress. We must, I believe, further conclude either that they are purely human contrivances, artificial and conventional schemes, for the promotion of desired results; or that they have their ground and justification in the eternal nature of things, that is, in the fundamental structure of the universe.

There is as much evidence that the universe itself has produced the dominating and shaping ideals of history as that the universe has produced electrons and protons, or that it has produced the amoeba and the salamander. History gives as plain evidence of a continual sifting and testing of ideals as biology does of the sifting and testing of species. There is all the way down, or rather up, the line of racial progress a stern selection of ideals. There are dead and effete ideals as surely as there are extinct trilobites and five-toed horses. The universe is just as busy weeding out unfit ideals as ever it has been locking up out-worn types of life in the buried strata of the "scarpéd cliff." There are ideals that are freakish and capricious. There are ideals that are artificial and conventional and which do not survive. They cannot pass the tests when the days of judgment come, when they are tried as by fire. There are other ideals which have stood the testings of the time-processes and the siftings of the ages. They endure through long periods and become contributory factors in shaping the course of history.

From *Pathways to the Reality of God,*
pp. 107–112.

-»>«<-

"ORTHODOXY" has been pitted against what it chose to call "heterodoxy," but in most instances the latter was as fervently, as intensely, *religious* as was the former. The alternative was always religion in another form. Today the pivotal issue has profoundly shifted. The religious attitude itself is challenged. The religious view of life as such is questioned. The validity of a spiritual outlook of any kind is put in jeopardy. The alternative to religious faith today is the acceptance of a naturalistic universe, a biologized man, a secularized society. Meantime the issues between the conservatives and the liberals, between the fundamentalists and the modernists, between the high church and the broad church wings seem like petty controversies, when the whole house in which the contestants are living is on fire and in deadly peril.

For a vast section of the human race religion today is declared to be "an opiate." It is thought of as a cunningly devised method of making the masses submissive to their overlords or their over-shepherds, and of lulling them into a dull acceptance of the hard present conditions of life by an imaginary vision of relief which is to be realized in a world to come. Religion is discounted as a scheme of drugging the victim with imaginary hopes and fears instead of with opium or with vodka.

This conception of religion as "opiate" is by no means confined to Russia. It has been caught up as a comfortable slogan by hosts of youth who are in a state of revolt from the inadequate interpretations of Christianity in their homes and in their childhood churches and Sunday schools. They have done almost no *thinking* about the deeper issues of life. They have blindly revolted against an inherited system that has lost its attraction, and they have caught up a popular "rationalization," which gives them a temporary relief from what seem to them the "burdens" of religion. Parents in their agony and ministers in their perplexity find themselves helpless. They are confronted by a "drift" like that which carries the sand of the desert over the vegetation of border countries. It is not a position which has been arrived at by intelligent processes of thought and which can consequently be answered by the reasoning mind. It is a confused "drift" of blind forces, urges, moods, inchoate attitudes, rather than a set of reasoned ideas which can be met in a stand-up, give and take, debate.

Then, again, we find ourselves today confronted with the central issue of what "civilization" is to mean in this post-war world. Have we perhaps left forever behind the comfortable world in which the free individual can be captain of his own soul, can think his own thoughts, plan his own career, and shape his own destiny as a person? Or is man—and woman too—to be a mechanized unit in a totalitarian state, to be regimented from outside, ruled as the wheel rules the spoke, and used as *a means,* as a passive instrument, for the ends of a completely secularized state? In a "civilization" of that latter type there can be no place for free, spontaneous, creative religion as a joyous response of the individual person to a higher invisible order of values and realities, for the totalitarian state is conceived already to be the highest reality and value, to which every knee must bow and every arm salute. The "civilization" is not a return to "paganism." It is not a "restoration" of the gods Odin and Thor. They—with paganism—belong to a past which is forever "dead." That primitive period of life was intensely, throbbingly, religious. It was alive with *faith* and *vision.* It was a crude faith, no doubt, and the vision was distorted, but it was nevertheless man's sincere attempt to adjust his life to invisible and eternal realities, greater than himself. That simple stage of life cannot be "restored." That early faith and that childlike vision do not fit the world-outlook of today.

The alternative tendency that is being adopted is, not to find the way down to a deeper faith, or to widen the vision to fit the whole field of reality, but to accept instead a social-economic theory of life as a substitute for religion, and to put the temporal state in the place of the eternal Fatherland of the soul. It is, again, not alone in one country that this severe "reduction" of life is under way. The "drift" toward a secularized world in one form or another is widespread, and it is an ominous mood. "Earth is enough" is one of its articles of confession. It is not enough. It will not do. We men cannot *live* that way. There is a "remainder"— a precious remnant of life— which needs to be explored. There are *implications* which our kind of life forces upon us. They need to be seriously dealt with. There is an interior *depth-life* in man that carries rich veins of wealth which should be carefully assayed. The historical trails to the headwaters of our faith are being profoundly searched today and these historical researches are accumulating stores of spiritual riches. We need not tremble for the preservation of the truth which History enshrines. It will not be lost.

From *The Testimony of the Soul,*
pp. 2–5.

⫸ VII ⫷

What Is True Mysticism?

VII

No definition of religious mysticism in general abstract terms is ever satisfactory. At its best it misses the vivid reality of a genuine mystical experience, somewhat as one misses the reality of motion when one stops a spinning top to see what motion is like! In both cases, what we are endeavoring to examine eludes us. In one instance we are examining an arrested object in order to find out what motion is like, and in the other instance we are putting an abstract theory in the place of a palpitating human experience which flowers or may flower into an almost endless variety of forms and types. It involves the fallacy of substitution—putting dry, congealed words for the live pluckings of the heart.

There will always be in any audience where one speaks of the mystic's way of life someone who will rise at the end of the lecture and say appealingly, "Will the speaker kindly tell us in two or three plain words what mysticism really is?" It is always possible to meet that demand by saying that religious mysticism is an immediate, intuitive, experimental knowledge of God, or one may say it is consciousness of a Beyond, or of transcendent Reality, or of Divine Presence. One can pack that phrase into his mind and take it home to Aunt Jane or to Grandmother Ann, but the phrase will mean much or little or nothing as it wakens or does not waken in consciousness some memory of high tide moments when the Spirit flooded in and changed the old levels of life. . . .

One of the most significant effects of experiences of this sort is the resulting deepening of life and a marked increase of joy. One feels as though his specific gravity were suddenly lightened by an incursion from Beyond the usual margins. The person concerned goes down to deeper foundations for the structure of life, somewhat as modern builders have learned to do for the stability of the present-day higher climbing type of steel and concrete structure, or those that may be tested by the force of earthquakes. The opening out of the depth-life of the soul is almost always in evidence in persons who have gained the conviction of direct contact with God. There comes that marked depth of calm and serenity which a touch of eternity brings to life. One is not taken out of the time-stream of change and process, but life is undergirded and steadied by a surer foundation which is deep-based in what is felt to be the eternal. So much of life is thin and gasping with rush and hurry that it is an immense asset to have these sub-basement resources which bring steadiness and assurance, even in the midst of change and turmoil. There can be a center of inward calm even while the affairs of life are going on in the time-stream.

It is, too, a very great advantage which the mystic has, that what we may call the Over-World—the World of Eternal Spiritual Reality—has become to him as certain and as much a part of the domain which he inhabits as is the world which he sees and touches and which gives him his daily food supplies. In the noble sense of the word "amphibian," he lives in two worlds and finds himself at home in both of them. Francis Thompson's words:

> O world invisible, I view thee;
> O world intangible, I touch thee;
> O world unknowable, I know thee;
> Inapprehensible, I clutch thee,

become as natural and normal expressions of his full life as the act of breathing or the act of swimming is. This Over-World is, of course, an essential feature of Plato's philosophy. It is for him the ground and home of truth and beauty and goodness; it is the realm in which all of our eternal values have their spire-top, and Platonism in all generations has borne faithful testimony to such an Over-World, though sometimes by too great depreciation of *this* world, and sometimes appearing to sunder the two worlds by too wide and unbridgeable a chasm.

It is another great advantage to discover, as the mystic does through his experience, that the human mind is not bound and limited to the world of matter and to the approach of the senses, but that it can be raised by divine assistance to an intimate correspondence with the transcendent and supersensuous realm of reality, and can become a transmissive organ of it— of a grace like that in Jesus Christ, a pure love like that in God, who is love, and a communion and fellowship with the Holy Spirit with whom our spirits, however feebly, are akin.

The mystic has found the bridge, the ladder, the scaling-wings, which make both worlds his. Sometimes he seems to break through or reach across, and sometimes he seems aware of a thrust from the Beyond into the now and here. In either case he finds himself no longer theorizing about the world of higher reality; he has found his way into it and partakes of it as his promised land. He is in vital communion with a larger world of Life that surrounds his temporal life. It brings with it the feeling of the essential grandeur of the soul, and it makes the moral purpose of life, which springs from this junction of our life here and the Eternal Over-World, the most august thing in the universe. Those great mystical books, the Upanishads, speak of the infinite personality of man, and the Cambridge Platonists said God is more in the mind of man than anywhere else in the universe.

But here we are confronted with the caveat of the psychologist that these experiences of the mystics are only subjective phenomena, lacking objective reference, and that they, further, are dubious because they are in many cases pathological phenomena and heavily weighted with illusion, hallucination, wishful thinking and autosuggestion.

I shall deal with the second point first, as it is the easier of the two to dispose of. It is true that there is a serious pathological factor to be faced in the biographies and autobiographies of many of the mystics of history. They often reveal in their lives a longer or shorter period of emotional intensity, with symptoms of hysteria and with tendencies toward mental instability. Mystics are, like most persons of genius, not tightly organized and they are inclined to be influenced by the fringe and marginal consciousness rather than by the focal and attentive center of consciousness. They tend to veer away from the habitual and to have novelty and freshness. This would mean that they might well be more subject to trance and ecstasy and hypnoidal conditions than are normal persons, but it might also mean that they would be more likely, when at their best, to be sensitive to an Over-World of Reality and more likely to be the organs of fresh revelations of it. It is a notable fact that their experiences, and their stabilized faith through what they believe to be their contacts with God, in many cases, in fact usually, result in a unification of personality, in a great increase of dynamic quality— a power to stand the universe—and in a recovery of health and normality. While it must be admitted that this pathological factor, which cannot be ignored, presents an element of liability in the mystic's testimony, there nevertheless seems to me on the whole to be an overwhelming balance of asset in favor of the significance of the mystic's life and message. Hysteria does not unify and construct life as mystical experience indubitably does do.

The fact that the mystic himself puts a heavy stress upon the testimony of *immediate consciousness* of reality, as contrasted with consciousness of objects mediated through sense contact or impact, seems at the take-off to give some ground for the claim of the critical psychologist that mystical experiences are infected, and "sicklied o'er," with the structural weakness of *subjectivity*, of a mere private buzzing in the head.

This charge of subjectivity, however, turns out to have much less ground of support than appears from the loudness of its roar. The purely empirical, or phenomenalist, psychologist, and it is he who is most apt to make this charge, finds *himself* admittedly, in his psychological method, shut up to a study of mental phenomena, that is to say, to *states* of mind which pass before the footlights of consciousness. He has no legitimate way, with his basic theory, of getting out of this "ego-centric predicament" and of establishing the validity of any objects beyond the "spectator mind." He lacks a sound philosophical basis for the objective validity of any kind of experience, even of the world of sense-experience. He needs a much sounder epistemology. If he proposes to treat psychology as confined to the study of "phenomena," i.e., to the study of mental processes, he is himself all the time sloughed in the bottomless bog of subjectivity. He usually fails to take adequate note of what Kant called the transcendental unity of self-consciousness, which is always involved in all perception of objects, and he takes too little note of the interpretative function of this unified and permanently *same self* in all processes of knowledge.

He furthermore has a far too superficial ground for the validity of our knowledge of our self, our assurance of the reality of other selves and our experience of the objective aspects of beauty, truth and moral significance. He has not yet adequately studied the depth-life of the inner self or its extra-sensory powers. There are in these lives of ours impalpables and intangibles, which determine the issues and destiny of life as surely as bread and other tactual objects do. They cannot be reduced to sense contacts, nor are they purely "subjective" phenomena. They have universal significance. They can be counted on and depended on as certainly as the Himalayas can be.

Finally these experiences of God, these mutual correspondences with the Over-World are *felt* by the mystic to be as objectively real, as genuinely a subject-object relationship—a self experiencing an Other—as is ever true of any event of life. The conviction of Presence, which attends these experiences, the affirmation of reality, is no whit weaker than is the case when one has an object in his clenched hand. It carries a triumphant sense of certitude. It enables the beholder to stand the universe. It organizes life on the profoundest levels. It wins the assent of the mind and will. It furnishes a dynamic of a unique sort and, again and again, this contact with the unseen in a man's life has been a determining factor in shaping the course of history. It has helped to build the world. In fact, the intuitions of the transcendent, insights of what ought to be and must be, convictions that the Eternal God shuts every door but *this one that opens,* have been a major factor in the course of human events, and must be taken into account as certainly as Alexander's conquests must be.

From *The Flowering of Mysticism,*
pp. 250–251; 258–263.

It should always be noted that the number of persons who are subject to mystical experiences—that is to say, persons who feel themselves brought into contact with an environing Presence and supplied with new energy to live by—is much larger than we usually suppose. We know only the mystics who were dowered with a literary gift and who could tell in impressive language what had come to them, but of the multitude of those who have felt and seen and who yet were unable to tell in words about their experience, of these we are ignorant. An undeveloped and uncultivated form of mystical consciousness is present, I think, in most religious souls, and whenever it is unusually awake and vivid the whole inner and outer life is intensified by such experiences, even though there may be little that can be put into explicit account in language. There are multitudes of men and women now living, often in out-of-the-way places, in remote hamlets or on isolated farms, who are the salt of the earth and the light of the world in their communities, because they have had vital experiences that revealed to them realities which their neighbors missed and that supplied them with energy to live by, which the mere "church-goers" failed to find.

I am more and more convinced, as I pursue my studies on the meaning and value of mysticism, with the conviction that religion, *i.e.*, religion when it is real, alive, vital, and transforming, is essentially and at bottom a mystical act, a direct response to an inner world of spiritual reality, an implicit relationship between the finite and infinite, between the part and the whole. The French philosopher, Émile Boutroux, has finely called this junction of finite and infinite in us, by which these mystical experiences are made possible, "the Beyond that is within"—"the Beyond," as he says, "with which man comes in touch on the inner side of his nature."

Whenever we go back to the fundamental mystical experience, to the soul's first-hand testimony, we come upon a conviction that the human spirit transcends itself and is environed by a spiritual world with which it holds commerce and vital relationship. The constructive mystics, not only of the Christian communions but also those of other religions, have explored higher levels of life than those on which men usually live, and they have given impressive demonstration through the heightened dynamic quality of their lives and service that they have been drawing upon and utilizing reservoirs of vital energy. They have revealed a peculiar aptitude for correspondence with the Beyond that is within, and they have exhibited a genius for living by their inner conviction of God, "of practicing God," as Jeremy Taylor called it.

From *The Inner Life,*
pp. 178–181.

->>><<<-

I AM not interested in mysticism as an *ism*. It turns out in most accounts to be a dry and abstract thing, hardly more like the warm and intimate experience than the color of a map is like the country for which it stands. "Canada is very pink," seems quite an inadequate description of the noble country north of our border. It is mystical experience and not mysticism that is worthy of our study. We are concerned with the experience itself, not with second-hand formulations of it. "The mystic," says Professor Royce, "is a thorough-going empiricist"; "God ceases to be an object and becomes an experience," says Professor Pringle-Pattison. If it is an experience, we want to find out what happens to the mystic himself inside where he lives. According to those who have been there the experience which we call mystical is charged with the conviction of real, direct contact and commerce with God. It is the almost universal testimony of those who are mystics that they find God through their experience. John Tauler says that in his best moments of "devout prayer and the uplifting of the mind to God," he experiences "the pure presence of God in his own soul," but he adds that all he can tell others about the experience is "as poor and unlike it as the point of a needle is to the heavens above us." "I have met with my God; I have met with my Savior. I have felt the healings drop upon my soul from under His wings," says Isaac Penington in the joy of his first mystical experience. Without needlessly multiplying such testimonies for data, we can say with considerable assurance that mystical experience is consciousness of direct and immediate relationship with some transcendent reality which in the moment of experience is believed to be God. "This is He, this is He," exclaims Isaac Penington, "there is no other: This is He whom I have waited for and sought after from my childhood." Angela of Foligno says that she experienced God, and saw that the whole world was full of God.

There are many different degrees of intensity, concentration and conviction in the experiences of different individual mystics, and also in the various experiences of the same individual from time to time. There has been a tendency in most studies of mysticism to regard the state of ecstasy as *par excellence* mystical experience. That is, however, a grave mistake. The calmer, more meditative, less emotional, less ecstatic experiences of God are not less convincing and possess greater constructive value for life and character than do ecstatic experiences which presuppose a peculiar psychical frame and disposition. The seasoned Quaker in the corporate hush and stillness of a silent meeting is far removed from ecstasy, but he is not the less convinced that he is meeting with God. For the *essentia* of mysticism we do not need to insist upon a certain "sacred" mystic way nor upon ecstasy, nor upon any peculiar type of rare psychic upheavals. We do need to insist, however, upon a consciousness of commerce with God amounting to conviction of his presence.

> Where one heard noise
> And one saw flame,
> I only knew He named my name.

Jacob Boehme calls the experience which came to him, "breaking through the gate," into "a new birth or resurrection from the dead," so that, he says, "I knew God." "I am certain," says Eckhart, "as certain as that I live, that nothing is so near to me as God. God is nearer to me than I am to myself." One of these experiences—the first one—was an ecstasy, and the other, so far as we can tell, was not. It was the flooding in of a moment of God-consciousness in the act of preaching a sermon to the common people of Cologne. The experience of Penington again, was not an ecstasy; it was the vital surge of fresh life on the first occasion of hearing George Fox preach after a long period of waiting silence. A simple normal case of a mild type is given in a little book of recent date, reprinted from the *Atlantic Monthly:* "After a long time of jangling conflict and inner misery, I one day, quite quietly and with no conscious effort, stopped doing the dis-ingenuous thing (I had been doing). Then the marvel happened. It was as if a great rubber band which had been stretched almost to the breaking point were suddenly released and snapped back to its normal condition. Heaven and earth were changed for me. Everything was glorious because of its relation to some great central life—nothing seemed to matter but that life." Brother Lawrence, a barefooted lay-brother of the seventeenth century, according to the testimony of the brotherhood, attained "an unbroken and undisturbed sense of the Presence of God." He was not an ecstatic; he was a quiet, faithful man who did his ordinary daily tasks with what seemed to his friends "an unclouded vision, an illuminated love and an uninterrupted joy." Simple and humble though he was, he nevertheless acquired, through his experience of God, "an extraordinary spaciousness of mind."

The more normal, expansive mystical experiences come apparently when the personal self is at its best. Its powers and capacities are raised to an unusual unity and fused together. The whole being, with its accumulated submerged life, *finds itself.* The process of preparing for any high achievement is a severe and laborious one, but nothing seems easier in the moment of success than is the accomplishment for which the life has been prepared. There comes to be formed within the person what Aristotle called "a dexterity of soul," so that the person does with ease what he has become skilled to do. Clement of Alexandria called a fully organized and spiritualized person "a harmonized man," that is, adjusted, organized and ready to be a transmissive organ for the revelation of God. Brother Lawrence, who was thus "harmonized" finely says, "The most excellent method which I found of going to God was that of *doing my common business,* purely for the love of God." An earlier mystic of the fourteenth century stated the same principle in these words: "It is my aim to be to the Eternal God what a man's hand is to a man."

There are many human experiences which carry a man up to levels where he has not usually been before and where he finds himself possessed of insight and energies he had hardly suspected were his until that moment. One leaps to his full height when the right inner spring is reached. We are quite familiar with the way in which instinctive tendencies in us and emotions both egoistic and social, become organized under a group of ideas and ideals into a single system which we call a sentiment, such as love, or patriotism, or devotion to truth. It forms slowly and one hardly realizes that it has formed until some occasion unexpectedly brings it into full operation, and we find ourselves able with perfect ease to overcome the most powerful inhibitory and opposing instincts and habits, which, until then, had usually controlled us. We are familiar, too, with the way in which a well-trained and disciplined mind, confronted by a concrete situation, will sometimes—alas, not always—in a sudden flash of imaginative insight, discover a universal law revealed there and then in the single phenomenon, as Sir Isaac Newton did and as, in a no less striking way, Sir William Rowan Hamilton did in his discovery of Quaternions. Literary and artistic geniuses supply us with many instances in which, in a sudden flash, the crude material at hand is shot through with vision, and the complicated plot of a drama, the full significance of a character, or the complete glory of a statue stands revealed, as though, to use R. L. Stevenson's illustration, a genie had brought it on a golden tray as a gift from another world. Abraham Lincoln, striking off in a few intense minutes his Gettysburg address, as beautiful in style and perfect in form as anything in human literature, is as good an illustration as we need of the way in which a highly organized person, by a kindling flash, has at his hand all the moral and spiritual gains of a lifetime.

There is a famous account of the flash of inspiration given by Philo, which can hardly be improved. It is as follows: "I am not ashamed to recount my own experience. At times, when I have proposed to enter upon my wonted task of writing on philosophical doctrines, with an exact knowledge of the materials which were to be put together, I have had to leave off without any work accomplished, finding my mind barren and fruitless, and upbraiding it for its self-complacency, while startled at the might of the Existent One, in whose power it lies to open and close the wombs of the soul. But at other times, when I had come empty, all of a sudden I have been filled with thoughts, showered down and sown upon me unseen from above, so that by Divine possession I have fallen into a rapture and become ignorant of everything, the place, those present, myself, what was spoken or written. For I have received a stream of interpretation, a fruition of light, the most clear-cut sharpness of vision, the most vividly distinct view of the matter before me, such as might be received through the eyes from the most luminous presentation."

The most important mystical experiences are something like that. They occur usually not at the beginning of the religious life but rather in the ripe and developed stage of it. They are the fruit of long-maturing processes. Clement's "the harmonized man" is always a person who has brought his soul into parallelism with divine currents, has habitually practiced his religious insights and has finally formed a unified central self, subtly sensitive, acutely responsive to the Beyond within him. In such experiences which may come suddenly or may come as a more gradual process, the whole self operates and masses all the culminations of a lifetime. They are no more emotional than they are rational and volitional. We have a total personality, awake, active, and "aware of his life's flow." Instead of seeing in a flash a law of gravitation, or the plot of Hamlet, or the uncarven form of Moses the Law-giver in a block of marble, one sees at such times the moral demonstrations of a lifetime and vividly feels the implications that are essentially involved in a spiritual life. In the high moment God is seen to be as sure as the soul is.

> I stood at Naples once, a night so dark
> I could have scarce conjectured there was earth
> Anywhere, sky or sea or world at all:
> But the night's black was burst through by a blaze—
> Thunder struck blow on blow, earth groaned and bore,
> Through her whole length of mountain visible:
> There lay the city thick and plain with spires,
> And, like a ghost disshrouded, white the sea.
> So may the truth be flashed out by one blow.

To some the truth of God never comes closer than a logical conclusion. He is held to be as a living item in a creed. To the mystic he becomes real in the same sense that experienced beauty is real, or the feel of spring is real, or that summer sunlight is real—he has been found, he has been met, he is present.

From *Spiritual Energies in Daily Life,*
pp. 135–144.

THE personality-building effect of mystical experience is one of the most notable results that flow from it. I am not thinking now merely of the effect on the physical health of the person. That in most cases is a striking result. Mystical experiences have in a multitude of instances been curative. It is what one would expect to happen. The calming of the mind, the increase of serenity within, would normally bring order and health to the body, and that is a usual sequence. But I am dealing here with the creative expansion of the entire personality. Eckhart glowed with the urge of a tremendous new life-impulse. He became quiveringly alive with powerful vitality. There was a gushing in, a welling up, of new and constructive life-forces—an *élan vital* plainly operating in him. St. Theresa speaks of the way her "actual dispositions" were changed so that the improvement was "palpable and brilliantly evident to all men." Porphyry bears witness to something similar in the daily life and personal bearing of Plotinus.

It is unmistakable in the lives of Jacob Boehme and George Fox. Of the latter William Penn wrote: "He was a new and heavenly-minded man—a divine and a naturalist and all of God Almighty's making." A contemporary says of Jacob Boehme that "his eyes lighted up like the windows of Solomon's Temple, and his spirit was highly illuminated of God beyond anything Nature could produce." The shining eyes we should expect—they are much in evidence too in the story of George Fox—but the slow formation of the inner spirit, and what Teresa calls the "dispositions" of the person, are the significant effects. . . .

As one would expect would be the case, mystics who attain this ripeness of experience, this amplitude of soul, this fathomless love, reveal a unique, converting influence over other lives. They carry a certain contagious influence. They do not strain or push to convert or to convince others. They become unconscious light-bringers. What they inherently *are* works powerfully, "breathing a beauteous order" of life. Madame Guyon has called this the quality of "spiritual fecundity." It is what one would expect, for the impact of faith is always dynamic and powerful, while the certitude of the possession of Reality carries one beyond the usual frontiers of "faith." The experiences I have been interpreting work transforming and permanent life-effects. They construct personality, equip for a mission, fuse persons into more dynamic groups and conduce to the increased power of the race. Energy to live by actually comes to these persons from somewhere. The universe in some sort backs and confirms their experience. The mystics even in the dark epochs in which they have usually flourished best have been, as one would expect they would be, strikingly optimistic or at least full of hope. We should all be living with a thrill and a sense of ultimate victory, if we had absolute assurance that the Eternal God is with us in our struggles and endeavors, is in fact "our Home," and everlasting Arms are underneath. Our difficulty in the midst of black-outs is our lack of conviction that the black squares are on a white background. The major mystics have that point settled in their minds. George Fox, in the sweep of his vivid experience, said: "I saw that there was an infinite Ocean of light and life and love that flows over the ocean of darkness. In that I saw the infinite love of God." In his vivid phrase, he felt that he was "atop of the devil and all his works," that "the Seed of God reigns." . . .

But the most striking effect of the sense of contact with God is the immensely heightened quality of personality that goes with the experience and the increased effectiveness of the person as an organ of spiritual service. Tennyson has King Arthur say of one of his Knights who saw the Holy Grail that "Leaving human wrongs to right themselves he cares but to pass into the silent life." The fact is that the effect of the discovery of God on the great mystics has been just the precise opposite of that. Under the creative impact of their experience they have become hundred-horse-power persons, with a unique striking force against gigantic forms of evil and with a remarkable quality of leadership in the Church and in the world. Eckhart is not alone in holding that active Martha is superior to passive, contemplative Mary, for Martha, he claims, has found what Mary is seeking, and her discovery has sent her into *action*. One of the monks of the desert came to his Abbot one day and said: "I do not know what is wrong with me, but something *is* wrong. I keep all the rules. I fast at all appointed times. I pray according to the prescribed regulations for perfect monks. And yet I am a complete failure. What is the matter with me?" The wise old Abbot held up his fingers to the sun and showed the monk the blood-red light between his fingers and said, "You must become a flame of fire." That is very different from "passing into the silent life" of inaction.

John Woolman expressed the true attitude of the mystic in his great words of dedication: "To turn all we possess into the channel of universal love becomes the business of our lives." It was this inward gale of the Spirit that made St. Paul say, "I have the strength to do all things through Him who gives me Power" (Phil. IV:13). It was this that sent St. Francis of Assisi out to visit the Soldan of the enemy Moslems, that sent St. Francis Xavier to the perils of China, India and Japan. It was this same waft of the Spirit that sent Mary Fisher to the Sultan of Turkey and Raymond Lull to martyrdom among the Moslems of North Africa. It was an inward power born of contact with God that made that quiet anonymous author of the Golden Book of the fourteenth century say: "I would fain be to the Eternal God what a man's hand is to the man"; that made James Nayler able to stand his immense sufferings and to say at the end: "There is a spirit which I feel, that delights to do no evil, nor to revenge any wrong, but delights to endure all things, in the hope to enjoy its own in the end. Its hope is to outlive all wrath and contention, and to weary out all exaltation and cruelty, or whatever is of a nature contrary to itself."

William James says of St. Teresa that through her mystical experiences there came within her "the formation of a new center of spiritual energy." It can be said with the same truth of Meister Eckhart, of Blessed Jan Ruysbroeck, of Gerard Groote, of that powerful human engine, St. Ignatius Loyola, and of scores of others, "who through faith wrought righteousness, obtained promises, out of weakness were made strong." This power to stand the world and to overcome it does not forthwith prove to everybody's satisfaction that the mystic's experience has the certainty of objective reference. For the pragmatist of the William James' type this proof of results and effects is proof enough. It *works* and that is demonstration of reality. I am impressed by the pragmatic test of the mystic's vision, but I am not satisfied with it, nor do I feel convinced that it is adequate proof of the reality of God. For the mystic himself who has *been there, yes!* He knows that he knows. But he cannot transmit his inner certainty to others. He cannot give a laboratory test-tube demonstration that convinces the beholder on the benches of the amphitheater.

> How can I tell or how can ye receive it,
> How, till He bringeth you where I have been?

The mathematician or the artist is just as helpless when he confronts persons who have no first-hand appreciation of the higher ranges of mathematics or of art. How can he tell until the listener has been brought to the level where he himself has been? The most the mystic can say in the last resort is that something in the very structure of the soul seems to be linked up with that higher world with which he feels himself in contact. He is committed to the faith that we can trust this highest verdict of the soul as surely as one can trust the testimony of mathematics or of beauty. It feels to him like the surest and safest cosmic investment. But to the non-beholder he can only cry in the wilderness: "I have seen and here are my tokens."

From New Eyes for Invisibles,
pp. 177–180; 182–185.

THERE are two very diverse types of mystical attitude which come out of this positive testimony of consciousness to the soul's relation to God. I shall call the two classes respectively *negation mystics* and *affirmation mystics*, though these words are used merely for purposes of description.

1. The sense of the divine presence will naturally work very different results upon different persons. If one discovers that he is a partaker of the divine Life, what shall he do next? Why, answers the mystic of our first class, he shall make it his goal to become absorbed in God—swallowed up in the Godhead.

Where can God be found? Not in our world of sense anywhere, answers this mystic. Every possible object in our world is a mere finite appearance. It may be as huge as the sun or even the milky way, or as minute as the dust speck in the sunbeam; it makes no difference. It is a form of finitude. It is, in contrast to the Absolute, an illusion, a thing of unreality. It cannot show God or take you to Him.

No better is the situation when you can fix upon some event of history or some deed of a person in his social relations. The event is a mere finite fact. Cut off and treated by itself, it is not a true reality. God cannot be found in it. The same thing applies to inner states. They are no better than finite activities. Every state of consciousness is sadly finite. It always seeks a beyond. Consciousness is the symbol of restlessness. It is like the flight of the bird which has not found its nest. When the soul is perfectly at home in God all thought will be quenched, all consciousness will cease.

"Believe not," cries one of these mystics, "those prattlers who boast that they know God. Who knows Him—is silent." He proceeds therefore by process of negation. Everything finite must be transcended. He must slough off not only the rags of his own righteousness, but the last vestige of his finitude. Union with God, absorption in His Being, so that "self" and "other" are unknown is the goal of his search.

> Some little talk awhile of Me and Thee
> There was—and then no more of Thee and Me.

He is seeking for an immediate experience which shall fulfill every finite purpose and leave nothing to be sought or desired—a now that shall hint of no beyond. One sees that this mystic is asking for something which cannot be granted, or at least for something which could not be known if it were attained. The Absolute who is postulated as precisely the negation of all finiteness turns out to be for us mortals only an absolute zero—a limitless sum-total of negations....

One sees at once the logical and practical outcome of the mysticism of negation. It ends in contraction and confusion or at least would so end if the person were faithful to his principle. "It is," as one of our rare American teachers has said, "as if the bud, knowing that its life is in the life of the parent tree, should seek to become one with the tree by withering and shrinking and letting its life ebb back into the common life. Seeing it we should not say, Behold how this bud has become one with the tree; we should say, The bud is dead."

Then, too, it has been the tendency of this type of mysticism to encourage men to live for the rare moment of ecstasy and beatific vision, to sacrifice the chance of winning spiritual victory for the hope of receiving an ineffable illumination which would quench all further search or desire.

2. We turn now to the *affirmation mystics*. They do not make *vision* the end of life, but rather the beginning. They are bent on having an immediate, first-hand sense of God—but not just for the joy of having it. More important than vision is obedience to the vision. There are battles to fight and victories to win. God's Kingdom is to be advanced. Error is to be attacked and truth to be established. Those who would have a closer view of the divine must seek it in a life of love and sacrifice.

Instead of seeking the Absolute by negating the finite, the mystic of this class finds the revelation of God *in* the finite. Nothing now can be unimportant. There is more in the least event than the ordinary eye sees. Everywhere in the world there is stuff to be transmuted into divine material. Every situation may be turned into an occasion for winning a nearer view of God. The most stubborn fact which fronts one in the path may be made a revelation of divine glory, for to this mystic every finite fact may become an open window into the divine.

It is a primary fact for him that he partakes of God, that his personal life has come out of the life of God and that he is never beyond the reach of God who is his source. But his true being is to be wrought out in the world where he can know only finite and imperfect things. His mission on earth is to be a fellow worker with God—contributing in a normal daily life his human powers to the divine Spirit who works in him and about him, bringing to reality a kingdom of God.

His life with its plainly visible tasks is always like the palimpsest which bears in underlying writing a sacred text. He is always more than any finite task declares, and yet he accepts this task because he has discovered that only *through* the finite is the Infinite to be found. His mystical insight gives him a unity which does not lie beyond the transitory and temporal, but which includes them and gives them their reality. The slenderest human task becomes glorious because God is in it. The simplest act of duty is good because it makes the Infinite God more real. The slightest deed of pure love is a holy thing because God shines through it and is revealed by it.

It is because beauty is a unity that any beautiful object whatever may suffice to show it and any object that does show it has an opening into the infinite. It is because God is a complete unity that any being who partakes of Him may in measure manifest Him. The whole purpose of the one who holds this view is to make his life the best possible organ of God.

He too, like our other mystics, seeks union with God, but not through loss of personality. The eye serves the body not by extinguishing itself but by increasing its power of discrimination; so too the soul is ever more one with the Lord of life as it identifies itself with Him and lets His being expand its human powers. . . .

The prayer of the affirmation mystic will be:

> Leave me not, God, until—nay, until when?
>   Not till I am with thee, one heart, one mind;
> Not till thy life is light in me, and then
>   Leaving is left behind.

From Social Law in the Spiritual World,
pp. 148–155; 156.

-»)«-

THERE is something at the very heart and center of the mystical life which calls for and demands self-denial and severe discipline. Mystical experience, like the edelweiss, is something which flourishes at its best only on the Alpine uplands. It is not a product of the prairie corn belt or the flat, potato plain. There must be some stiff mountain-climbing, the spirit of adventure, a scorn of ease, and a defiance of peril. But the only forms of ascetic practice which are legitimate for a sound-minded mystic are forms that minister self-discipline and that have to do with the athletic training of the soul for its daring adventures in the heights. As one climbs a great mountain, the paths which one can choose decrease in number as one approaches the top. There in the heights, divergent ways and by-paths disappear. At last, near the top, only *one* way is left, and that goes straight up toward the peak from which vast things can be seen.

All excellence is difficult. Mystical experience, by which I mean capacity to see the invisible, personal discovery of God, and joyous consciousness of divine presence, is no more difficult than any other supreme achievement. Holman Hunt once said to a lady who asked him how she could learn to make perfectly drawn, free-hand circles like his, that all she had to do was to practice eight hours a day for forty years! Then it would be as easy as breathing! ...

The mystic's asceticism, in so far as it is legitimate self-denial, is nothing more and nothing less than the "cost" of his way of life—the inherent price which must be paid for the "goods" upon which he has set his soul. It is involved in the very nature of self-conquest. The highest life is sure to call for all that a man hath. Nobody can help to build the Kingdom of God in the soul, and then in the world of men, without a stern elimination of all the unnecessary baggage which we mortals usually carry.

There have, of course, been so-called mystics in almost all centuries who have used ascetic methods to produce desirable states which they sought. They wanted to have visions and ecstasies and marvelous occurrences. They had discovered the psychological fact that long periods of abstinence— semi-starvation—bring an individual into a condition favorable to trance and ecstasy. So, too, do lacerations of the body and all assaults upon it which tend to produce temperature and fever. With the breaking-down of health, the weakening of vital forces, and of the tang and vigor of blood and muscle, suggestion operates more easily, and psychic concentration occurs almost without effort. The result is that when mystics, or pseudo-mystics as I should prefer to call them, have been eager for these phenomena, they have pushed mortification to an excess, and have welcomed that pitiful state of body which would let the soul have its swoons and raptures. This mistaken course naturally carries with it as severe risks as does drinking wood alcohol in order to get a moment of fullness of life.

The greater mystics have always seen that this is a false track. They have discounted visions and ecstasies. St. Teresa and St. John of the Cross spoke very sound and sensible words against all tendency to strain after morbid signs and supernatural marks of union with God, and they discounted every type of experience which did not add to the permanent moral and spiritual power of the life and character. Smaller mystics, who have given themselves periods of gruelling torture and long stretches of hunger to secure the spectacular results of the mystical way, have, in many cases, come to a deeper wisdom, and have given up, often at what seemed to them to be the command of God, all unnecessary austerities and all longing for these superficial signs of holiness. ...

All the mystics of the Middle Ages saw Christ in distorted perspective. They failed to see the happy, joyous, normal side of His life. The shadows of Gethsamane and Golgotha stretch back upon Him in their minds, and cover all His years of life. The prophet's phrase, "a man of sorrows," had become for them a character description for Christ, which colored all the gospel narratives. They could not believe that His contemporaries ever thought of Him as a happy diner at feasts, or as one who enjoyed nature and social life, and felt at home with all kinds and conditions of men and women. It was over-easy for anyone in the thirteenth or fourteenth century to neglect the vivid details of the gospels where these dealt with the human side of the story, and to focus upon the supernatural birth and the death and suffering which had won their redemption. The obvious natural result of this was that one who set out to imitate Christ invariably felt that he must walk the hard path of agony and crucifixion. The figure of the suffering Christ was prominent in every church, and it hung in the room of every person who made religion the sum and substance of his life. The constant thought of Christ as a sufferer, and the readiness to follow Him in the way of the Cross, tended, no doubt, to give depth and seriousness to life; but it also tended to shift the balance of life, to distort the perspective, to glorify suffering as an end in itself, and to induce the mystic expert to contrive artificial sufferings rather than to go into the world of men, to take up and to share the burden of actual necessary human suffering. . . .

There is still, however, something more to say on the subject. The true mystic has, once for all, settled for himself the issues of life. He has ceased to "halt" between two aims. He has resolved to be a citizen of the spiritual kingdom—the city with foundations whose builder is God.

When a person has thus finally balanced his accounts and knows that all his important assets are in the spiritual world, it is natural to care intensely for that. To seek, to find, to love, and to be in union with God is his serious business. All rivalries are at an end. All secondary appeals become subordinate to the main concern. The ancient apostolic word is the mystic's battle-cry: "This one thing I do." The mystic, like St. Paul, is a "one-thinger" person. That means, as both William James and Evelyn Underhill tell us, that to be a genuine mystic one must form "new pathways of neural discharge." New habit tracks must be plowed. The wild jungle of the instincts and passions must be organized. The old springs of energy and action must be sublimated and turned in new directions. The disordered life must be brought into order. Its strife and jar must be changed to peace and harmony. In short, at whatever price, there must be a conquest of the self. The old negation mystics call this process a "noughting of the self," self-annihilation. "Nothing burneth in hell but self-will," says the *Theologia Germanica*, "and therefore, it hath been said, put off thine own will and there will be no hell.". . .

The important mystics are men and women who have washed their souls clean of the hedonistic taint. They have a wholly different estimate of life. Pleasure, here or hereafter, is for them neither the aim nor the test of life.

If one wants to see a man who has climbed clear above the pleasure line, and who lives in a height in which the pleasure spur is forgotten and has been left behind as though it did not exist, let him read St. John of the Cross. I admit that it sometimes seems to me as though, in leaving behind all reference to aspects of preference, of like and dislike, St. John of the Cross has also left behind our human way of life, and has withdrawn almost into a vacuum where exists very little of the air we mortals breathe. I feel the same way about Madame Guyon and Fenelon, who propose to themselves to attain to a state of absolute "indifference," in which they would pass beyond all consideration of the qualities of good and evil, of pleasure and pain, as inducements. Acts and situations cease to be considered in reference to those well-known coefficients. Every act is to be done solely for the love of God, not for any other reason whatsoever. I feel a sense of hush and awe in the presence of these tremendous lovers of God, but in my critical moments I am convinced that they are endeavoring to do what cannot be done, and, I am bound to add, what ought not to be done. They propose to eliminate all the springs of action which characterize us as men, to obliterate all the concrete clues from human experience which serve as practical guides for us, and to walk only by a supernatural pillar of cloud and fire from above.

Nevertheless, I verily believe that their way of life is sounder than the way of hedonism is. A pleasure theory sheds no light. It tells no one where to get on or where to get off. It gives no guidance on the problem of where we are going. It is dumb on all fundamental issues. It leaves one focused on a pure abstraction. It is like trying to kill a bear by aiming at him "all over." Pleasure? Yes, but what kind of pleasure, and attached to what aims and ends of life? If we are ever to get on with life-issues, we must neither be *indifferent* nor must we talk that silly rubbish of aiming at pleasure—which means aiming at nothing in particular—as though one should say, "I am going to be a professional man, but I am never going to choose a *specific* profession! I am going to marry, but I am never going to fall in love with anyone in particular."

What the mystic means to say is, that he is out on a quest for "the shining table-lands to which our God himself is moon and sun," and having set his face to that business, no "toil of knees or heart or hands" terrifies him or turns him back. The man who sets out to climb unconquered mountains, or who proposes to fight his way over ice and through pitiless northern blizzards to the pole of the earth, trains for it, makes himself fit, and, absorbed as he is in an overmastering purpose, he forgets to consider what the butterfly and the dilettante call pleasure. It is not killed or annihilated; it is raised, sublimated, and fused in with the total purposes of the life. Pain is there too, but pain is forgotten. The agony of cold and hunger, the toil and weariness of climbing, the loneliness of days and nights, are merely an inherent part of the cost of this quest. So, too, with the mystic. He does not crucify himself, as though suffering were good in itself. He does not suppose that bludgeonings will win him merit. He is simply going a way of life which involves discipline, endurance, control. He becomes a spiritual athlete; he trains for his task. He pays the price for what seems to him a glorious venture. Pleasure goes out of his thought, because something much better and worthier of life comes in. Here is the testimony of St. Catherine of Siena: "I would rather exert myself for Christ crucified, feeling pain, darkness and inner conflict, than not to exert myself and feel repose."

From *New Studies in Mystical Religion*,
pp. 71–84.

⋙ VIII ⋘

What Does Prayer Mean?

VIII

RELIGION is primarily and at heart the personal meeting of the soul with God and conscious communion with Him. To give up the cultivation of prayer would mean in the long run the loss of the central thing in religion; it would involve the surrender of the priceless jewel of the soul. We might try in its stead to perfect the other aspects of religion. We might make our form of divine service very artistic or very popular; we might speak with the tongues of men and sing with the tongues almost of angels, but if we lose the power to discover and appreciate the real presence of God and if we miss the supreme joy of feeling ourselves environed by the Spirit of the living and present God, we have made a bad exchange and have dropped from a higher to a lower type of religion.

Prayer, no doubt, is a great deal more than this inner act of discovery and appreciation of God, but the joy of communion and intercourse with God is the central feature of prayer and it is one of the most impressive facts of life.

The early Franciscans remained on their knees rapt in ardent contemplation praying with their hearts rather than with their lips. It was a prayer of quiet rather than a specific request. Francis thought of prayer as a time of storing up grace and power through union with God. He called it in his happy phrase, sharing the life of the angels—a needed preparation for the life of action and service which was to follow it.

Fortunately we do not need to *understand* vital processes and energies of life before we utilize them and start living by them. The child would die in unconscious infancy if he refused to turn to his mother's breast for nourishment until he had acquired a good working theory of the value and efficacy of mother's milk. Long before our modern laboratories succeeded in explaining why the combination of bread and butter is well adapted to be a staff of life for the race, primitive man had hit upon it by some happy accident of the trial and error method, and had selected it out of a multitude of other possible combinations. We watch with a kind of awe the marvelous accuracy of the homing instinct of birds and the guiding urge which brings the migratory fish and eel from their winter feeding-grounds in the central deeps of ocean back to the identical spawning place where their lives began. There are vital springs and life-urges in us all that baffle our capacity for analysis or rationalization, and the history of human development has revealed and demonstrated which of these subtle deep-lying forces and energies minister to the increase and furtherance of life and which ones must be checked and controlled as life marches forward from lower stages to higher levels.

One of these deep constructive energies of life is prayer. It is a way of life that is as old as the human race is, and it is as difficult to "explain" as is our joy over love and beauty. It came into power in man's early life and it has persisted through all the stages of it because it has proved to be essential to spiritual health and growth and life-advance. Like all other great springs of life, it has sometimes been turned to cheap ends and brought down to low levels, but on the whole it has been a pretty steady uplifting power in the long story of human progress. The only way we could completely understand it would be to understand the eternal nature of God and man. Then we should no doubt comprehend why He and we seek one another and why we are unsatisfied until we mutually find one another.

The two dangers that always beset prayer and threaten to deaden or stifle its vitalizing power are (1) the danger of making prayer a utilitarian scheme and (2) the danger of being caught in one of those thin rationalizing tendencies which recur frequently in human history, and of having as a result religious faith itself drop to a level of low potency.

The first danger has beset prayer in all generations. The *ego* aspect of life is very strong in the primitive stages of development as it is also in the early period of the formation of the child's aims and ideals. It was in every way natural that primitive man, as soon as he discovered that prayer was a real power, should have inclined to use it as an easy way to get the "things" he wanted, and especially that he should have used it as a magic method of protection from the things he feared. This utilitarian aspect ramifies the early religion of almost all races and when once it has become embedded in the fundamental religious habits of a people it is extremely difficult to dislodge it. The result is that this note of self-seeking has formed a subtle overtone in much of the world's praying, even when it has not been the major chord of it.

It is of all things important that prayer should be raised far above this short-cut scheme of self-seeking and of utilitarian aspirations. We have reached an ethical stage when we are slowly learning to dispense with the appeal of rewards and punishments as a religious motive. We feel, at least many of us feel, that it is a drop to lower religious levels to endeavor to push a person toward religion by scaring him with the fear of hell or by emotionally moving him with vivid pictures of heavenly bliss. We want him to love God because of God's own grace and loveliness, not because he can use Him for selfish ends, and we want him to turn to religion not because it is a path of safety from threatening danger, or a way to crowns and diadems, but because it is man's noblest adventure and the way to the completest fulfillment of life's meaning and significance, and because it enables man to become girded and equipped for the richest human service. So, too, prayer, if it is to be kept, as man moves up to higher ethical levels of life, must be sublimated from its lower and more egoistic traits and must be purified with a passion of love and cooperation.

The second danger is only too well known in this period through which we are passing. We are in the grip of a tremendous scientific current. The scientific method has been so successful in banishing mystery from the world and in organizing and controlling the forces of nature that we have easily assumed that there are no limits to its domain or to its sway. The authority of the laboratory has superseded all other types of authority. The method of explaining by antecedent "causes" is so direct and effective that it has made all other ways of interpretation seem weak and antiquated. Those who have become fascinated with the achievements and triumphs of science have grown somewhat disillusioned over the less exact and less compelling methods of religion. Their rationalized and causally explained world seems to need no God and to leave no place for Him.

It is, however, becoming pretty obvious that the successes of science are somewhat misleading. The practical effects are plain enough and they are real achievements. But when one asks how far science has been successful in making the universe rationally intelligible or in conserving those intrinsic values by which men live, the answer halts. A modern writer, in *The Glass of Fashion,* has very soberly diagnosed human life as it is to-day in these words: "The present depression of humanity has its ground, I believe, solely in man's degraded sense of his origin. The human race feels itself like a rat in a trap. We began in mud and we shall end in mud. Life is reaching the end of its tether. Humanity rots for a new definition of life." I should prefer to say a new interpretation of life rather than a new "definition" of it, but that need not matter. The point of importance is that the scientific method has severe limits which are now plainly in evidence. It can only do what it is equipped to do and we ought not to expect the impossible of it. . . .

There is no solution for our present poverty of life or for our feebleness of vision except to wake up to the fact that methods of exact description and of causal explanation can apply only to certain parts and levels of our universe and that the values of life and realities attaching to them call for quite a different way of approach. Already the tide has turned, the deeper currents of life are circulating and there are signs of a return to richer and more adequate ways of interpreting the values and spiritual issues of life. With these fresher discoveries will come new faith in God and that will carry with it an increase in the reality and power of prayer.

Everybody who reads or studies psychology is ready to admit that the prayer of faith has at least a *subjective* effect, often to a profound degree. The soul's aspiration for purity of heart helps immensely to make the heart pure. The vivid suggestion of ideal aims, whether audibly uttered or only breathed as a wish, *works* in almost marvelous fashion. There are high moments of faith when the whole being, including even the body and its functions, is extraordinarily responsive to interior suggestions. Any wish or hope or faith that rises to expression and which meets no contra-suggestion or inhibition is sure to be more or less creative and constructive in its effects. The period just before sleep begins or the time at waking is a moment when suggestion is peculiarly effective and dynamic, and so are moments of hush and silence in periods of corporate worship.

Noting the recognized fact of the extensive range of suggestion, its curative power and its moral effects, some modern students of the phenomena of prayer have been inclined to reduce it to a purely subjective aspect. They admit that prayer is a type of power, but that it works solely as a well-known form of auto-suggestion. I am quite ready to recognize the importance of this subjective aspect of prayer and I am thankful for it. We may well be grateful for all those features of life that can be brought under well-known laws and can be explained by principles with which we have grown familiar. But there is much more involved in the experience and power of prayer than can be attributed to its subjective effects.

In the first place the subjective power of prayer would quickly wane and die away the moment prayer were actually reduced to that aspect of it. We can pray with dynamic effect on ourselves only when we pray with living faith in Something more than ourselves. When I become convinced that prayer is a *one-way* affair, a single-minded communication, I can no longer bring myself into the state of mind that makes it work creatively. The power has oozed away and left me weak and ineffective. I can no longer close the circuit and set the current of power free. In order to make prayer work even in the sphere of my own life-area, I must rise to a faith in a Beyond. But that is by no means the only ground for a belief in the objective reality of prayer. Men have prayed in all generations and they have done so primarily because they have felt themselves to be in living relations with higher realities than themselves. They have prayed because they needed to pray as much as they needed to breathe or to eat. They have flung out their souls with the same kind of confidence that they had when they risked their bodies to the buoyant character of the water as they launched out to swim, and they found something happening in the process that refreshed and buoyed their souls. Praying is a life-creative method that has its own essential evidence in the act itself.

Clement of Alexandria, an uncanonized saint of the third century who comes very close to being my ideal of a Christian man, thought of prayer as a "kind of divine mutual and reciprocal *correspondence.*" It is a double-sided operation, due to an attractive drawing power at work above us and at the same time to a homing tendency in us. We are so made that we cannot live as egocentric beings. We are not contented with our success in conjugating the verb to *eat.* We natively reach out beyond our fragmentary self for completion, and we aspire to find springs and sources of life of a wholly different order from our daily food and drink for the body.

That is, I think, where prayer *begins.* It is born of our need for spiritual fellowship. That kind of prayer would abide and last on, even if we ceased to have what might be called formal or conventional prayer and if we gave up asking God for desirable "things" of life. In our best moments of hush and quiet, especially in those high-tide occasions when many human hearts together are fused in silent communion, there often is a palpitating sense of divine presence, an overbrimming consciousness of healing, vivifying currents of life circulating underneath our little lives, and we are thereupon filled with joy and wonder. That is the very substance and essence of prayer as "mutual correspondence."

But prayer is both less and more than that. We all know only too well how easy it is to have prayer drop to a lower level than that of vital correspondence with God. We are, alas, very familiar with prayers which consist of words, words, words. The eyes are closed, the face is turned upward, God is addressed, but in every other particular the exercise belongs to this earthly world-order of events. Habits, prejudices, natural interests, the old, well-known stock of ideas, the familiar *"patois* of Canaan," get expression, but the heart is not on fire with a passion for something that is felt to be essential to life itself. The words are spoken because a prayer is expected at that time, or on that occasion. The newspaper report on a famous occasion of "the most eloquent prayer ever *addressed to a Boston audience"* is familiar to us, and it unconsciously reveals the essential weakness of much formal and conventional praying. It is intended for an audience rather than for God, and it lacks too often the quiver and urgency of the soul's sincere desire and overmastering need. It just wanders on.

It is a pity to see such a transcendent thrill of life drop to a dull ordinary stream of talk, but it sometimes happens. "I hope you will not offer a very long prayer," a nervous university president said to me once as I was about to conduct a chapel service in his university, "the students will be sure to become restless and I cannot guarantee what they will do." My sympathy was all with the poor, long-suffering students, for I could easily realize what they had endured before they reached the stage of protest and revolt. No persons are more quick to feel the note of reality than are college and university students.

So, too, prayer is, or may be, *more* than wordless and aimless communion and correspondence. It may and often does rise to a clear apprehension in thought and word of some experience or event or attainment that seems to be absolutely essential to life itself. The soul in its need throws itself unperplexed on God in a yearning of love and faith and confidence, and asks for what seems to be absolutely indispensable to its complete being. These goals toward which the soul strains forward in prayer, these yearning needs, are, however, by no means always selfish aims; on the contrary, they usually are unselfish and stretch out to ends that mainly concern others. It is usually obvious enough that we can be of little service in the world to others unless we are raised in quality and power ourselves. But all great prayer is born out of intense earnestness and out of a consciousness that only God through us as a feeble organ of His will, can accomplish what we seek and what we need.

> From him who desireth greatly
> No wisdom shall be concealed.
> To him the future is present—
> All secrets shall be revealed.

Prayer at its highest reach climbs up to a vicarious exercise of the soul. I mean by that somewhat abused word, "vicarious," that we can, and do, lend our souls out as organs of love and suffering in fellowship-prayer for others who are in need of help and comfort. There are mysteries no doubt attached to intercessory prayer which we cannot solve with our intellect or by our efforts at rationalization. So, too, there are unsolved mysteries connected with the radio-mechanism which brings the voice of a friend from a distant city into our room where we sit tuning in to catch invisible vibrations. We do not wait until we can explain these energies before we use them, and so, too, there is no good reason why we should forego "lifting hands of prayer" for those who call us friends, until we completely understand how our human longing and our voice of prayer can affect the eternal divine Heart. If God is our Great Companion, as we believe He is, then we and He are "bound together in one bundle of life," as a woman believed centuries ago when the world was younger. It may well be as philosophers and poets have said, that the whole round earth is bound in vital union with the life of God. In any case, we certainly must know much more than we know now before we have any proof that true prayer for others is vain and fruitless.

We may well feel hesitation, I think, in extending the range of prayer so as to include effects upon inanimate things. There are grave dangers in sight whenever prayer drops to a level that identifies it with a method of *magic*. The startling, the spectacular, the marvelous, the miraculous, has always fascinated the primitive and infantile mind, and probably always will do so, and it was of all things natural and to be expected that child-minded men would stretch after quick and easy ways of controlling nature, and of getting desired results by the use of sacred words and mighty phrases that were believed to have magical power over the nature divinities. Spiritual religion feels the degrading and superstitious character of all such tendencies and it moves away from them with a keen desire to employ only moral and spiritual methods in relation with the God who is Spirit and with a worship which must be in spirit and in truth to be real. Each person must of course in all these matters decide what for him is actually "in spirit and in truth."

Meantime those of us who pray have the best of all evidence that prayer is a vital breath of life, for we come back from it quickened and vitalized, refreshed and restored, and we are happy to believe and trust that our intercourse with the Companion of our lives has helped to fill with love the cup which some friend of ours with agonizing hands was holding up in some hour of need.

From *Pathways to the Reality of God,*
pp. 241–253.

→»×«←

Is not the advance of science making prayer impossible? In unscientific ages the universe presented no rigid order. It was easy to believe that the ordinary course of material processes might be altered or reversed. The world was conceived as full of invisible beings who could affect the course of events at will, while above all, there was a being who might change things at any moment, in any way.

Our world today is not so conceived. Our universe is organized and linked. Every event is *caused*. Caprice is banished. There is believed to be no such thing, in the physical world, as an uncaused event. If we met a person who told us that he had seen a train of cars drawn along with no couplings and held together by the mutual affection of the passengers in the different cars we should know that he was an escaped lunatic, and we should go on pinning our faith to couplings as before. Even the weather is no more capricious than the course of a planet in space. Every change of wind and the course of every flying cloud is determined by previous conditions. Complex these combinations of circumstances certainly are, but if the weather man could get data enough he could foretell the storm, the rain, the drought exactly as well as the astronomer can foretell the eclipse. There is no little demon, there is no tall, bright angel, who holds back the shower or who pushes the cloud before him; no being good or bad, who will capriciously alter the march of molecules because it suits our fancy to ask that the chain of causes be interrupted. What is true of the weather is true in every physical realm. Our universe has no caprice in it. Everything is linked, and the forked lightning never consults our preferences, nor do cyclones travel exclusively where bad men live. As of old the rain falls on just and unjust alike, on saint and sinner. The knowledge of this iron situation has had a desolating effect upon many minds. The heavens have become as brass and the earth bars of iron. To ask for the interruption of the march of atoms seems to the scientific thinker the absurdest of delusions and all fanes of prayer appear fruitless.

This physical universe is a stubborn affair. It is not loose and adjustable, and worked, for our private convenience, by wires or strings at a central station. It is a world of order, a realm of discipline. It is our business to discover a possible line of march in the world *as it is*, to find how to triumph over obstacles and difficulty, if we meet them—not to resort to "shun pikes" or cries for "exception in our particular case."

William James, in the nineties of the last century, said the right word in his great psychology about prayer in this scientific world. I have often quoted his words to my students. They are as follows: "We hear, in these days of scientific enlightenment, a great deal of discussion about the efficacy of prayer; and many reasons are given us why we should not pray, whilst others are given us why we should. But in all this very little is said of the reason why we *do* pray, which is simply that we cannot help praying. It seems probable that, in spite of all that 'science' may do to the contrary, men will continue to pray to the end of time, unless their mental nature changes in a manner which nothing we know should lead us to expect. The impulse to pray is a necessary consequence of the fact that whilst the innermost of the empirical selves of a man is a Self of the *social* sort, it yet can find its only adequate *Socius* in an ideal world."

William James said much later in his life that "the real backbone of the religious life—I mean prayer, guidance and all that sort of thing immediately and privately felt . . . is mankind's most important function." He added: "Prayer is Religion in act: that is, Prayer is real Religion."

The real difficulty is that our generation has been conceiving of prayer on too low a plane. Faith is not endangered by the advance of science. It is endangered by the stagnation of religious conceptions. If religion halts at some primitive level and science marches on to new conquests, of course there will be difficulty. But let us not fetter science, let us rather *promote* religion. We need to rise to a truer view of God and to a loftier idea of prayer. It is another case of "leveling up." On the higher religious plane no collision between prayer and science will be found. There will be no sealing of the lips in the presence of the discovery that all is law.

The prayer which science *has* affected is the spurious kind of prayer, which can be reduced to a utilitarian bread-and-butter basis. Most enlightened persons now are shocked to hear "patriotic" ministers asking God to direct the bullets of their country's army so as to kill their enemies in battle, and we all hesitate to use prayer for the attainment of low, selfish ends, but we need to cleanse our sight still farther and rise above the conception of prayer as an easy means to a desired end. I have heard of a minister on the sea-coast of Maine who was asked by his congregation to pray for rain. This is what he said in his prayer: "Thy servant has been importuned to pray for rain, but Thou knowest, O Lord, that it is not so much rain that is needed on these coast farms as it is good old barn manure for the success of the crops of this community."

It is a fact that there are *valid prayer effects* and there is plenty of experimental evidence to prove the *energy of prayer*. It is literally true that "more things are wrought by prayer than this world dreams of." There are no assignable bounds to the effects upon mind and body of the prayer of living faith. No doubt many a man has come back from his closet where the turmoil of life was hushed and where all the inward currents set toward God, many of us I say, have come back with a new energy and with cleared vision and we can grasp what before eluded us, we can see farther into the spiritual meaning of any of God's revelations. There is perhaps never a sweep of the soul out into the wider regions of the spiritual world which does not heighten the powers of the person who experiences it. Profound changes in physical condition, almost as profound as the stigmata of St. Francis, have in our own times followed the prayer of faith, and many of us in our daily problems and perplexities have seen the light break through as we prayed, and shine out, like a searchlight, on some plain path of duty or of service. There is unmistakable evidence of incoming energy from beyond the margin of what we usually call "ourselves."

There are no known limits to the creative and transforming effects of this cooperation of the spirit of a believing person with our great divine companion. The influence of the energy of faith over body conditions goes beyond all usual limits and seems to carry us into the realm of what used to be called "miracle." I am compelled to believe that its range is not confined to the body of the person who has the original faith, but it may reach out by a divine telepathy and work extraordinary effects in the lives of others. I have many friends who report to me prayer-effects of an amazing sort, and I am bound to believe their testimony.

We have not to do with a God who is "off there" above the sky, who can deal with us only through "the violation of physical law." We have instead a God "in whom we live and move and are," whose being opens into ours, and ours into His, who is the very life of our lives, the matrix of our personality; and there is no separation between us unless we make it ourselves. No man, scientist or layman, knows where the curve is to be drawn about the personal "self." No man can say with authority that the circulation of divine currents into the soul's inward life is impossible. On the contrary, energy does come in. In our highest moments we find ourselves in contact with wider spiritual life than belongs to our normal *me*.

There is nothing quite so much needed now in the realm of religion as an adequate conception of the ultimate nature of man's *soul*, and its relation to the eternal spiritual Reality in the universe. Every new advance in the range of our knowledge makes it more certain that mind, spirit, and not matter, is ultimate. And it becomes equally certain, I think, that something of ultimate Spirit finds expression in our souls. This is the very core of the original Quaker faith, as well as the poet's creed: "Closer is He than breathing and nearer than hands or feet."

True prayer is immediate spiritual fellowship . Even if science could demonstrate that prayer could never effect any kind of utilitarian results, still prayer on its loftier side would remain untouched, and persons of spiritual reach would go on praying as before. If we could say nothing more we could at least affirm that prayer, like faith, is itself the victory. The seeking is the finding. The wrestling is the blessing. It is no more a means to something else than love is. It is an end in itself. It is its own excuse for being. It is a kind of first fruit of the mystical nature of personality. The edge of the self is always touching a circle of life beyond itself to which it responds. The human heart is sensitive to God as the retina is to light waves. The soul possesses a native yearning for intercourse and companionship which takes it to God as naturally as the homing instinct of the pigeon takes it to the place of its birth. There is in every normal soul a spontaneous outreach, a free play of spirit which gives it onward yearning of unstilled desire.

It is no mere subjective instinct—no blind outreach. If it met no response, no answer, it would soon be weeded out of the race. It would shrivel like the functionless organ. We could not long continue to pray in faith if we lost the assurance that there is a person who cares, and who actually corresponds with us. Prayer has stood the test of experience. In fact the very desire to pray is in itself prophetic of a heavenly friend. A subjective need always carries an implication of an objective stimulus which has provoked the need. There is no hunger, as Fiske has well shown, for anything not tasted; there is no search for anything which is not in the environment, for the environment has always produced the appetite. So this native need of the soul rose out of the divine origin of the soul, and it has steadily verified itself as a safe guide to reality.

From *A Call to What Is Vital,*
pp. 133–140.

->>><<<-

It seems to me very clear that there is a native, elemental homing instinct in our souls which turns us to God as naturally as the flower turns to the sun. Apparently everybody in intense moments of human need reaches out for some great source of life and help beyond himself. That is one reason why we can pray and do pray, however conditions alter. It is further clear that persons who pray in living faith, in some way unlock reservoirs of energy and release great sources of power within their interior depths. There is an experimental energy in prayer as certainly as there is a force of gravitation or of electricity. In a recent investigation of the value of prayer, nearly seventy per cent of the persons questioned declared that they felt the presence of a higher power while in the act of praying. As one of these personal testimonies puts it: prayer makes it possible to carry heavy burdens with serenity; it produces an atmosphere of spirit which triumphs over difficulties.

It certainly is true that a door opens into a larger life and a new dimension when the soul flings itself out in real prayer, and incomes of power are experienced which heighten all capacities and which enable the recipient to withstand temptation, endure trial, and conquer obstacles. But prayer has always meant vastly more than that to the saints of past ages. It was assuredly to them a homing instinct and it was the occasion of refreshed and quickened life, but, more than that, it meant to them a time of intimate personal intercourse and fellowship with a divine Companion. It was two-sided, and not a solitary and one-sided heightening of energy and of functions. Nor was that all. To the great host of spiritual and triumphant souls who are behind us prayer was an *effective and operative power.* It accomplished results and wrought effects beyond the range of the inner life of the person who was praying. It was a way of setting vast spiritual currents into circulation which worked mightily through the world and upon the lives of men. It was believed to be an operation of grace by which the fervent human will could influence the course of divine action in the secret channels of the universe.

Is this two-sided and objective view of prayer, as real intercourse and as effective power, still tenable? Can men who accept the conclusions of science still pray in living faith and with real expectation of results? I see no ground against an affirmative answer. Science has furnished no evidence which compels us to give up believing in the reality of a personal conscious self which has a certain area of power over its own acts and its own destiny, and which is capable of intercourse, fellowship, friendship, and love with other personal selves. Science has discovered no method of describing this spiritual reality, which we call a self, nor can it explain what its ultimate nature is, or how it creatively acts and reacts in love and fellowship toward other beings like itself. This lies beyond the sphere and purview of science.

Science, again, has furnished no evidence whatever against the reality of a great spiritual universe, at the heart and center of which is a living, loving Person who is capable of intercourse and fellowship and friendship and love with finite spirits like us. That is also a field into which science has no *entrée;* it is a matter which none of her conclusions touch. Her business is to tell how natural phenomena act and what their unvarying laws are. She has nothing to say and can have nothing to say about the reality of a divine Person in a sphere within or above or beyond the phenomenal realm, *i.e.,* the realm where things appear in the describable terms of space and time and causality.

Real and convincing intimations have broken into our world that there actually is a spiritual universe and a divine Person at the heart and center of it who is in living and personal correspondence with us. This is the most solid substance, the very warp and woof, of Christ's entire revelation. The universe is not a mere play of forces, nor limited to things we see and touch and measure. Above, beyond, within, or rather in a way transcending all worlds of space, there is a Father-God who is Love and Life and Light and Spirit, and who is as open of access to us as the lungs to the air. Nothing in our world of space disproves the truth of Christ's report. Our hearts tell us that it might be true, that it ought to be true, that it is true. And if it is true, prayer, in all the senses in which I have used it, may still be real and still be operative.

There is no doubt a region where events occur under the play of describable forces, where consequent follows antecedents and where law and causality appear rigid and unvarying. In that narrow, limited realm of space particles we shall perhaps not expect interruptions or interferences. We shall rather learn how to adjust to what is there, and to respect it as the highest will of the deepest nature and wisdom of things. But in the realm of personal relationships, in all that touches the hidden springs of life, in the stress and strain of human strivings, in the interconnections of man with man, and group with group, in the vital matters by which we live or die, in the weaving of personal and national issues and destinies, we may well throw ourselves unperplexed on God, and believe implicitly that what we pray for affects the heart of God and influences the course and current of this Deeper Life that makes the world.

From *The Inner Life,*
pp. 111–116.

-»>«<-

PRAYER releases energy as certainly as the closing of an electric circuit does. It heightens all human capacities. It refreshes and quickens life. It unlocks reservoirs of power. It opens invisible doors into new storehouses of spiritual force for the person to live by, and, as I believe, for others to live by as well. It is effective and operative as surely as are the forces of steam and gravitation.

The recent important psychological studies of prayer all agree in this one point, that most persons while engaged in earnest, sincere prayer feel an inflow or invasion of greater power than they were conscious of before they prayed, and Christians of all types and communions, of all lands and of all periods, unite in bearing testimony to this truth. "Energy," as William James says, *"which but for prayer would be bound, is by prayer set free and operates."*

Frederick Myers was drawing upon his own experience when he wrote: "Our spirits are supported by a perpetual indrawal of energy and the vigor of that indrawal is perpetually changing.... Plainly we must endeavor to draw in as much spiritual life as possible and we must place our minds in any attitude which experience shows to be favorable to such indrawal. *Prayer* is the general name for that attitude of open and earnest expectancy."

There can be no question that all effective dynamic prayer rises out of living faith. A person cannot let himself go and pour out his soul as he knocks at the great doors of the divine world unless he believes that there is a divine world that will be reached by his cry of need. We hear much talk in these days of the subjective character of prayer, but you cannot cut the subjective aspect of prayer away from the objective aspect and keep the former a thing of value and power by itself any more than you can cut the convex side of a curve away from the concave side and keep either a reality by itself alone. In order to have subjective results there must be live faith in an objective reality. A person cannot in this present world of gravitation lift himself by his belt or by his boot-straps, nor can he any more easily, in the inner world of spiritual facts, lift himself or others out of sin or sorrow or loneliness or failure or littleness by subjective strivings which attach to no objective support beyond the margin of his own personal area. The moment the objective side drops out or is assumed to be illusory, the moment we convince ourselves that our Great Companion is only a dream of our own, we immediately fail to get dynamic effects from our subjective strivings. Brother Lawrence was right when he said: "It is into *the soul permeated with living faith* that God pours his graces and his favors plenteously. Into the soul they flow like an impetuous torrent, when it finds a passage for its pent-up flood after being dammed back from its ordinary course by some obstacle."

We cannot live constructively toward any end of life as our operative goal or ideal until we can make that goal or ideal seem real to ourselves. It must not be vain or illusory if it is to hold us fixed and pointed toward it. It must not seem to us a will-o'-the-wisp, a mirage, if it is to control us and steer us forward through the storms and waterspouts of life. We build our lives by visions of real goals that are worth our venture and only so can we rise above the level of instinct, the dull bread-and-butter life. But what is true here in the field of ethics is also true in the realm of prayer. We must have faith in the Beyond. We need not wait until we can demonstrate the certainty of what the far-reaching tentacles of our heart feel to be real, but at least we must have a soul's vision of a More Than Ourselves to whom we turn, on whom we rely and from whom we expect what we need for ourselves and others to live by. The wonderful praying of the great mystics is due to their wonderful faith. They get what they seek because they expect to get it. They absolutely trust the far-flung tentacles of their soul.

Our surface life of effort and conscious striving is split up into many fragmentary aims and into many conflicting activities. We are carried about by shifting winds and by the drive of cross-currents. When we "return home," as the mystics say, to our deeper self and enter into our inner sanctuary we are borne along and unified by one great ground-swell longing for the life that is Life. We fall away from and lose our little self—our selfish self—and find a deep-lying conjunct or comprehensive self that is always more than we. In these truest moments of prayer a man comes upon that rock-bottom experience which a great ancient soul had met when he said: "Underneath are the everlasting arms."

The unification of the usually scattered forces of our inner self, the concentration of all our powers toward one perfect end, the focussing of the soul's aspiration and loyalty upon one central reality that is adequate for us, the surrender of our own will to a holier and mightier will, produce just the inner conditions that are essential for the flooding in of spiritual energy, and for the release of it for others who are in need of it. Everybody knows what it is suddenly to lose all fears and fear-thoughts that have obsessed one and to rise up with courage to face the tasks that are waiting to be done. We have all some time seen the shadows flee away or we have seen them pierced by a light that obliterated the shadow and left us in possession of insight and a forward-looking attitude which conquered the difficulty in advance. The literature of conversion is full of records of men and women, beaten and defeated, suddenly lifted to new levels of experience, put in reach of transforming forces, flooded with transfiguring light, convinced of new possibilities and becoming in the strength of the experience "twice-born" persons. When I speak of "unification" and "concentration" I do not mean that they are the result of conscious effort. Quite the opposite is generally the case. There is no thought of what is happening to one's self in genuine prayer. The worshiper is utterly absorbed with God and with the joy and wonder of His Presence, and thus the usual strain and tension of thought fall away as they do also in the presence of an object of perfect beauty or when one is listening to great music. Just that cessation of conscious direction, that absence of conscious effort is probably the best way to secure that release of hidden energies within the subconscious life. Even the physical attitude of prayer, the release of all muscle strain in the eyes, the momentary exclusion of the whole sensible universe from the field of consciousness assist the worshiper to relax, to let go of time and space and to break through into the region where fresh currents of life are stored and circulate. Richard Cabot is undoubtedly right when he says in his splendid book, *What Men Live By,* that prayer fulfills what play and art and love attempt. It heightens, as those other higher attitudes and activities of life do, all our forces; it fortifies and reintegrates the self, restores the depleted energies, orientates us when we are lost, confused, or perplexed and it renews and heartens the soul, as sleep does the body. Prayer is beyond question an energy-releasing function of life. It is as important for the health of the soul as exercise is for the body or as the fresh search after truth is for the mind.

From *The World Within,*
pp. 102–109.

->>)<<-

RELIGION is too rich and complex to be reduced to any one act or attitude or aspect of life. In so far as our religion is real and genuine, it will touch, heighten, and transform every feature of our lives, and, if that is so, we must not expect that we can pick out one feature and say here or nowhere the consummate blossom of religion is to be seen. But there is one act of life which does bring us in a special and peculiar way into the holy of holies of religion—a central act without which any person's religion will always remain dwarfed and unfulfilled. This central act is worship. By worship I mean the act of rising to a personal, experimental consciousness of the real presence of God which floods the soul with joy and bathes the whole inward spirit with refreshing streams of life. Never to have felt that, never to have opened the life to these incoming divine tides, never to have experienced the joy of personal fellowship with God, is surely to have missed the richest privilege and the highest beatitude of religion. Almost all of our modern forms of Christianity make too little of this central act, and, with some truth, it has been called "the lost art of worship." The main reason for the decline of worship is the excessive desire, so common to-day, to have something always happening or, as we often say, to have something "doing." Hush, waiting, meditation, concentration of spirit, are just the reverse of our busy, driving, modern temper. The person who meditates, we are apt to think, will lose an opportunity to do something; while he muses, the procession will go on and leave him behind.

Another tendency into which we easily fall is that of making religion consist of words, words, words. Talking about God, expounding the experiences of them of old time, saying apt and lovely things about religion, occupy us much when we come together, and quite rightly so. But to what purpose do we "talk about God" if none of us can pause in our inward rush and find him, actually meet with him and enter into the joy of the Lord? What have we gained by recounting the "experiences" of past ages if nobody now is to have similar experiences? It is melancholy to hear of Bethels in the dim, far past if we are to conclude that that ladder between the soul and God has been pulled up, or pulled down, and that direct divine intercourse has ceased. The apt and lovely words about religion have place and meaning only if they create in us the passion and the positive intention to go ourselves on the spiritual pilgrimage, the goal of which is this holy of holies, where words about God fall away, since we have entered into the joy of His real presence.

In the right place and in the proper degree we may well consider what are the great truths of our religion, what are the structural ideas of our faith, and it is essential that we should work out, and work out intelligently, the ways and means, the plans and methods, of social service—the practical application of our spiritual insight to the society of our time—but in all these matters do not let us make the fatal mistake of supposing that religion is primarily either words or service. Religion is primarily, and at heart, the personal meeting of the soul with God. If that experience ceases in the world, religion, in its first intention, is doomed. We may still have ideas about the God whom men once knew intimately, and we may still continue to work for human betterment, but there can be living religion only so long as the soul of man is capable of experiencing the fresh bubbling of the living water within and can know for himself that a heart of eternal love beats in the central deeps of the universe within his reach.

To give up the cultivation of worship, then, means in the long run the loss of the central thing in religion; it involves the surrender of the priceless jewel of the soul. In its stead we may perfect many other things; we may make our form of divine service, as we call it, very artistic and very popular; we may speak with the tongues of men and sing with the tongues almost of angels, but if we lose the power to discover and appreciate the real presence of God and if we miss the supreme joy of feeling ourselves environed by the Spirit of the living and present God, we have made a bad exchange and have dropped from a higher to a lower type of religion.

There is no doubt that, as with all the supremely great things, the act of worship calls for intense devotion, for unusual concentration, for long-continued spiritual preparation. If it is, as I believe, the very goal and pinnacle of religion—the flowering of the tree of life—then we must not expect that it will cost nothing or that it will be reached along the lines of least resistance. Religion has always demanded, for its best things, the absolute price. There is no finding without losing; there is no getting without giving; there is no living without dying. For a few dollars we can get a book on religion; for a few more dollars we can get someone to talk to us about the things of religion; but what we cannot get for dollars, however high we heap them, is this experience which is the heart of religion, this experience of God, this practice of the divine presence, this joy of being ourselves in the holy of holies.

From *The World Within,*
pp. 18–22.

->>)<(<-

WORSHIP, like love, unites; speculation and argumentation divide. The moment we try to formulate doctrines, or to construct a theory of Church organization, we discover that we are handling explosive material and we are sure to arouse disagreement if not dissension. We are moving here in the field of debate, and however plausible our position may seem to us, there are always other ways of viewing that same position of ours which we usually overlook. In all matters of life and thought the problems are intricate and complex, and no formulation of terms can exhaust the possibilities of any situation. There is something about the "inner life" of a black beetle which escapes the wisest entomologist. He describes the outside appearance, the look of the beast. He reports on legs and wings and speed of motion, but when he is all done with his description the beetle might well say, if it could utter itself, "You really do not know me at all as I am in myself!" How much more does our knowledge fall short of the mark when we are dealing with the inner life of a man, and how hopeless is the task of telling all the infinite truth about Christ, about God, about the universe and about eternal destiny! No, it cannot be done. There is more to be said than any of us say. And when anyone tries to make us take his account, we want the privilege of saying it over in our own way and of supplementing his way of saying it.

But worship is different. As I have already said, it is like love, and therefore it draws together and unites. Worship is not theory; it is not speculation; it is not thinking; it is not talking—it is discovery, adoration, joy, peace, communion, fellowship. There are deeper strata within us than come up to light in our ideas, or decisions, or declarations. The roots of our life—our real life—lie in this subsoil of our innermost being. We need to feed and fructify this deeper buried region, and to liberate its energies. That is what genuine worship does. It opens the avenues of the interior life and lets the spiritual currents from beyond us flow in and circulate about the roots of our being. Whittier was declaring this truth in his fine lines:

> And all the windows of my heart
> I open to the day.

It is, too, what William Watson is expressing when he

> Hears the bubbling of the springs
> That feed the world.

All truly spiritual persons in all ages have known, at least dimly, that there is some junction of the soul with God in the deeps of the inner self, and they have practiced silent communion and concentration of mind as a way of discovering the Beyond within themselves. Prayer was joyous correspondence and fellowship of spirit with Spirit before it came to be thought of as a way of getting things from a Superior Power.

Professor Friedrich Heiler of Marburg, who has written one of the most important books on prayer that has appeared in modern times—*Das Gebet*—says that "prayer is a living communion of the religious man with God, conceived as personal and present in experience." He thinks of prayer as the heart of religion and always as a direct approach to God and a way of fellowship with Him. It is this experience, he believes, which keeps religion alive, fresh and dynamic. With this vital contact gone, religion becomes a theoretical affair, a formal system. "Prayer," declared the holy nun, Mechthild von Magdeburg, "draws a great God down into a little heart; it raises the hungry soul to God who holds all things."

Genuine prayer of this deeper and truer type is as old as smiling and weeping, as old as love and death. Men pray still, as William James so well said, "because they cannot help praying." ... If all this is true, which I believe it is, it would naturally be asked why prayer of this deeper, communion type might not perfectly well be carried on in a quiet retreat by each worshiper in his own room at home. Why join with others and take the pains of going to churches and assembly rooms for what can be done just as well in a garden or in a house? Well, the answer is, first, that we come together in meetings and churches for other things beside worship, prayer and communion; and, secondly, because it is not possible to worship as effectually in the quiet at home—assuming that one could find it there—as in a larger group where many join together for the same exalted purpose.

It is psychologically a sound principle that group silence is much more effective than solitary silence. Robert Barclay was drawing upon the fruits of his experience when he said: "As when many candles lighted and put in one place do greatly augment the light, and make it more to shine forth, so when many are gathered together *into the same life* there is more of the glory of God and His power appears to the refreshment of each individual, for each partakes not only of the light and life raised up in himself, but in all the rest." There is certainly a cumulative power where many persons together are fused and expectant. It amounts to team work. Each one "lends his soul out" to help the rest, and the corporate hush assists each individual in turn to open the avenues of his soul. The outpouring of Pentecost came when the first Christians were "of one accord in one place." It did not happen and could not have happened, when they were having a divisive debate over the status of the law, or the value of circumcision.

Very few churches are organized today for this deeper type of corporate worship, and far too little or no provision is made for group hush. Congregations frequently, perhaps usually, take some part in religious services. They join in responsive readings from Scripture, in the Lord's prayer, in reciting the Creed, in singing hymns and, in the Anglican or Episcopal system, in corporate prayer and communal service. The difficulty is that all these ways of worship so easily become formal and almost mechanical. *They do not draw upon the deeps of the soul.* They do not demand any personal effort, any first-hand creative contribution. Gladstone spoke once of "the work of worship." I do not very much like the word "work" in this connection, but in any case we ought to realize that this supreme business of life cannot be truly done when we are sliding along a groove of habit, or running through a performance which perhaps once cost the precious life-blood of some ancient saint, but which costs us nothing now. ...

It would be well for us to reduce the amount of talk, of words, or argument, of question-asking, reduce also what is formal and mechanical, and greatly increase the living, silent, penetrating corporate activity of worship of which Whittier wrote those great words of his—the meaning of which he had experienced:

> Without spoken words low breathing stole
> Of a diviner life from soul to soul,
> Baptizing in one tender thought the whole.

From *The New Quest*,
pp. 114–122.

↠ IX ↞

What Is the Matter With the Church?

IX

THE disturbing thing is the present widespread *attitude of mind* in the world around us toward organized religion. There is a serious loss of interest in it. It is treated as negligible by a great many persons who, except for this attitude, are thoroughly good persons. It seems obvious, however, at the same time that there is no slackening of interest in vital religion, in a religion of life. When a book appears which presents in a fresh and living way the essential features of religious faith, or which interprets the personality of Jesus Christ in warm and appealing fashion, it immediately becomes the "best seller." The rank and file of people are keenly interested as soon as a famous writer, or a prominent person in any field, tells about his personal religion. It is always good "copy." Any fresh note on the old subject is hailed with enthusiasm. Any person who shakes himself free from conventions and breaks forth with a straightforward and sincere interpretation of practical religion gets all the hearing he wants. There is a good deal of evidence that religion is a *live* topic in our busy world of to-day and that it holds its place of high importance as a real issue of life to fully as great a degree as in any one of the last nineteen centuries. If it is true, as I believe it is, that religion as a fundamental trait of human life is still quick and vital, while there is at the same time a prevailing lack of interest in the organized Church, in its ministries, its offices and its services, there is good reason for supposing that the Churches of our time need to undergo a profound transformation, if they are to interpret God and if they are to minister to life in the world today.

When we seriously ask what is the matter with the Churches, we raise a question which cannot receive any easy, simple answer. We are confronted, as I have said, not alone by an intellectual issue, but by a more or less inarticulate *attitude of mind*. To use the famous phrase of George Fox, the Churches do not "speak to the condition" of the time. They are organized and equipped for a different generation than the one that happens just now to be here. It is something like an army with bows and arrows suddenly called upon to meet an army furnished with mauser rifles, machine guns and "big Berthas"; or like a teacher prepared for teaching multiplication and subtraction who is unexpectedly confronted with a class of students wanting to learn calculus, or fluxions. The debates which occur in most Church conferences and councils show how little the leaders comprehend the situation. They contend over matters which seem to the onlookers from without to be trivial and futile. It looks from an outside point of view like a Lilliputian battle over the question of whether eggs should be opened at the big end or the little end—a contest betwen "big-endians" and "little-endians." Brought up, as so many theologians and churchmen are from their earliest days in a certain atmosphere and habit of thought, they find it wellnigh impossible to stand off and to see the situation from the outside, or to get that first-hand feel of the utter inadequacy of these Church issues, which is so strong a feature in the lives of the great majority of people today.

In the first place, the Churches are bound to face, in a more adequate way than has yet been done, the intellectual reinterpretation of the universe. Christianity is, of course, vastly more than a theory of the universe. But at the same time, it cannot be right to hamper the freedom of the spiritual life of man by trying to keep it fitted into the intellectual framework of apostolic ages, or dark ages, or middle ages, or the reformation age. What one is asked to believe, or to think, or to hold, must fit in with and conform to one's whole system of thinking. Religious truth must always first of all be *truth*. It must not be *determined* by the views which prevailed in religious circles in some particular former century, any more than medical truth, or truth in physics, should be so determined. Every truth that has been discovered, verified and demonstrated, is thereby orthodox. Truth in this sphere and field, as in all other fields, grows, expands and enlarges. It must not be limited to what was in stock in the ages when creeds were formed. It is not enough, then, to debate a change of phrase here and there in an ancient formulation of faith. The person who is to be genuinely religious, who is to be a follower of Christ, must be free to believe what his deepest being finds to be true and he must not be asked to say that he believes what he cannot square with the facts of his universe, or with the testimony of his soul.

Every spiritual experience which those great Christian souls before our day have passed through, every word of prophetic insight which has come from them to us, is still precious and will assist us to find our way onward toward the fullness of truth and life, but the thoughtful person of this age feels that he should not be called upon to take over unchanged their world outlook or their intellectual findings. We need a type of Christianity that is brave enough to crown and mitre the individual in his search for truth and light, and which will use the conclusions and formulations of the past only as historical illustrations of the great spiritual adventure and as marked stages in the progress of the soul.

There is very widespread dissatisfaction with the type of preaching which for the most part prevails. It is built too much on antiquated models. It does not speak to the times. The sermon usually begins with a Scripture phrase or incident, and a large amount of time is often spent expounding the phrase or the incident. This may be done in a way that is valuable, but it is very apt to be dull and trivial. Where the dramatic issues of life stand out, or where great human traits come to light, or where the work of God through men of an earlier time is clear and vivid, then the exposition positively *counts*, but how often it is abstract or wooden! Where, as in many instances, the preacher leaves exposition of Scripture and turns to deal with social and economic problems, the gain is slight. It often ceases to be preaching and becomes lecturing, and often enough it is lecturing by one who is ill-equipped for the field with which he is dealing. Men are not going to the churches in this busy world, crowded with calls and interests, to hear weak lectures. Nor are they going to church to be entertained. As soon as a church drops to the level of purveyor of entertainment, its doom is near and "mene" is written on it.

The Church, if it is to hold men, and keep its influence in the march of life, must be nothing less than a revealing place for God. It is *prophetic* ministry that serious people want—prophetic in the deepest sense. I mean by that a ministry that reveals God and interprets life in its nobler and diviner possibilities. People everywhere, especially young people, are confused in their thought of God. They have lost their sense of His reality. They discuss and seek and grope and doubt. They have little guidance and help. The old-fashioned answers and evidences do not convince. The problems are new ones. The questions come in different form. They cannot be answered by formula or by phrases. The young seekers want honest, sincere guides who understand the issues, who have travelled through the fog and the shadows and who have come out on the hill-top into the light.

A minister ought to be to all of us in our religious strivings what the artist is to those who are eager for beauty, or what the musician is to those who love music. The artist interprets beauty. He presents it in its convincing reality.

> Art was given for that;
> God uses us to help each other so,
> Lending our minds out.

And what is true of the artist's mission is no less true of the minister's. His business is making God real to men here—not entertaining them, or giving them a theory of society. It is no easy mission, that is clear enough, but it is the greatest one on earth, and there are many persons who have divine gifts for it. Let the Church become a revealing place and it will no longer need to apologize or advertise, its standing will be immediately settled....

Faith, Experience, and Service should be the great sacred words of our new Christianity. It is no doubt much more difficult to initiate a person into the Christian life on the basis of faith, experience and service than it is on the basis of a creed or a catechism. We pass over here from something fixed, definite and external—something to be learned by rote—to something more vague, shifting and inward. The task of training a Christian becomes more like that of training a person in art and music. The *soul* must now be trained as well as the memory. The individual must now work out his own salvation. He must win spiritual insight and not merely learn to recite something. He must face the fact that God is not a being to be read about in a book, but *a reality to be found and loved and worshipped*. He must discover that religion underlies all life and is not an appendix or addendum to it. Religion becomes the inspiration and spring that raises daily living to a new and wonderful stage of joy and power. On this basis, the organization would become something that the Church *is*, not something that it *has*, or has inherited and must maintain.

This brings us to a new difficulty that confronts the Church as it is today. Its organization is antiquated, as is its system of thought. It seems, no doubt, to many Christians that the antiquity of the structure of the Church is one of its greatest claims to reverence. Has it not come down unchanged from a divine and hoary past? Does it not bear the marks of a divine origin and is not its *authority* due to just this glorious beginning? Each one must answer such questions as that for himself, but the serious and thoughtful person of our time does not look for his evidence of divinity in origins. He looks for it in processes, in development, in achievement, in effectiveness. We do not find it easy to settle the origin of conscience. We estimate its worth and claim by its moral illumination and power, not by its primitive origin—by what it does, not by where it came from.

There is very little to indicate that Christ was concerned with founding an institution. His interest in the kingdom of God, and in a way of life, completely overtops His interest in the construction of a Church. The first stages of the life of the Church are dim and uncertain. There was a fellowship at first, rather than an authoritative organization. There was group life and power of growth, rather than system and structure. All through the formative period, what we call the apostolic period, the leaders are feeling their way. They have no map or plan. They meet emergencies and work through them in the wisest way possible. They give no hint or intimation that their solution is the only possible one. They do not claim that the road forward is on a divine chart which they have in their hands. Early churches had more than one form of organization, just as early interpreters of Christian truth gave more than one form of interpretation. There was large freedom and leeway and scope. They were all searching for the best and most effective way to transmit the precious truth and life committed to them. . . .

There are two well-known ways of dealing with the spiritual contribution of the past, both of which ways are inadequate. There is (1) the way of the *authoritarian*. He assumes that the past settles what is to be accepted, received and venerated. There is, he believes, a matchless authority in the structure which has been built by the bold hands of the fathers. We turn to it as to a sacred ark of heavenly origin. It is not to be changed, it is to be preserved in its purity and transmitted to the future. Every feature of it is essential to its structure. Nothing must be added or subtracted. Every jot and tittle must be kept. We should lose the possibility of salvation if we lost "the efficacy and validity" that have come from the divine founders and transmitters. The criterion of spiritual truth and certainty is not in our own souls; it is in the immemorial authority of the institution.

On the other hand, there is a strong alternative view. It is (2) the view of the *rationalist*. He makes little of the authority of the past. The past has no more authority than the present. Antiquity supplies no title-deeds to truth. Everything must run the gauntlet of scientific enlightenment. We must have verifiable facts. We must build only on what we know and can prove. The rationalist plays havoc with sacred writings and with venerable institutions. He insists on their writ of *quo warranto*. He analyzes and dissects the most revered inheritances. He abhors superstition and he has a deep antipathy for dogmatism and underground assertion. He is in irreconcilable opposition to the authoritarian.

It seems hardly likely that the Church of the future—the spiritual Church which we are seeking—will be either the Church of the authoritarian or of the rationalist. Each of them represents a half-truth, each looks out on life with a large blind spot. The Church of the future will certainly not be of this old-fashioned authoritarian type. Its authority will be inward rather than outward. It will be due to a *present* quality of life and power and not to something in a remote past. But the new Christianity will not be clipped and pared down to the *cold residuum* of the rationalist. It will not fly in the face of facts. It will not defy rationality, as Tertullian did. It will respect history and science and the splendor of the mind. But it will insist on the recognition of the whole life and not merely on the rights of the intellect. A man's emotions and sentiments are as deep and significant as his power of reasoning. We are what we are as much because we *feel* as because we *think*, and when we clap down the lid on our feelings we have wrecked our capabilities as men. We not only argue and prove, but we build ideals, we overpass what we see and touch. We live in the unseen and forecast what ought to be. We want a religion that *knows,* but we also want one that *loves and believes and appreciates.* Our new Church which is to speak to the condition of the time must have an authority, but that authority must be the authority of spiritual life and transforming power. It must have wisdom and insight, but it should be the wisdom and insight of experience rather than of formal logic and of reasoning.

From *Faith and Practice of the Quakers,*
pp. 2–13.

→»)«←

THE primary thing for Christ was the attainment of an inner spirit, the seed-spirit of the Kingdom, the spirit of the beatitudes—the attainment of a type of life to which blessedness inherently attaches.

The question at once arises, how shall this inner spirit be spread and propagated? How is religion of the inner type to grow and expand? There are two characteristic ways of propagating religious ideas, of carrying spiritual discoveries into the life of the world. One way is the way of *organization;* the other way is the way of *contagion.* The way of organization, which is as old as human history, is too familiar to need any description. Our age has almost unlimited faith in it. If we wish to carry a live idea into action, we *organize.* We select officials. We make "motions." We pass resolutions. We appoint committees or boards or commissions. We hold endless conferences. We issue propaganda material. We have street processions. We use placards and billboards. We found institutions, and devise machinery. We have collisions between "pros" and "antis" and stir up enthusiasm and passion for our "cause." The Christian Church is probably the most impressive instance of organization in the entire history of man's undertakings. It has become, in its historical development, almost infinitely complex, with organizations within organizations and suborganizations within suborganizations. It has employed every known expedient, even the sword, for the advancement of its "cause," it has created a perfect maze of institutions and it has originated a vast variety of educational methods for carrying forward its truth.

But great as has been the historical emphasis on organization, it nevertheless occupies a very slender place in the consciousness of Christ. There is no clear indication that He appointed any officials, or organized any society, or founded any institution. There are two "sayings" in Matthew which use the word "Church," but they almost certainly bear the mark and coloring of a later time, when the Church had already come into existence and had formed its practices and its traditions. And even though the great "saying" at Caesarea Philippi were accepted as the actual words of Jesus, it is still quite possible to see in it the announcement of a spiritual fellowship, spreading by inspiration and contagion, rather than the founding of an official institution. It is, no doubt, fortunate on the whole that the Church was organized, and that the great *idea* found a visible body through which to express itself, though nobody can fail to see that the Church, while meaning to propagate the gospel, has always profoundly modified and transformed it, and that it has brought into play a great many tendencies foreign to the original gospel.

Christ's way of propagating the truth—the way that inherently fits the inner life and spirit of the gospel of the Kingdom—was the way of personal *contagion*. Instead of founding an institution, or organizing an official society, or forming a system, or creating external machinery, He counted almost wholly upon the spontaneous and dynamic influence of life upon life, of personality upon personality. He would produce a new world, a new social order, through the contagious and transmissive character of personal goodness. He practically ignored, or positively rejected, the method of *restraint*, and trusted absolutely to the conquering power of loyalty and consecration. It was His faith that, if you get into the world anywhere a *seed* of the Kingdom, a nucleus of persons who exhibit the blessed life, who are dedicated to expanding goodness, who rely implicitly on love and sympathy, who try in meek patience the slow method that is right, who still feel the clasping hands of love even when they go through pain and trial and loss, this seed-spirit will spread, this nucleus will enlarge and create a society. If the new spirit of passionate love, and of uncalculating goodness gets formed in one person, by a silent alchemy a group of persons will soon become permeated and charged with the same spirit, new conditions will be formed, and in time children will be born into a new social environment and will suck in new ideals with their mother's milk.

From *The Inner Life*
pp. 23–27.

-->><<<-

MANY years ago Walter Rauschenbusch wrote: "When we compare the Church with all other human institutions we rejoice, for there is none like her. But when we judge her by the mind of the Master, we bow in pity and contrition."

The first principle of life with Christ was freshness and vitality. He was always going on before the religious interpreters of His time, breaking new ground and announcing new insights of life and truth. The Church, on the other hand, has shown a tendency to be conformed to the creeds and interpretations and forms which earlier times had created and transmitted. It has always carried a heavy load of ancient and dead conceptions, because they were sacred once to founders or reformers. This tendency has led the Church, or at least many of its representatives, to oppose again and again the verified conclusions of science and to go on talking about a great many things that were "not so." The conflict has been a tragedy, but almost uniformly science has won and the Church has lost the issue.

To a great extent, especially here in America, the preaching has been timid and has conformed in large degree to the mental attitude of the conservative element in the pews, and too often has not brought a vital and convincing message to the trained minds of the persons who looked up and were not fed. There can be no question that a great deal of the preaching in our American churches is dull and unconvincing, and about matters that have little meaning for those who have been trained in laboratory science. The professor with his test-tubes speaks with absolute authority, for the result which he announces will follow when he pours the two tubes together. All this occurs before the eyes of the spectators in complete demonstration. The laboratory persons are accustomed to seeing words verified by corresponding effects. Too often the sermon ends in words, and nothing follows in terms of results. The words lack verification.

The time has come—it is long overdue—for a Christianity that is fresh and vital and in conformity with established truth, but, what is no less important, proves its reality by the test-tube method of corresponding results. Too long our Christianity has consisted of words—has begun and ended in words. We must have a Christianity that is self-demonstrative in results. Too long the Church has seen the world sag down to the pagan level and fight the wars which it has blessed and furnished its youth to go out to fight, instead of being the organ of that divine love—that *agapé*—which Christ lived and died to illustrate and transmit. And when these disastrous wars were over the Church has contented itself once more with pious words and talk instead of organizing a crusade of love to feed the hungry and rebuild the world on nobler lines. Every local church in Christendom ought to be a creative center of transforming life and love in its community and if it presented this test-tube demonstration of a unique dynamic for life it would *convince* the scientists and their students. We should then have a Christianity of power and not one of ancient statements and present-day talk.

There are Christians of this dynamic and demonstrative type in the world today, but there are not enough of them to convince the scientists and their disciples, to infuse the rank and file of people, absorbed with "busyness" and with the things of the world, caught in a moving tread-mill, so that they no longer respond to the inward whispers of the divine Spirit in their souls. It is, then, not just the scientists who are responsible for the wave of materialism and naturalism that has dimmed the light and truth of Christianity in our times. The cause is widespread and the blame is broadly diffused. What most concerns us in this extreme crisis of human history is not the discovery of who is essentially to blame, but the concentration of all our energies to the fresh re-interpretation of the essential spirit and truth of vital Christianity, and above everything else the translation of it in practical application to the sores and illnesses of our present civilization.

The most impressive feature of the testimony of history is the way a new burst of religious faith has lifted the civilizations of the past to a new dynamic level, with a unique marching power. What had looked like a terminus suddenly became a thoroughfare for a new advance. We need above everything else in this crisis of history a fresh burst of faith, a new discovery of the dynamic of religion, and a vivid consciousness of the eternal reality vitally present in our world of thought and events.

From *A Call to What Is Vital*,
pp. 7–10.

-»>«<-

SECULARISM, naturalism, materialism, and in some parts of the world, communism, stand out in intrenched hostility to the Christian way of life and to the Christian body of ideas and ideals. In one form or another, by silence or by settled opposition, they all deny the reality of God and they leave human life stripped almost bare of spiritual significance and transcendent meaning.

But there is another obstacle to be found within the Christian movement itself, which perhaps presents a graver difficulty to the spread of Christianity than any one of those militant foes on the outside. No one of these temporary formulations of thought, which for the moment seem to be a menace to the spread of Christianity, would present any serious obstacle if the forces of organized Christianity were united in heart and purpose and if the Church of Christ were in truth and in reality a living organ of His Spirit. The divisions in the Church itself and its failure to confront its tasks with vision and leadership and creative power constitute, if the truth were frankly uttered, the supreme difficulty which confronts the Christian interpretation of life in the world today. Organization in a subtle, more or less unconscious way tends to become an end in itself and may even defeat the very ideals and aims it exists to promote and foster. The power and authority of a great system, made august and sacred by time and perspective, fit rather badly with the spiritual demands of personal freedom, initiative and fresh creative leadership. Ecclesiasticism does not easily keep house on friendly terms with a growing faith of first-hand experience and inward vision. The natural conservatism of a great historic religious body is bound to produce a dampening effect on glowing and original minds, and it makes it difficult for the prophets of a new age, when they appear, to find scope for their transforming work. The importance of the preservation of the inheritance from the past cultivates an attitude of caution and inclines an ancient organization to defend the *status quo*, to stand sponsor for outgrown customs, and to protect forms of worship and systems of thought which have become inadequate for the expanding life of the race. We are only too familiar with the tendency to compromise, the lack of social vision, the failure to see, as from a mountain-top, the dawn of new epochs and to give prophetic leadership in times of moral crisis.

For these and other reasons the organized Church often seems to social and economic reformers a main obstacle to human progress. That attitude today is widespread and it is wellnigh irreconcilable. It is a primary item in the Soviet creed and it dominates the modern culture of most countries in Europe and Latin America. In the United States and Canada the lines are not quite so sharply drawn. The hostility to the Church, except in the ranks of organized labor, is moderate and tempered. It is an attitude of neglect rather than positive opposition. A great many of the educated youth of these countries have lost faith in the Church as an instrument of progress and have gradually, often reluctantly, turned away from it because it does not minister to their highest needs and because it seems to them so hesitant in its championship of the ideals of life with which they are kindled and possessed. They find it difficult to understand how a Church founded by Christ can show such feeble loyalty to the principles of truth, the way of life and the spirit of love to which His life was dedicated. Their very loyalty to the Christ of the Gospels often makes it difficult for them to be enthusiastically loyal to the Church which bears His name. The inability of the Church to meet the intellectual issues of modern times and to rise to a convincing spiritual interpretation of the world, which laboratory science has been discovering, has left many minds stranded in doubt and many more persons suspicious and lethargic toward it. Its pronouncements often seem to them helpless and futile. It spends time on issues and problems that are remote from the ones that are central in the minds of the youth of today.

They come from their books and class-rooms and laboratories, and are asked to listen to matters which have no vital interest for them. They look up and are not fed. It is not altogether the fault of the Church. There is a certain element of perversity and caprice of attitude to which no amount of wisdom and insight would probably bring health and healing. But in the main the present generation of youth are sound in their fundamental aims and keen for reality and truth. They are ready for great adventure when they are summoned to it and they would go the whole costly way with a Church genuinely pledged to Christ's program. Whenever the Church has taken a position of creative leadership and has summoned its youth to some great spiritual adventure significant enough to draw forth the potential capacities of its youthful members, they have always responded with zeal and alacrity, as they would do once more if the call reached them with kindling power. . . .

In spite of the dangers, however, which beset organizations, institutions and systems, and in spite of their tendency to smother the truth they carry, there appears to be no solution of the problems of the transmission of the Life and Love and Truth of God revealed in Christ without the existence of a visible corporate body in the world as the organ of its apprehension and transmission. The most urgent problem before us today, if we are eager to carry spiritual vision and power into the life of our present-day world, is the task of drawing the branches of the Christian Church together into one living whole, sufficiently unified to be an organ of the Spirit, and possessed of wisdom and power enough to attract into its wide family life the multitude of spiritually minded persons who at present have no religious home and no group fellowship. . . .

There will almost certainly always be many persons in the world who feel the need of a Church which possesses august authority. For persons of that type the Church *is* a Church precisely because it is something more than a collection and aggregation of religiously minded persons. It is something more than an empirical congregation of truth-seekers. Its authority to their minds is due, not merely to its antiquity and its immense service to humanity through the power of its message and ministry, nor alone to its array of saints and martyrs. They think of it, and feel bound to think of it, as a supernatural institution, divinely inaugurated at a specific moment in history, miraculously endowed from above with efficacious sacraments and with a God-given ordination for effective ministry. . . .

But just as certainly there are and always will be persons who feel assured in their own soul's experience that there is a divine light planted in man's inmost being which makes it possible for persons like us to have direct intimate communion and fellowship with God here and now. Those who live and work in the joy of that faith and experience look for and desire no other kind of authority than the authority of inner light and the demonstration of life and love and truth. They do not feel like aliens and foreigners here in the world of time, who need special ambassadors commissioned to speak for a distant Sovereign. Their hearts burn with the consciousness of a living Presence here and now. They live their lives and do their work with a sense of unsundered correspondence with their Great Companion. For them a Church is a Fellowship of those who believe in, live by, and share in this presence of God. It is a "blessed community" of persons joining together in the life of the Spirit for the service of Christ and His Kingdom. Life and organism, union in the spirit of love, are for such persons more important and more essential than are great organizations and imperial institutions.

Persons who share that outlook for the most part welcome fresh light and the advance of knowledge. They expect more truth to break forth under the guidance of the Spirit of Truth. They welcome, too, the social and ethical tests of group-experience by which what is capricious and erratic can be weeded out and the precious gold be recognized and preserved.

This mystical position, which in substance is the Quaker position, is far more widespread than the membership of the Society of Friends. That Society has gathered up and transmitted a mystical attitude as old and as continuous as the Christian Church. The Society of Friends has never been a wholly adequate organ of these ideas and ideals, and at its best it has had in its membership only a fraction of the persons who are of that type of mind. The Society of Friends as a separate body may decrease, and may even cease to exist as a bearer of these ideals. But even so they will find a new incarnation as they have done many times in the past, and there will continue to be what may be called a Church of the Spirit—a body of persons who are satisfied with a very simple organic form of organization and who find their spiritual life inwardly fed by the bread and water of life.

These two types of Church are strikingly unlike, but neither type alone would ever satisfy all those who are religiously minded and who want to belong to the Household of God. Neither one has any right or claim to set itself up as God's only channel of love and grace or as the only way that men can find their spiritual need met. The varieties of human need are great and the aspects of divine truth are so multiform that the Great Church of which Christ is the Head must include these two and many more characteristic family types.

From *A Preface to Christian Faith in a New Age,*
pp. 137–140; 145–146; 153–157.

->>)<(<-

Do we as self-conscious human persons reveal ourselves at our best and completest when we act "habitually," when we follow repeatable moulds of reaction, *or* when we act spontaneously, creatively and with fresh initiative? It is a question which cannot be answered in terms of either alternative. We should never expect to "discover" any person in either one of these halves of himself. "Character" is the very apex of human life. It is *both* "habitual" and "spontaneous." It is impossible to have character without continuity. It is a result of the conservation of life-gains. It carries a predictable element. Heraclitus was wise when he said that "a man's character is his destiny." And William James was sound when he said that "character is a rightly fashioned will to act." But no one would ever praise a man's character if it were to become *nothing but* the dull rattle of the chains of life that had been forged by the formation of habits. Raphael's habits as a painter were extremely important attainments, and there was always a predictable factor in his artistic work. But, after all, it is just the unique aspect, the unexpected burst, the creative touch which makes us feel that the Sistine Madonna is an immortal revelation of genius.

Something similar, I think, must be said about the revelation of the Spirit in and through the Church. Its tendency to conserve what the past experienced, to hold its creeds unaltered and unaffected by the changing processes of life and thought and to keep faithfully to the sacred channels which habit has plowed, often seems to be overmuch in evidence. The habitual, repeatable traits of the Church are stronger than were needed for the purpose of continuity and for the preservation of what is essential to historic life. But we may well say with profound assurance that the Church has been an organ of the Spirit and the transmitter of the Eternal Gospel even in its periods of quiet insistence on continuity and order and the preservation of the faith. It has never been wholly free from the contaminations of that other city which St. Augustine contrasted with the City of God. It has always been enfeebled by its worldliness, by its bent for politics and by its love of power and control. But throughout its checkered history it has preserved for us a community life through which, even in the static periods, the Spirit has been revealed. We may wish, as many of us do wish, that it had followed more closely the teaching and spirit of the Master, that it had preserved more fully "the Galilean accent," that it had been more responsive to the eternal Spirit whose habitation it was meant to be. But nowhere else in the world through these nineteen centuries has God been manifested more convincingly than in the life of the Church.

Fortunately there have also been great mutation epochs in the life of the Church, when the note of an Eternal Gospel seemed much clearer and more vivid than at other times. These times are always "critical." The two alternative tendencies of life come then into collision. The guardians of the past, the defenders of unvarying order, can find the Spirit only in undeviating forms. And the champions of change and freshness and novelty see only superstition and spiritual sterility in the preservation of the old system. Too often the collision of the two types produces what seems like a break of continuity, a catastrophe of division. But, even so, in the long run of History, the epochs of transition prove to be epochs of fresh revelation. Truth is often pounded out in the shocks of controversy. I have always believed with Tennyson that:

> Life is not as idle ore,
>
> But iron, dug from central gloom,
> And heated hot with burning fears,
> And dipt in baths of hissing tears,
> And batter'd with the shocks of doom
>
> To shape and use.

The Church we know historically has passed through many cyclones and waterspouts. Its current has not run smoothly. The turbulent swirls and the Niagara plunges are as much a part of its History as are the calm and placid levels when it seemed hardly to move at all. If we are to think of it as the Beloved Community of the Spirit we must accept the difficult challenge of believing that the Spirit is revealed both in the calm processes of continuity and in the turbulent periods of break and transition. The breakup of the unity of the Church in the sixteenth century was inevitable. There had been, ever since the opening of the thirteenth century, a succession of powerful *pushes* which threatened to disrupt the unity of the western Church. Finally the immense forces which were liberated in the epoch of the Renaissance, with the new emphasis on individual liberty and the importance of personal insight, were bound to bring on a crisis for the type of authority which the Church had claimed, and had achieved. On the whole the tragic collision and break of unity set free new spiritual energies, brought new births of life, and gave fresh impetus for the tasks of modern History. The schism was unmistakably a tragedy, "the wars of religion," so-called, were even darker tragedies, but in spite of all that stands on the debit side of the events, the Reformation and the Counter-Reformation are facts of major significance for the spiritual life and development of the western world.

Every person who thinks that it is the spiritual mission of the Church to become the most refreshing and healing stream of life which flows through the modern world must hope for the recovery of the unity of it. But that unity, we may be sure, cannot be restored in any superficial way, certainly not in any artificially constructed way of patching up a *scheme* of unity. It can come only through deepening processes of life and growth. A superficial unity brought about by the formulation of a common creed and order would mark no great advance in spirit and creative power. What is needed most is a rediscovery of the message and mission of Christianity, the Galilean way of life, the depth and power of Christ's life, and the significance of life and sacrifice for the world today. The Church must once more, as in the days of its glory and radiance, take its place of spiritual leadership in bringing the Kingdom of God into reality.

From *The Eternal Gospel*,
pp. 125–129.

-»)«-

WHAT ought to have happened long ago, and what must happen now as soon as possible, is that the leaders of the Church and the leaders of the Christian forces generally should joyously welcome all freshly discovered truth as from God, and should reinterpret Christianity in the light of all the truth that can be demonstrated as truth. That is what Clement of Alexandria insisted upon when Christianity was still young. "Truth by whomever spoken," he declared, "is from God." For him the great Greek philosophers were forerunners of Christ, as were the Hebrew prophets. In his mind there was no conflict between the demonstrations of knowledge and the testimony of faith, which is the assent of the soul to truths that for the moment transcend knowledge though they are essential for the whole of life.

In an even more striking way St. Augustine brought over into Christianity the immense contribution of the Neo-Platonists of the third and fourth centuries. Instead of fighting these influential schools of Greece as rivals, he absorbed into his formulation of Christianity all that could be used in their systems for the richer interpretation of the faith of the Church. Dean Inge is quite right in insisting that historic Christianity is profoundly Platonic, and it can be shown that it was largely through St. Augustine's genius that the Platonic stream came in full flood into the Christian stream. There can, I think, be no question that Christianity was enriched by the process, and there is no doubt that multitudes of thoughtful persons were won to the Church by this absorption of the intellectual gains of Greece, which would have been lost to the Church and to the world if the lines had been sharply drawn and Neo-Platonism had remained a stubborn outside rival of Christianity—a hostile interpretation of life.

An even greater service was rendered by that remarkable genius of the thirteenth century, Thomas Aquinas. The works of Aristotle were discovered and brought into Europe at the close of the twelfth century. They were almost at once declared dangerous by the Church, and in 1209 and again in 1215 they were proscribed and forbidden to be read. But great Christian scholars found out by patient study that they had a very important contribution to make for the enrichment and expansion of the Christian faith, and Thomas Aquinas (1224–1274) devoted his superb genius to this task of interpretation. Instead of forcing the students of Aristotle into rivalry with the Church, Thomas showed that there could be a fusion of Aristotelian thought with the basic conceptions of Christianity, and that the two together could meet the growing intellectual needs of the world. The Church gradually recognized the truth of the claim and Aquinas wrought out his mighty system of thought which formed the intellectual basis of Dante's "medieval miracle of song" and furnished a fundamental scheme of Christian thought until the modern world was born.

The most important single spiritual task before the religious world today is the discovery of a similar use of the present-day intellectual conquests of thought for the enrichment and expansion of our Christian faith. To pit Christian faith against the onward march of science is to drive a wedge into the very center of the structure of truth. It means a division of the forces which alone can build the new civilization for which we wait. It would make rivals of two currents of culture both of which are needed for a complete and vital whole of life. For better or for worse, science has come to stay. It has won, as we have already seen, the allegiance of the institutions of learning almost everywhere in all lands. It has captured the minds of the thoughtful youth of today. They have lost their interest in a Christianity which sets itself into rivalry with the facts which science is discovering and verifying, or which insists on interpretations of life and thought out of harmony with those facts. This situation of rivalry in a very acute degree confronts the Christian missionary in Japan, China, and India, where the institutions of higher learning, both secular and Christian, have accepted the scientific method of explanation. The students of these countries are at the present moment in a striking way under the spell of science. They pin their faith unreservedly to its method of explanation. They accept its conclusions with finality. Its authority overtops all other authority. In contrast with the truth of science, religion, whether native or foreign, seems to them in their hearts to be only superstition. The missionary who is unequipped with scientific knowledge and insight seems to them an inferior teacher and he carries little weight or authority when he endeavors to speak to such students. I am inclined to think that there is no one thing that more impresses a man as he travels through country after country around the world than the spell which science has thrown over the minds of youth today.

At the same time the way of life which Christ has revealed is so infinitely precious that it cannot be surrendered without giving up the priceless jewel of our souls. The central faiths of Christianity are realities by which men can *live* today as certainly as in the first century. They cannot be dropped without tragic and irreparable loss to the human race. We could quickly recover if we lost our warehouses, our railroads, and our office buildings. We could come back to a new prosperity with most of our visible assets gone. But there is no substitute for these invisible assets which form the spiritual wealth and health of our souls.

There is a power, a saving and constructive force, in the eternal Gospel of Christ, which is more essential to the health and life of a nation than all its armaments and battleships, or even than all its means of transportation. We must not belittle the faith of the ages. We must not let any sweep of scientific thought blind us to the incomparable worth of that spiritual truth which constitutes our inheritance from Christ and the Fellowship of the saints. Our ultimate victory for the faith will certainly not come through surrender, or through a weak compromise of vital principles. The eternally precious treasure must be saved at all cost and kept for the life and health of coming generations.

With that point settled in our minds, we can boldly take up what I have called "our most important spiritual task." That does not mean the defeat, or the suppression, of science and criticism. It does not involve a proclamation to the leaders of research saying: "Thus far shalt thou go and no farther; here shall thy proud triumph come to a halt." There is no end to investigation and question-asking. The returns are not all in and they will not all be in while men like us remain on earth. We cannot limit the desire to know. We cannot issue "bulls" against the fearless pursuit of facts or of truth. Our Christian task is a different one. It must consist in a fresh and living interpretation of our faith in the light of and by means of all discovered and verified truth, through science or history. Professor A. N. Whitehead is right when he maintains that religion, in so far as it is made coherent and rational, is "the wider reaction of men to the universe in which they find themselves."

It is an immense undertaking. This process is a monumental task, like that of building the cathedrals of Europe, or constructing the creeds of Christendom, or reforming the Church in the sixteenth century. It will take the same kind of patience, perseverance, indomitable spirit, adventurous courage, and constructive insight that pioneered the continent of America, won it for agriculture from the primeval forests, and made it a land of plenty. It will not be easier than has been the creation of the immense systems of railroad lines, of banks, of telegraph and telephone networks by which the nations of the West have achieved and secured wealth and commercial prosperity. It could be successfully done if Christian leaders would go to work with the same patience, coöperation, and marvelous devotion to truth that have characterized the men who have in the last quarter of a century discovered the internal nature of the atom and reinterpreted the structure and character of physical matter.

It should be recognized, of course, that there are many prominent and steadfast Christian believers and workers among scientists and among historical-research scholars. In fact the leaders and first-hand experts in these fields are probably no more "secularized" than are the men and women in the foremost ranks of any other pursuits of life. The cooling of faith and the drift away from religion are more apt to appear among those who are less tremendously in earnest than are the greatest leaders, and who have discovered enough to unsettle them but not enough to carry them through to a constructive basis of thought and life. But in any case those who are borne along in the sweep of scientific conclusions need more help, and a different kind of help, from the leaders of religious thought, than they have yet received. Debate and argument and dogmatic assertion will not be enough. There must be a clear comprehension of the issues involved. An illuminating and convincing presentation of the spiritual basis of reality and of the Christian way of life must be given. This entire review of secular civilization makes the fact very evident that Christianity is confronted with a vast body of persons who exhibit rival interests and who are influenced by the appeal of values quite different from those which are expressed in and through the Church. These persons are largely impervious to warnings concerning the dangers that threaten their souls in the next world. They are cold toward the whole content of what is known as eschatology—the world beyond death. If they are to be reached and moved and transformed, it must be through an interpretation of life which raises it to a new dynamic quality, which increases its intrinsic richness, and which opens out within the man himself unsuspected interior dimensions of life. A keen-sighted, present-day prophet in the Far East has seen that men natively, naturally love Christ and want to follow Him when they really *see* Him in His true beauty and loveliness. He declares that the personality of Christ has everywhere an almost irresistible attraction. He declares that Christ who has been overlaid with theological and ecclesiastical interpretations repels many of those who have formed their ideas and ideals in the atmosphere of the present time, whether in the home field or in the foreign field, but the Christ of Galilee and Gethsemane, the personal Christ of the evangelists, makes an instant appeal to their hearts and minds. "The Christ of the Indian Road" is also, I believe, the Christ of the Chinese Road, and the Christ of the Philippine Road, and the Christ of the American Road. To see Him is to love Him.

There never was, again, a generation more eager for adventure than the one passing across the stage of life at the present moment. This spirit of adventure often carries men and women into absurd undertakings and sometimes sets them toward bizarre goals. But the spirit of adventure itself is in the main a great spirit. It merely needs direction and guidance. It needs to be shown an end worthy of the deep-lying inner urge. Let Christianity learn once more how to present the appeal of the abundant life, and men who die endeavoring to beat records of height in the air, or who defy the hazards of ocean flight, will with the same enthusiasm face the hardest perils for the sake of truth and goodness. We have tried to make the religion of Christ soft and easy. We have dangled before men's eyes the appeal of a sure reward. We have promised a *quid pro quo*. We have cried, "This way safety lies." We have called the Church an Ark. But all the time the fact remains that real men are not seeking "safety." They want to discover how to live the fullest and completest life, and that always means risk and danger and the perilous edge. Let us present again now, as at the first, the Christian way of life as its own sufficient prize.

Above everything else we must insist on a Christianity that stands first, last, and all the time for the truth. In this respect, too, we must lose our fears. We have tried by far-fetched schemes and methods to safeguard "our" truth, to hedge it about, and to keep it insulated within its safe defenses. We have thought of "Christian" truth as something above and beyond "truth in general," as though there were levels and strata in the domain of truth. We must come to see that we gain nothing by insisting on private standards of truth, and by setting apart our peculiar truths as though they belonged in a sphere where the normal tests of truth could be avoided or evaded. There is only one set of scales for truth, and our Christian claims to truth must be tested on those scales and must stand or fall by the way in which these claims conform to the eternal nature of things.

One needs hardly to say that if the secular-minded man of today is to be convinced of the higher spiritual values of Christianity, we who profess it as our faith must take its lofty ethical standards very seriously. The weakest spot in our Christian armor is our failure to live the life about which we talk and preach. Everybody admits without question or debate that the Galilean way of life is the most beautiful ideal that has yet been proposed. But Christianity cannot win the world by a reference to the glory of a past epoch. It stands or falls, not by what it was in primitive vision, but by what it is in actual fact. We who profess it and who hope to propagate it are its supreme evidences. It is not the miracles of two thousand years ago that prove it now to this scientifically-minded age; it is the present miracle of spiritual grace and power triumphant in a human life that has all the effect of a laboratory experiment.

> From *The Jerusalem Meeting of the International Missionary Council*, March 24–April 8, 1928, "Secular Civilization and the Christian Task."

->>><<<-

LIBERALISM in a peculiar way from the very nature of the case is in danger of having its *vision* change into a *restrospect*. It came to birth with a battle program. Its mission was to "set free" minds and souls that were hemmed in. It was a revolt against all forms of traditional authoritarianism. It aimed to lift off the yokes that were too heavy to be borne. It was eager to remove shackles, not from legs and arms, but from human spirits. It was in its essential significance a movement in behalf of freedom. A liberal is primarily a person who wants to "set at liberty those who are bound." He wants to "enlarge the empire of man's spiritual estate." In addition to that, he stands for the method of free inquiry, the right to think boldly and honestly.

Well, when the specific battle is won, what is easier or more natural than to rest in the glory of the famous victory? The particular issue becomes a *fait-accompli*. The great stream of life sweeps on, but the liberal who has won his fight is always in danger of being left in a back-wash, in a dead end. He is always in danger of being a disciple of Lot's wife. He can shake off "the heavy and weary weight" transmitted from the past, but can he accomplish the still greater task of creatively shaping the future, which can be done only by those who are living in the current of the central stream of life, not by those who are backward-looking or are stranded on a midway shoal?

It is just now a bad moment for liberals. It is the open season for hunting and trapping all types of them. I found not long ago this news item in a provincial Canadian paper: "Sam Higgins was accidentally shot yesterday while hunting. One of the wounds is pronounced to be fatal, but his friends will be glad to hear that the other wounds are not considered dangerous." There are many persons today who think that liberalism has received at least one mortal wound and many less dangerous ones. . . .

Let me quote the words of T. S. Eliot, of London, which express a somewhat characteristic attitude of this present generation of youth. This interesting poet and literary critic recently said: "Our present-day society is worm-eaten with liberalism." There you have a keen writer and thinker, speaking for the new generation. He uses his pen as a deadly weapon, and though the wound he makes with it may not be quite mortal, his words, revealing an existing state of mind, will at least make liberals feel nervous.

Eliot's pen is polite and gentle compared with the fiery darts that are aimed at liberals by Reinhold Niebuhr and other leaders of radical thought, both in England and America. They think of liberal views as soft and mushy. They want something hard to bite on. They much prefer the stern apocalyptic message of the darker prophets, the pessimism of Koheleth, the vertical dividing line of "crisis theology," to this thin food for babes which they impute to liberals. "Liberalism" for these stern men means shallow diagnosis of social diseases. It denotes expansive sentimentality, uncritical faith in progress, naïve idealism; in a word, inability to see facts as they really are and as by the nature of things they *must be*. There is a loud cry today for realism and the liberal must heed it. The thin optimism of old-fashioned liberalism is well scored in Hilaire Belloc's little poem:

> I said to heart
> How goes it?
> Heart replied
> Right as a Ribstone Pippin,
> *But it lied.*

It won't quite do to scorn this onslaught of the new radicals against the liberals. It is a more deadly onset than that old one, now nearly spent, made by the conservatives. The liberal always stands in bad perspective. The radicals see him over in the dead-end with the unmoving conservatives and the conservatives see him in bad fellowship with the unshorn radicals.

Liberalism, if it is to have a signal future, must have a well-matured philosophy of life, it must have a program to be accomplished, and it must reveal a propulsive dynamic which is powerful enough to change the line of march and to bring into play new energies to live by. But above everything one must insist that liberalism is first of all a spirit, an attitude, a state of mind, rather than a body of ideas. Liberals are not known by their conformity to a set of views, or by their fidelity to a system of thought. They are known rather by their loyalty to the unending *pursuit* of truth and by their obedience to the enlarging vision of the soul. What Henri Bergson has happily called "open religion," by which he means religion kept vital by fresh contact with the central stream of Life, is typically the religion of a genuine liberal. The befitting frame and temper of mind for a liberal is that attitude now so characteristic of a great scientist, the determination to be free from prejudices, to seek, to find and not to settle down upon any frontier already *won*.

Religious liberalism in the epoch of its birth was powerfully influenced by the rationalism of the age of enlightenment. That was beyond question a world-shaking movement. It broke down age-old superstitions. It set minds free. It looked straight at facts. It hated mysteries and mysticisms. It was suspicious of enthusiasms. Truth was to be emancipated from tradition and inherited faiths, and from the dominance of emotions. Man's unique trait, rationalism held, is *reason*. Religion, therefore, must be pruned of its wilder growths and be brought within the bounds of pure reason. This was no doubt a liberating tendency. It ended many outgrown tyrannies. But at the same time this rationalism was too thin for the whole rich life of man. It left the soul gasping for breath. It produced striking reactions and revolts in the direction of romanticism and in various forms of mysticism. It was an inadequate philosophy of life.

The new liberalism cannot flourish on the basis of that stark, thin "rationalism" of the past. It is as unreal as the Jabberwock. Man's true and essential nature includes vastly more than his capacity to describe and explain, more than his power to "categorize" facts. The moment he lives and acts he reveals preferences and values and brings ideals into play. His loyalties, his sentiments, his aspirations, are as inherently a part of his being as are his logic or his categories. A true liberalism must deal with man as a whole, not with a truncated and reduced "reason."

It is no less true that the liberalism of the future must be positive rather than merely negative. It must have affirmations as well as denials. There are times when the most important task in hand is a severe stripping away of antiquated survivals from the past. But the stripping process must be only a preparation for creative construction. It is impossible to live in a vacuum, or to keep house in the rooms of the mind that are "empty, swept and garnished." There is a well-known story of a woman who was found in the fourteenth century, going about the streets of Strasbourg with a pail of water in one hand and a blazing torch in the other. She was asked to explain her strange symbolism. "I am going to put out hell fire with the pail of water," she said, "and with the torch I am going to burn up Heaven, so that men will stop pretending to love God because of their fear of Hell or of their desire for the joys of Heaven."

It is all very well to eliminate these crude utilitarian incentives from religion. But what urge does one propose as a substitute for the ancient ones? There can be no great philosophy of life constructed on the foundation of mere negations. It is not what peradventure one does not believe that matters most, but what fiery positive faith dominates one's soul.

From *Re-Thinking Religious Liberalism*,
pp. 2–8.

X

What Is the Christian Way of Life?

X

In many great American cities the electric light and power companies display at night on their lofty skyscraper buildings brilliant electric signs which flash out across the city the words, "Public Service; Light and Power." Our desire is that all our local churches, whether in city or country, may make that their motto and their constant aim, that they all may aspire to fulfill their double mission for which Christ wrought and for which He died— that each church may be a *live centre* in the world "for public service, light and power."

From *Report of the Social Service Commission
to the Five Years Meeting of the Religious
Society of Friends in America, 1912.*

Our theology has made us extremely individualistic. The great stress has been put on the attainment of certain individual states of experience. The look has been turned too exclusively inward. This is a reversal of Christ's emphasis. His "sacred words" are service, ministry, fellowship, love, doing God's will in daily life. That outreaching spirit was, too, the dominant feature of early Quakerism. If we are to become a people of the Lord in this century we must once more embody that spirit.

The great problems of our age are social problems: problems of wealth and poverty, problems of housing the poor, of correcting the criminal, of moral education for children, problems of changing the social environment for multitudes of our fellows so that they can have something like a fair chance in life. Nobody today can live a Christian life and dodge these practical issues. To withdraw from the human press and struggle and seek only the selfish thrill of individual salvation is the way of spiritual danger.

Few heresies are worse than the heresy that the Kingdom of God is to come in a far-off sky, or by a sudden miracle. It is coming now as fast as we become sons of God and practise human brotherhood. It is a society in which the will of God is done—a fellowship of joyous love and service. The least in it is greater than the greatest who has only the passport of sound theology in his lean hands.

The coming Church is the one which best takes up its social mission and proves most efficient in carrying light into the actual social conditions about us. We must widen "divine service" until it means something more than sitting for an hour once a week in a comfortable seat. It is our task, our business, to save the world, to carry goodness and love, light and joy into all the hidden corners of it. If we expect working men and thinking men to be impressed with the reality of our religion, it must be practical—it must work itself out in actual life; it must verify itself.

This does not mean that we are to take a short cut and run into theories. The Kingdom of God is not going to come by the proclamation of socialism or any other cure-all scheme. As Herbert Spencer has well said: You cannot get a golden conduct out of leaden instincts. You cannot bring a golden age by any shuffling of the poor old material. It is the aim of the Church to produce a new kind of person. We ourselves are to be those persons—a society of sons of God, practising love and brotherhood, exhibiting fellowship and service, and carrying out the Gospel of the Kingdom of God in our Christian lives. But history clearly proves that the spirit of love, the eagerness to help, is not enough. With the best intentions and with even complete consecration we shall fail to reconstruct the social life of the world unless we can strike sound principles. In the work of bettering the world and of spiritualizing humanity we can no more ignore the structural principles of society than a bridge builder can ignore the laws of mechanics in his work. We must shun all easy methods which aim to produce a perfect world by fiat, and go to work to produce persons who will make a pure family life, who will make their own homes training places for patience, obedience, reverence and unselfishness, persons who will consider it a part of their Christian business to understand the social conditions of their own immediate neighborhood and to carry out the principles of love and service in that neighborhood. The Gospel idea is not indiscriminate alms-giving, not a common purse, nothing which lessens individual aspiration and personal responsibility. It calls for nothing less than a membership, or brotherhood, of persons who will take time and pains to know the needs of the little world close about them and to apply to that world the wisest ministry within their power, at the same time permeating themselves with that spirit of consecration and service which carried Christ to Calvary.

This means that we must feel now, as our founders felt, the call to a holy life. Our message from first to last must be grounded in experience, not built on theory. It is an axiom of our faith that God and man meet within the soul, and the Quaker of power—the hundred candle-power Quaker, the hundred horse-power Quaker—will be the person who knows in his own experience that God and man do meet, because he himself has found the divine tides beating into his own personal inlet. From the very initial stage we must have a religion of the first-hand type. Its supreme transactions are transactions which occur within the soul itself. It is not an affair of heavenly bookkeeping; it is concerned with an actual transformation of the life, inner and outer.

Complete salvation on this basis therefore means that the person is delivered from sin and from the love of it and turned into a positive spiritual being, living in joy and freedom and sharing with Christ in the triumphant experience of overcoming the world. This is not an experience which can be had for the easy asking. No one will be caught up by the angels and carried into it. It can come only in line with the conditions of the spiritual life. It is reached, as all high things are reached, by coöperation with God, by a steady, progressive response to His revelations, by a loss of the old, narrow, selfish will and gaining of that kind of will which Christ exhibited.

But let nobody suppose that "holiness" is a static, fixed and final state, a sort of mountain peak to be reached once for all, with no peaks beyond. Once again we must deal with experience, not with theories. Actual life cannot be arrested at a point without being destroyed. To live is to go on. No person is holy who is not stretching on to be more holy. To say "Behold in me the goal and summit of holiness" is to make any real and genuine holiness impossible, for there is no fixed goal this side of the perfectness and fulness of God Himself. There is, too, no holiness which is an end in itself, which is sought for its own sake. It is once more a practical matter, a question of horse-power and candle-power. Saints are not made for haloes and for inward thrills. They are made to become focus points of light and power. The true saint is a good mother, a good neighbor, a good constructive force in society, a fragrance and a blessing. The true saint is a dynamic Christian who exhibits in some definite spot the type of life which is fully realized in heaven.

From *Our Social Task and the Life Which It Demands,*
a pamphlet.

→»«←

IN putting the emphasis for the moment on the inner way of religion, we must be very careful not to encourage the heresy of treating religion as a withdrawal from the world, or as a retreat from the press and strain of the practical issues and problems of the social order. That is the road to spiritual disaster, not to spiritual power. Christ gives no encouragement to the view that the spiritual ideal—the Kingdom of God—can ever be achieved apart from the conquest of the whole of life or without the victory that overcomes the world. Religion can no more be cut apart from the intellectual currents, or from the moral undertakings, or from the social tasks of an age, than any other form of life can be isolated from its native environment. To desert this world, which presses close around us, for the sake of some remote world of our dreams, is to neglect our one chance to get a real religion.

But at the same time the only possible way to realize a Kingdom of God in this world, or in any other world, is to begin by getting an inner spirit, the spirit of the Kingdom, formed within the lives of the few or many who are to be the "seed" of it. The "beatitudes" furnish one of these extraordinary pin-hole peeps through which this whole inner world can be seen. Here in a few lines, loaded with insight, the seed-spirit of the Kingdom comes full into sight. We are given no new code, no new set of rules, no legal system at all. It is the proclamation of a new spirit, a new way of living, a new type of person. To have a world of persons of this type, to have this spirit prevail, would mean the actual presence of the Kingdom of God, because this spirit would produce not only a new inner world, but a new outer world as well.

The first thing to note about the *blessedness* proclaimed in the beatitudes is that it is not a prize held out or promised as a final reward for a certain kind of conduct; it attaches by the inherent nature of things to a type of life, as light attaches to a luminous body, as motion attaches to a spinning top, as gravitation attaches to every particle of matter. To be this type of person is to be living the happy, blessed life, whatever the outward conditions may be. And the next thing to note is that this type of life carries in itself a principle of advance. One reason why it is a blessed type of life is that it cannot be arrested, it cannot be static. The beatitude lies not in attainment, not in the arrival at a goal, but in the *way*, in the spirit, in the search, in the march.

I suspect that the nature of "the happy life" of the beatitudes can be adequately grasped only when it is seen in contrast to that of the Pharisee who is obviously in the background as a foil to bring out the portrait of the new type. The pity of the Pharisee's aim was that it could be reached—he gets his reward. He has a definite limit in view—the keeping of a fixed law. Beyond this there are no worlds to conquer. Once the near finite goal is touched there is nothing to pursue. The immediate effect of this achievement is conceit and self-satisfaction. The trail of calculation and barter lies over all his righteousness. There is in his mind an equation between goodness and prosperity, between righteousness and success: "If thou hast made the most High thy habitation there shall no evil befall thee; neither shall any plague come nigh thy dwelling." The person who has loss or trouble or suffering must have been an overt or a secret sinner, as the question about the blind man indicates.

The goodness portrayed in the "beatitudes" is different from this by the width of the sky. Christ does not call the *righteous person* the happy man. He does not pronounce the attainment of righteousness blessed, because a "righteousness" that gets attained is always external and conventional; it is a kind that has definable, quantitative limits—"How many times must I forgive my brother?" "Who is my neighbor?" The beatitude attaches rather to hunger and thirst for goodness. The aspiration, and not the attainment, is singled out for blessing. In the popular estimate, happiness consists in getting desires satisfied. For Christ the real concern is to get new and greater desires—desires for infinite things. The reach must always exceed the grasp. The heart must forever be throbbing for an attainment that lies beyond any present consummation. It is the "glory of going on," the joy of discovering un-won territory beyond the margin of each spiritual conquest.

Poverty of spirit—another beatitude-trait—is bound up with hunger for goodness as the convex side of a curve is bound up with the concave side. They are different aspects of the same attitude. The poor in spirit are by no means poor-spirited. They are persons who see so much to be, so much to do, such limitless reaches to life and goodness that they are profoundly conscious of their insufficiency and incompleteness. Self-satisfaction and pride of spiritual achievement are washed clean out of their nature. They are open-hearted, open-windowed to all truth, possessed of an abiding dis-position to receive, impressed with a sense of inner need and of childlike dependence. Just that attitude is its own sure reward. By an unescapable spiritual gravitation the best things in the universe belong to open-hearted, open-windowed souls.

Again, in the beatitude on the mourner, He reverses the Pharisaic and popular judgment. Losses and crosses, pains and burdens, heartaches and bereavements, empty chairs and darkened windows, are the antipodes of our desires and last of all things to be expected in the list of beatitudes. They were then, and still often are, counted as visitations of divine disapproval. Christ rejects the superficial way of measuring the success of a life by the smoothness of its road or by its freedom from trial, and He will not allow the false view to stand: namely, that success is the reward of piety, and trouble the return for lack of righteousness. There is no way to depth of life, to richness of spirit, by shun-pikes that go around hard experiences. The very discovery of the nearness of God, of the sustaining power of His love, of the sufficiency of His grace, has come to men in all ages through pain, and suffering and loss. We always go for comfort to those who have passed through deeps of life and we may well trust Christ when He tells us that it is not the lotus-eater but the sufferer who is in the way of blessing and is forming the spirit of the Kingdom.

Meekness and mercy and peace-making are high among the qualities that characterize the inner spirit of the kingdom. Patience, endurance, steadfastness, confidence in the eternal nature of things, determination to win by the slow method that is right rather than by the quick and strenuous method that is wrong are other ways of naming meekness. Mercy is tenderness of heart, ability to put oneself in another's place, confidence in the power of love and gentleness, the practice of forgiveness and the joyous bestowal of sympathy. Peace-making is the divine business of drawing men together into unity of spirit and purpose, teaching them to live the love-way, and forming in the very warp and woof of human society the spirit of altruism and loyalty to the higher interests of the group. These traits belong to the inmost nature of God and of course those who have them are blessed, and it is equally clear that the Kingdom is theirs. There is furthermore, in this happy way of life, a condition of heart to which the vision of God inherently attaches. He is no longer argued about and speculated upon. He is seen and felt. He becomes as sure as the sky above us or our pulse beat within us. We spoil our vision with selfishness, we cloud it with prejudices, we blur it with impure aims. We cast our own shadow across the field of view and make a dark eclipse. It is not better spectacles we need. It is a pure, clean, sincere, loving, forgiving, passionately devoted heart. God who is love can be *seen*, can be found, only by a heart that intensely loves and that hates everything that hinders love. . . .

It is the modern custom to talk much about the ethics of Jesus and to see in the Sermon on the Mount an ideal of human personality and a program for an ideal social order. But a careful reader cannot fail to feel in Christ's teaching the complete fusion of His ideal for the individual and for society with His consciousness of the world of unseen realities. The new person and the new society are possible in His thought, only through unbroken *correspondence* with the world of higher forces and of perfect conditions. The only way to be perfect is to be on the way toward likeness to the heavenly Father, the only moral dynamic that will work is a love, like that of God's love, which expels all selfishness and all tendency to stop at partial and inadequate goods. If any kingdom of heavenly conditions is ever to be expected on earth, if ever we may hope for a day to dawn when the divine will is to be exhibited among men and they are to live the love-way of goodness, it is because God is our Father and we have the possibilities of His nature.

The ethical ideals of the Kingdom are inherently attached to the prayer experience of Jesus. The kind of human world which His faith builds for men is one forever linked to the kind of God to whom He prays. Cut the link and both worlds fall away. We cannot shuffle the cold, hard, loveless atoms of our social world into lovely forms of coöperative relationship. The atoms must be changed. In some way we must learn how to lift men into the faith which Christ had, that God is the Father who is seeking to draw us all into correspondence with His unseen world of Life and Love. "After this manner pray ye. Our heavenly Father of the holy name, Thy Kingdom come, Thy will be done on earth as it is in heaven." The two faiths make one faith—the faith in a Father-God who cares, and the faith in the realization of an ideal society based on coöperative love.

"And as He was praying, the fashion of His countenance was altered and His raiment became white and dazzling." This is a simple, synoptic account of an experience attaching to a supreme crisis of personal decision in the life of Jesus. His so-called ethics, as I have been insisting, is indivisibly bound up with His attitude toward the unseen, with His experience of a realm where what ought to be, really is. So, too, it is because He has found His inward relation with God that He makes His great decision to go forward toward Jerusalem, to meet the onset of opposition, to see His work frustrated by the rulers of the nation, to suffer and to die at the hands of His enemies. The transfiguration has been treated as a myth and again as a misplaced resurrection story. But it is certainly best to treat it as a genuine psychological narrative which fits reality and life at every point. As the clouds darken and the danger threatens and the successful issue of His mission seems impossible, Jesus falls back upon God, brings His spirit into absolute parallelism with the heavenly will and accepts whatever may be involved in the pursuit of the course to which He is committed. When He pushes back into the inner experiences of relation with His Father and the circuit of connection closes and living faith floods through Him and fixes His decision unalterably to go forward, His face and form are transfigured and illuminated through the experience of union. This prayer of illumination, reported in the gospels, is not an isolated instance, a solitary experience. The altered face, the changed body, the glorified figure, the radiation of light, have marked many a subordinate saint, and may well have characterized the Master as He found the true attitude of soul toward the unseen and formed His momentous decision to be faithful unto death in His manifestation of love.

In Gethsemane, as the awful moment came nearer, once more we catch a glimpse of His attitude to the unseen. In place of illuminated form and shining garments, we hear now of a face covered with the sweat and blood of agony. Just in front are the shouting rabble, the cross and the nails, the defeat of lifelong hopes and the defection of the inner fellowship, but the triumphant spirit within Him unites with the infinite will that is steering the world and piloting all lives, and calmly acquiesces with it. But to this suffering soul, battling in the dark night of agony, the infinite will is no abstract Power, no blind fate, to be dumbly yielded to. The great word which breaks out from these quivering lips is the dear word for "Father" that the little child's lips have learned to say: "Abba." The will above is His will now and He goes forward to the pain and death in the strength of communion and fellowship with His Abba-Father. There may have been a single moment of desolation in the agony of the next day when the cry escaped, "My God, why hast thou forsaken me?" but immediately the inner spirit recovers its connection and its confidence, and the crucifixion ends, as it should, with words of triumphant faith, "Father, into thy hands I intrust my spirit."

The most important fact of this Life, which has ever since poured Alpine streams of power into the life of the world, is its attitude toward the unseen. We miss the heart of things when we reduce the gospel to ethics or when we transform it into dry theology. Through all the story and behind all the teaching is the mighty inner fact of an intimate personal *experience* of God as Father. To live is to be about the "Father's business." In great moments of intercourse there comes to Him a flooding consciousness of sonship, joyous both to Father and Son: "In Him I am well pleased," and in times of strain and tragedy the onward course is possible because the inner bond holds fast and the Abba-experience abides.

It is not strange that a synoptic writer reports the saying: "No man knoweth the Father but the Son." The passage as it stands reported in Matthew may be colored by later theology, but there is a nucleus of absolute truth hidden in the saying. There is no other way to know God but this way of inner love-experience. Only a son can know a Father. Only one who has trodden the wine-press in anguish and pain, and through it all has felt the enfolding love of an Abba-Father really *knows*. Mysticism has its pitfalls and its limitations, but this much is sound and true, that the way to know God is to have inner heart's experience of Him, like the experience of the Son.

From *The Inner Life*,
pp. 14–22; 62–69.

❧❧❧

THERE are few more awe-inspiring events than the budding of self-affirmation in the little child. Blindly his instincts have pushed him toward the mother's breast and have guarded his slender thread of life when nobody could have saved him, if he had not, without knowing it, saved himself. His eyes have obediently followed the bright light, the striking color, and, by a tendency more primitive than will, he has found out how to perceive objects. Through imitation, which underlay all conscious acts, he has caught the first meanings of personality, and has won the little stock with which he can begin life's business for himself. One fine day, not announced beforehand, he makes his surprising debut. He asserts his *will*. "I am somebody and I am resolved to be more of a somebody," is what he is trying to say. He is no longer a center of instincts. He has begun to *affirm* himself. All the mysteries of self-direction and self-assertion have appeared in the little life. He will never again quite passively let the world make him as it wishes. He has become a factor in his own making. He has started out with sufficient stubbornness to assert and maintain his own uniqueness. This will to be is the very core of ethics, and without it life would lose its significant and dramatic element.

But by itself it would be a self-destructive principle. Made into a universal law it would produce a monster—a bare, isolated individual. No amount of planing or shaving ever gets a board so thin that it has but one side! A board with only one side is an absurdity! But that is no more absurd than an isolated individual who has solely and exclusively *asserted himself*, who has aimed at solitary self-realization. Only the maddest insanity could exhibit such a specimen. Involved in the very heart of life itself is another principle as fundamental as self-assertion. It may be called self-surrender or self-sacrifice. Whatever it is named, it is the altruistic attitude and endeavor. It is not a late reversal of nature's primary law, struggle for existence, as some have supposed. It is not something which has come in "afterwards." It is structural like the other principle. Without surrender and sacrifice nobody could be a person at all. The world through and through has its centripetal and centrifugal forces, and chaos would come if either force vanished.

Those who have called self-sacrifice irrational or supra-rational have failed to note that bare self-assertion is just as irrational. No real personal qualities could be won on either tack pursued alone. Without gravitation, William James says, the world would be "an insane sand-heap." Yes, and without centrifugal force it would be an insane undifferentiated lump. If self-sacrifice is, as we are told, "glorious madness," then certainly undeviating self-assertion is inglorious madness. Either path leads alike to annihilation. Both end alike "in the dark night where all cows are black." We have come upon one of those deep paradoxes of life. To become a person one must both affirm and deny himself. One involves the other. They are not totally different things. They are diverse aspects of the same thing. They belong together as indissolubly as the two sides of the board do.

To get we must also give, to advance we must surrender, to gain we must lose, to attain we must resign. From the nature of things life means choice and selection, and every positive choice negates all other possibilities.... To go north limits one from going south. To enter the spiritual contest for an incorruptible crown limits one from being an easy pleasure-seeker. As of old, so to the end of time, it is impossible to serve both God and Mammon. Now in all these choices we get what we want, but at the same time we often, perhaps generally, give up what we also want. Our choice entails a real loss, and this hard fact, that each choice strips off a whole world of possibilities, has often figured in the pessimist's list of woes. Whether it shall be reckoned among the evils or the goods of life—as a debit or a credit in our earthly stock-taking—will depend on the further question, whether we fix our thought on what we are getting, or on what we are losing—on our self-realization or on the things which it forces us to drop.

From this approach, self-sacrifice makes us dwell on our finiteness, it compels us to note that we reach any goal whatever through an endless process of limitations, over a path strewn with dead possibilities. From another approach, as we shall see, it carries with it the implications of an infinite relationship. The person who seriously aims at any end which can be called good must surrender something and must reach beyond the bare "I" and "me."

Nothing at all can be achieved within the solitary circle of the self. Such an undertaking is as impossible as the gymnastic feat of lifting oneself by the boot-straps. The life of a person is a bundle of relationships. He has received from everybody, living and dead, who by any possibility could open a line of communication or influence with him. There is undoubtedly something personal, private and unique in his selfhood. Environment does not account for him. But he can *find* nothing in himself which he has not received. There is another's mark on every good which he possesses. Nebuchadnezzar's boast he may never apply to himself, "See this great person that I have builded." The self-made man is harder to find than the missing link. There simply cannot be such a "creature." All other lives have helped constitute his self. Strip him of what he has received and he would perish with poverty and nakedness. . . .

The "isolated self" is no more real than the "conjunct self." Cut apart, they are both abstractions. Neither can be, nor be realized, without the other. To live for the isolated self would be to lose the conjunct self, but at the same time to lose the isolated self too! The complete egoist annihilates himself. It is therefore not irrational to prefer the conjunct self to the isolated self—it is the height of rationality. We lose one self to save another self. The mother's sacrifice illustrates it. She is not herself with her child gone. The sacrifice that saves the child is for her the only path by which she can realize the self which she wants. Here is the pathetic story of a little boy who was picked up in the water, from the burning steamer "General Slocum": "My mother gave me a life-preserver, that's how I got saved," said the little fellow, whose name was Muller. "I guess she did not have none for herself, 'cause they can't find her." The patriot carries us a step farther. He finds his real self in a country free and united. Without this his isolated self is of little worth. He dies to the one to win the other. The martyr does not care for his life if it is to be cut apart from the truth he loves, i.e., from the ideal society to which through his truth he belongs. He dies to the one in the hope of saving the other. The saint has become a member of an invisible kingdom which is his supreme reality, he dies to the existence of sense that he may live to his conjunct self where life is full.

Every instance of self-sacrifice, which is calm and full of purpose, is of this nature. To the sympathetic spirit every child is in some sense an own child. One cannot see it lost without losing something of his real self. To the true citizen of a state every situation which affects the welfare of the state makes its call upon him and he must decide where his duty lies. In every age there comes the immemorial contest "betwixt old systems and the *word*." Each one of us must side with truth as we see it, and in these choices the free soul must always have his taste of martyrdom. But here again he prefers his self plus this truth to his narrow, shrunk self without it. . . .

Nobody can have the gains of friendship, the glorious gift of love, who cannot surrender. He who stubbornly stands guard over the "me" and the "mine" is forever denied these supreme blessings. The friend, the lover, loses his isolated self and finds himself anew in a conjunct self, which "neither two nor one is called."

From *Social Law in the Spiritual World*,
pp. 89–97.

→»)«‹←

GARFIELD was pointing in the line of truth when he preferred to have President Hopkins sitting with him on the other end of a log to any other college he knew. There would be occasions when he would need laboratories and test-tubes and lecture-rooms and a library, but the best moments would undoubtedly be those when he had his rendezvous with President Hopkins on the traditional log.

John Colet visited Florence in his youth and felt the spell of Savonarola's life and words. He returned to England and passed the kindling torch on to Erasmus. Erasmus found Thomas Bilny in his university days and left him "another man." It was Thomas Bilny who awakened Hugh Latimer and kindled the burning passion in his soul. It was Hugh Latimer who in the street at Oxford lighted a fire in England—a martyr fire—which by the grace of God has never gone out. In such ways, from life to life, the torch passes on, though not often, as in the above chain, can the linkages be traced. It has been my lot throughout life to be the receiver and the giver of great friendships. There is nothing else in this world more rich and wonderful than such friendships and there is no way of transmitting the spiritual fruitage of a life which is quite so effective. It, however, baffles description and defies all methods of cataloguing. One might as well try to photograph and describe the aurora borealis. Nor, again, is there any technique by which one can contrive and achieve friendships. They just *come*. They are by-products of life, not ends to be aimed at. . . .

It was from St. Francis of Assisi more than from any living person that I learned the full significance of the power of this silent transmission and the infinite importance of gentleness, humility, simplicity and tenderness. Evelyn Underhill has a beautiful poem which begins: "I come in the little things, saith the Lord." God certainly does come that way; and up to a point, I always knew that He did. But St. Francis gave me a unique sense of it. . . . We probably romanticize and sublimate the story of "God's poor little man," but there is in him a spontaneity of joy and wonder that seems like a fresh stream of life bursting forth from the immortal Fount of Life itself. Religion here in him changes from debate and argument, from doctrine and system, from calculation and utility schemes, to a sheer *élan vital*, a thrill and burst of joyous life and love. His poverty is not an ascetic cross to be carried, nor is it a costly method of purchasing salvation; it is a way of relief from complication and competition, a leap into freedom and simple living. *His* way cannot be repeated now, nor can we find our simplicities by imitating him seven hundred years afterward. He is not a *pattern*, he is an inspiration, a kindling life, that can awaken us and help us to find our own simplicities which fit this age, and to become in our day transmitters of a spirit like his.

About this same time I read John Woolman's *Journal*, edited by Whittier, who was, in his later life, one of Woolman's disciples. Here again was simplicity of style, of life and of thought. . . . He was poor in spirit, meek, a mourner, pure in heart, a peacemaker, ready to be persecuted for righteousness' sake, and he hungered and thirsted with a passion for what was eternally right and good. But what impressed me most in him was his gentleness, his tenderness, his absolute simplicity. The divided will, which is so much in evidence even in most good persons, did not appear in him. There was no duplicity, no doubleness, no utilitarian aims; self-seeking was as completely washed out of his heart as it can possibly be washed out and have any life of personality left. Perhaps the most striking passage in the *Journal* is the one in which he heard a divine voice say: "John Woolman is dead," and discovered that it meant, "I [John Woolman] am crucified with Christ, nevertheless I live, yet not I, but Christ liveth in me," and in the same experience he found himself *merged* indistinguishably with the suffering, toiling laborers of the world.

The richest lesson I got from him was his absolute faith that a man could plant himself on an eternal principle of Right and Truth and then calmly stand the world. The meek man who does not bluster, or strive, or cry, or lift up his voice, or get nervous, fussy or fidgety, but quietly stands on the Truth which his pure soul apprehends, he in the end inherits the land of promise, the goal of his hope. The Lamb, as of old, makes war with the beast and overcomes him. The armor of light is, as in the first century, the surest panoply for victory. That *principle* of warfare is the great message of Woolman's life, beautifully transmitted in his *Journal*. . . .

The Roman soldier could aways compel any man whom he met on the road to carry his military "kit" for an even mile, but for no more than that measured mile. Jesus must often have seen an event like that happen on the great Roman road that ran near Nazareth, and He may in his carpenter days have Himself carried a soldier's burden to the next milestone. He seized upon this Roman custom as a vivid parable of a great spiritual ideal of the way of life. Everywhere He turned He saw religion and the moral life reduced to calculation and spoiled by the fact that they were thought of as compulsions laid upon men's souls as burdens which they *had* to carry. Religion was "cluttered" with commandments, with customs, with weary performances which had to be gone through whether one liked them or not, what St. Paul called "a yoke too heavy to be borne." There was great temptation to wear the pedometer, to measure the mile of compulsion, and to stop short when the "must-limit" was reached. Jesus looking on and watching this religion of the compelled mile said once: "When you have done all these things that are required of you, count yourselves unprofitable servants"—you have hardly begun yet to find the real path of life.

Religion in its first intention as a way of life begins only when one goes out beyond that first milestone of compulsion, stops counting milestones altogether and contributes a mile and more for the sheer joy of it. If anybody —the legal system of your time, or the conventions of society and organized religion—compel you to go a mile, well, take up the load, and carry it with what grace or grin you can show, but after that, go of your own accord the mile which is not compelled, the one you add by the promptings of your own free spirit. . . .

It may, perhaps, be supposed by some who count themselves to be "redblooded men" that such a soft and gentle type of religion will produce only milksops, spineless Uriah Heeps, apologizing for their existence and lacking all that characterizes the fibre of a real man. One cannot of course testify here in his own behalf that he is "a hundred per cent man." But there is "a great cloud of witnesses" made up of persons who were tender and gentle in spirit, in whom "the grace of the Lord Jesus" had come to abide, who did go the "second mile" with a love that would not let go, and who yet had the manliness and virility of the old heroes of chivalry. The reserve force and staying power of persons who have "dug" in and settled upon the deepest resources of the spiritual life are truly remarkable phenomena in human history. There are other kinds of power besides. that of fists and bluster, besides that of bombs and "big Berthas"—there is a terrible might of meekness. Whittier has a strong stanza in which he characterizes the strength of Joseph Sturge:

> Tender as woman, manliness and meekness
> In him were so allied
> That they who judged him by his strength or weakness
> Saw but a single side.

Perhaps some day we shall see it demonstrated that truth needs no panoply except its own, and that love is the strongest, as well as the greatest thing in the world.

From The Trail of Life in the Middle Years,
pp. 122–128; 132–135.

→»«←

OUR generation does things. It is essentially practical. If it constructs theories it is for the purpose of getting its tasks done more adequately. It is impatient of theoretical web-spinning, and it meets every thinker with the question: "What can you coin your thoughts into; can you make your ideas march and conquer some field of practical life?" The sage in the arm-chair, who constructs pretty ideals of life out of his head, has lost his audience, and can no longer live upon the sales of his books. If he is to be listened to as a sage, he must do something and arrive at his wisdom in the practical field of tasks.

This situation, which is of course not altogether new, but only more emphatic than in most earlier periods, presents some very real difficulties for the person of sensitive moral conscience and of lofty ethical ideals. It is fairly easy to be morally "good" if it only means *holding* fine ethical ideals, but it is quite another matter to be "good" when you mean by it the actual practice of your goodness in the stress and strain and complications of a world of other men. The test comes when you insist that a person who is to be "good" must be *good for something,* and not merely good in the abstract. The hard test comes, I say, because in the actual world of men, duties are not the plain, simple, unconflicting things which they appear to be in the mind of the man who stands apart and spins theories about them. As we sit apart in the hush and listen to the august voice of conscience, there is no question in our minds that lying is utterly, absolutely wrong, and we feel that this ideal of truth-telling has the supreme right of way. Before this tribunal, there are no limits to the moral obligation to respect the personal rights of others, to treat their property and their lives and their reputations as sacred things. One of the most imperative commands that utters itself in the solitude within us is: "Thou shalt not do evil to bring about good."

But in the world of society where our duties must be wrought out, it is rare that we find a situation in which duties do not conflict and interlace. He is a happy man indeed who can follow his shining ideal without having it collide head on with another ideal as shining. What doctor has not found himself at the moral junction where he must decide whether to tell the absolute truth to his patient or whether in the interest of saving his life he is under obligation to keep the truth from him? Is a maiden's highest duty to stay and care for a dependent parent or shall she follow the call of love and go where she can realize the fullness of her life? If loyalty to a country, which seems to us unspeakably precious, and which, still more, seems to us to be the guardian of the best ideals and hopes of humanity, comes into collision with some fixed moral ideal that we also cherish, which of the two shall we choose to follow? Are we ever justified in toning down our ideal so that we may make it march and conquer in a stubborn world that is not yet ready for the perfect thing to which our inmost soul is consecrated? These and a thousand more like them are some of the questions which confront the person of moral ideals who goes into practical life today.

There are two possible ways—both of them, I think, moral ways—of meeting this situation. One way, a very heroic way, of meeting it is to focus the conscience upon the ideal line of action and then to refuse utterly any other course whatever. You nail your colors to the mast, and there they are to fly, whether your ship floats or goes to the bottom. There is to be no compromise though the sky fall on you. If you hold an official position which conflicts in any way with the ideals of conscience, you instantly withdraw from the position. You will not shave one iota from your complete ideal though your stubborn refusal to do so may imperil a million other interests. In this class are to be counted some of the world's finest moral heroes, who have finally won, if they win at all, not by yielding, but by dying at their hard post and giving the world the legacy of their faith.

The other way of meeting the moral crisis, the moral junction, as I have called it, is the more "practical" way of facing the stubborn conditions of a complicated world of human society, getting what can be got under the circumstances, and postponing the ideal and perfect achievement until times are more ripe for it. The person of this type may be just as loyal to his soul's vision, just as consecrated to that which is eternally and absolutely right and good; but not being able to force events and circumstances to fit his vision and his ideal, he submits to the slower method of getting, now a little gain here and now a little there, and instead of leaping at a bound to his height, he goes up the almost imperceptible slope of progress, sometimes by yielding to obstacles, sometimes by gracefully bending round them, but always aiming at a good which lies in front which he intends to reach as fast as possible. He accepts a half good if that is all he can get at the present, and he makes his slow advance by demanding only what he sees is within the range of practical possibility. Where his moral ends are in conflict and he cannot achieve both, he takes the one which seems to him higher and lets the other go by.

This type, no doubt, looks less heroic and robust than the other, and the champion of it will always seem in the eyes of the idealist of the first type, to be a compromiser, an inconsistent reformer, and he will receive attacks both from sinners and saints. But he is often a hero of the first rank, and if he is clear grained at heart, unswervingly honest in purpose, and does not surrender the central loyalty of his soul for any returns whatever, his moral rank may be just as high as that of the moralist who insists upon all or nothing. The two types will never be reconciled to each other, but as a matter of fact, the men of both types are valiant servants of the truth, and they both advance the precious causes of the race, though I am sure that I should rather be reckoned in the first camp.

I saw many times this summer one of the supreme creations of art— Botticelli's wonderful picture of Judith as she returns to the camp of Israel after slaying Holofernes. She has no thought of the dark aspect of her deed, she does not look at the severed head of the tyrant which her servant carries; she dwells only on the triumphant fact that Israel has been delivered and her hand has done it, because God selected her to do it. The victory to our minds is mixed and marred by the manner of its winning, but she focusses attention alone upon the gain for her race, God's chosen people, and she walks in a conscious triumph which is apparent even in the folds of her dress. She is of my second type.

I saw many times this summer Giotto's St. Francis, kneeling by the cross of his Saviour, the fire of love shining from his face, and streaming from the wounds in his hands and feet and side, intense, passionate, dedicated to the one idea which possessed him. You see here a man who has ventured neck or nothing, who loses himself and all he has to find himself. He can endure pain and loss, he can die at a moment's notice, but he cannot compromise or barter, he cannot take the world's way of progress, he cannot accommodate his ideal to practical demands nor to the stubborn circumstances of a slow old world. He is of my first type. Most persons belong to one or the other of these types, and each is likely to feel that the other is unsuited to the accomplishment of moral ends. My claim is that they both minister to the coming of that better humanity for which we pray.

From *The Friend,* London, Vol. 51 (1911), pp. 706–707.

Pacifism means *peace-making*. The pacifist is literally a peace-maker. He is not a passive or negative person who proposes to lie back and do nothing in the face of injustice, unrighteousness and rampant evil. He stands for "the fiery positive." Pacifism is not a theory; it is a way of life. It is something you *are and do*.

I am a good deal disillusioned over the value of propaganda as a method of achieving moral and spiritual ends. It is no doubt immensely successful as a means of advertising commodities or of accomplishing utilitarian purposes. If you say a thing often enough, and if you say it emphatically enough, vast numbers of people will believe it. Practically any theory about life or about society will accumulate a following if vivid writers write it up, and if "peppy" speakers proclaim it as a panacea for the ills of the world. But theories, like good resolutions, are very thin and abstract until they are put into operation and tried in practice. . . .

St. Paul knew enough about the forces of evil to know that they could be conquered only by greater *forces,* and so he set forth his famous method— "overcome evil with good." There is no other way to overcome it. Something else, something better, must be put in its place. Something strong and positive must put it down, conquer it and make it cease to be. The evil that concerns us, the evil that really matters, is always embodied; it is incarnate in a person, or in a social institution, and consequently our new way of life, our pacifism, to meet it and overcome it, must be incarnate, too, and must have the dynamic of personal lives in it and behind it.

We shall not get very far with phrases like "passive resistance" or "nonresistance," or "the use of force is immoral." One can neither train a life nor build a world on those or any other slogans. In the last analysis children are trained and worlds are built by persons who are living concrete and positive lives, whose theories have taken on flesh and blood and have behind them the attractive power of a strong personality. There would be little use having our Government and all the other governments of the world adopt abstract resolutions to the effect that military force shall be outlawed and shall never be resorted to again, if at the same time all the selfish and unjust methods of life and business and social relations were left to work just as they are now working. War is a fruit which grows and ripens like other fruit. No magic phrase, no written scrap of paper, will stop the ripening of it if the tree which bears it is planted and watered and kept in the sunshine and warm air. The axe must first be laid to the root of the tree. The old way of life must be abolished and a new way of life must be produced and made to flourish. We shall never succeed in stopping war until we have a human society permeated with persons who practice a way of life which removes and abolishes the grounds and occasions of war, and which at the same time matures and ripens a spirit of mutual understanding and personal co-operation. . . .

If we are to be effective peace-makers we must be vastly more than propagandists. We must demonstrate the power of the kind of life which conquers evil and produces the fruits of peace and good will. Under the old system, armies invaded countries and conquered them with force. Our method, too, must be one of *invasion*. God invaded Africa through David Livingstone and He has invaded Labrador through Sir Wilfred Grenfell. Both these men are types of the overcoming way of life. They conquer men as surely as Alexander or Napoleon did, only their force is different. It is good will and kindness, it is love and gentleness, it is health and strength, it is light and healing. It invades and conquers, overcomes, transforms, rebuilds and inaugurates the new day. Let us join the ranks of the "invaders."

From *The New Quest,*
pp. 97–100; 105.

->>><<<-

THE deepest cleavage in our modern society is the cleavage between the rich and the poor—a wide gash which cuts straight down through humanity. Most of us have *neighbors* who get hardly more out of life than did the primitive cave-dwellers—human fellows so low down that they have to reach up to touch bottom, and neighbors at the other extreme, among "the unemployed rich" who, like lotus eaters,

> Live and lie reclined
> On the hills, like gods together,
> Careless of mankind.

We have learned, after centuries of experiment, that this social trouble is too deep to be cured by the easy methods of flinging alms to poor beggars, or by systems of organized charity. The millionaire who, in his business, fosters iniquitous social conditions and turns men into cogs in the vast machinery of industry, and then tries to wash his soul and his reputation by enormous gifts to charity, philanthropy and education, is not solving the problem. The woman who gives freely to vagrants and to public charity, and then does nothing to show her own human personal interest in those who labor and are heavy laden in the circle of her own household, and the wider circle of her neighborhood, is not helping to solve the problem.

But we must not take the short cut and shipwreck on the shoals of abstract theories. The society toward which we are toiling and aspiring will not come by the proclamation of socialism or by any other cure-all scheme. No system of sharing goods, or of sharing profits, *in itself*, will accomplish the end in view; nothing short of the sharing of life, the spirit of love and brotherhood, the personal consecration, not only of our wealth but of ourselves, to our fellows, will make a good society. The millennium will not come by express tomorrow.

Any sharing of goods that is to be effective must spring out of a genuine spirit of love and brotherhood, a spirit that finds *joy* in sharing. No quick panacea will transform society, no reshuffling of leaden atoms will make a golden group. We must, to be sure, make use of every sound economic and sociological principle which comes to light to change the *conditions* of life and the *social environment* of men. In the work of bettering the world and of spiritualizing humanity, we can no more ignore the structural principles of society than a bridge builder can ignore the laws of mechanics in his work, but there is no sane and efficient program which does not include the old-fashioned Quaker faith in the personal worth of the individual, a faith that a man is more precious than the gold of Ophir, a vision of the potential child of God in the submerged toiler and, with that faith and that vision, the readiness to identify ourselves as friend with those who need us, the bestowal of personal care and sympathy, the sharing of the self as well as the sharing of money, the cultivation of the spirit of consecration to the tasks and needs of the neighborhood group in which we live. In the great words of the Quaker prophet, John Woolman: "We must make it the business of our lives to turn all we possess into the channel of universal love."

We must meet the problem of "the submerged tenth" with "a vicarious tenth," steadily growing into a *vicarious church*. Instead of being content with preaching about a God who *once* vicariously suffered for man's redemption, it is rather our task so to live in the life and power of that Divine love, that Divine self-giving, that our lives, kindled and aflame with that passion, shall again make Christian love real, practical and dynamic, and shall exhibit the beauty and joy of service, as the Master did.

From Quakerism: A Religion of Life,
pp. 34–40.

-->>><<<-

WILLIAM JAMES, in *Varieties of Religious Experience,* defined religion as "the feelings, acts and experiences of individual men *in their solitude,* so far as they apprehend themselves to stand in relation to whatever they may consider the Divine." Speaking a little earlier in the same book of the contribution which the Quaker, George Fox, made to modern religious life, James speaks of it as "a religion of veracity *rooted in spiritual inwardness."* He makes no account of the Quaker contribution to social transformations. Religion is "inwardness," not efforts to make a better "outwardness."

In a similar strain, Professor Whitehead has in quite recent times boldly defined religion "as what the individual does with his own solitariness." In an earlier sentence Whitehead says with equally emphatic stress: "Religion is the art and the theory of the internal life of man, so far as it depends on the man himself, and on what is permanent in the nature of things," which last phrase we may assume means God. "This Doctrine," Whitehead comments, "is the direct negation of the theory that religion is primarily a social fact."

There is, of course, a certain element of truth in this extreme position of Whitehead and James. Rudolf Otto with his theory of religion as the unique numinous feeling aroused in the soul, and Karl Barth with his conception of man's soul miraculously confronted in an utterly perpendicular way by the recreative act of a Divine Other, would both of them, I think, give backing to this view that religion, in its *essentia* is what man does, or what is done to him as "a *solitary* being," alone with God. . . .

But, nevertheless, there is only a tiny fraction of truth in this attempt to reduce religion to what one does alone with God in one's solitariness. The primary fact of human life is not the lonely individual, but the group that makes the individual possible. There can no self emerge in this world without a mother, without a purveyor of food; there can be no acquisition of language, no nurture of mind or spirit, no formation of ideals, no basis of reality without some kind of background society. Society of some sort is the primitive fact. One person alone is simply nobody at all. An isolated being with no relationships would be more difficult to find than the "missing link," and when found would contribute nothing to the meaning of life. Only in a madhouse can one find a completely isolated self. It is no more insane to conceive oneself composed of glass, or to be Ursa Major, than it is to expect to arrive at any goals of life apart from others. The unit-member is dependent at almost every point upon the community, upon the social group, that is, upon the life of the whole.

Religion, which is as immemorial as smiling and weeping, does not begin with a St. Stylites alone on the top of a pillar. If it had so begun the saint would soon have perished without a sympathetic community to feed him— or what is more important, to admire him. It is foolish for us to waste any precious time trying to settle the issue whether religion originates with the individual or the group. It is as absurd as trying to find a stick which has only one end. Individual and group cannot be cut apart and be treated as though either were real as a sundered existent.

The moment an individual has arrived on the scene with a capacity for the mystical, that is, the direct personal apprehension of God and capacity to interpret his experience, there is bound to be behind this individual the long molding processes of history, the accumulations of the experiences and transmissions of many generations. If the given individual runs on ahead of the group, as a prophet-genius does do, it will be along the lines and in the direction for which the group has long been preparing the line of march. And the individual does not possess his insight with a permanent assurance until he has interpreted it and carried others along with his conviction. In short, however important the creative insight of the rare soul may be, religion does not count as a contribution to the race until a beloved community is formed and the discovery is interpreted and transmuted into a social movement. As far as its *significance* is concerned, religion is essentially *social*. It is an affair of a beloved community. Here I align myself with Josiah Royce rather than with William James, both of whom gave me their guidance and friendship.

St. Paul was not exaggerating when he declared that the church-group is Christ's body—the new body which is to be the living expression and growing interpretation in the world of the mind and spirit of Christ through the ages. And St. John is only stating what was literally the truth when he has Christ say of the new fellowship, "I am the vine-stock and you are the vine-branches of one living organism." There never was a time when Christianity was a disembodied idea, or ideal, or spirit. The Gospel itself was formulated and came to the world through the beloved community, and Christianity has always lived on and has always been transmitted through the Body of believers we call the Church.

I mean, then, by *the Church*, the Body of Christian believers and trans-mitters of Christ's mind and spirit through the centuries, rather than a specific organization, or institution, or a single concrete communion, however extensive or historically important. This larger, all-inclusive body of believers has sometimes been called the Church Universal, or what the Spiritual Reformers in the sixteenth century called the "Invisible Church," or in St. Augustine's famous phrase the *Civitas dei qualis nunc in terra*—the City of God as it now is on earth.

This continuous unbroken invisible Church of the Ages as the total Body of Believers has always been a social and socializing force in the world. It has always expressed its truth, its spiritual message, in terms of a society. Its saints have not usually been "exhibits" on lonely pillars; they have been men and women living in the world and expressing in life and action the ideals of their faith as they held it at the time. The Church has always been a society of people living in the midst of the world, penetrated by certain convictions about life. Even in periods when no one yet talked of a "social gospel" in the modern sense, Christianity was nevertheless an immense constructive and socializing force in the reconstruction of the Western World after the overthrow of the Roman Empire by the hordes of the barbarian invaders. The *Civitas dei* went right on as an operative power when the visible empire was submerged, and built the new epoch. . . .

The Church of the ages is a stream which began in mighty Head-waters, and it has until today kept its onward flow more or less influenced on great occasions by its fontal tides of the Spirit. It can continue its mission, its divine function in the world, only as it discovers how to minister in some adequate way both to the souls and the bodies of men. There can be no significant continuing Church, which is concerned solely with what is to happen eschatologically in a post-mortem sphere beyond the glimpses of the moon. The Church must face the real issues of life and make a practical difference in the lives of actual men and women and children, or it is doomed to become a disappearing affair. That does not mean that it is to become secularized. A completely secularized Church has already reached its terminus, and its mission as a Church of Christ is over.

The primary function of a Church, if it is to be a continuing Body of Christ in the world, is to raise human life out of its secular drift and to give reality to the eternal here in the midst of time. When it ceases to bear witness to the real presence of an eternal reality operating in and upon the lives of men, its race is run; it has missed its mission. But just as certainly the Church is commissioned as the organ of the Spirit to bring health and healing to the human lives of men and to the social order in which these lives are formed and molded.

It may be true, as the realistic higher critics tell us, that the Kingdom of God as presented in the Gospels is not a new social order to be slowly, painfully, and creatively realized here in the furrows of our world through the coöperation of God and man together. On the other hand, there is most assuredly a type of life presented in the Gospels which, when it appears, seems to be already the Kingdom of God—a type of life in which love is the supreme spring and motive, in which the spirit of forgiveness has come to ripeness, and which aims to do the will of God on earth as it is done in heaven. In so far as the Church carries on and incarnates that commission it becomes the sower of the seeds of the Kingdom of God and the bearer of a new order for human society.

There is a proverb which says that God empties the nest not by breaking the eggs, but by hatching them. Not by the violent method of revolution will the new social order of life come, not by the legal enforcement of ancient commands, or by the formal application of texts and sayings, but by the vital infusion of a new spirit, the propagation of a passion of love like Christ's, the continuation through the Church of the real presence of Eternity in the midst of time, will something come more like the order of life which we love to call the Kingdom of God. It is the role of the Church, I maintain, to be the fellow laborer with God for this harvest of life. The true Church will be proved to be the true Church, not by its legalistic conformity to the laws and practices of the first century, but by its spirit of love and service, its vision and insight of eternal realities, and its transmission of the Mind, the Spirit, and the Will of Christ here in the world of men.

From *University of Pennsylvania Bicentennial Conference,*
"The Church as an Organ of Social Ideals," from
Religion and the Modern World.

⇒ XI ⇐

How Deal With Dark Days?

XI

ONE of the first passages in the Bible I ever learned was the Prologue to St. John's Gospel "In the beginning was the Word and the Word was with God and the Word was God. All things were made by Him and without Him was not anything made that was made. In Him was life and the life was the light of men. And the light shines in the darkness and the darkness comprehended it not."

The phrase in Greek, *Logos,* is untranslatable. It had been current in philosophical circles for five hundred years, as Mind, Reason, Spirit, Wisdom, but in this Gospel the famous phrase is used with a new and fresh meaning, as "authentic tidings" of ultimate Reality. St. John is saying that this Logos of God, this utterance of the divine purpose, this expression of God, took visible form in a Person and dwelt among us, so that we saw with our eyes, and heard with our own ears and our very hands handled this Word of Life.

We now know that the mysterious saying that "the darkness comprehended it not" ought to be translated: "The darkness does not put it out!" If it is true that the darkness does not put God's light out, it is one of our greatest truths. We need to hold on to it just now—the darkness, even this sevenfold darkness, does not put out the Light. We need not try to protect it by hiding it under a bushel against the storm, for no storm can put it out. The man who wrote this passage claims to have seen the crucifixion. It looked as though the Light was put out, but across the years the beloved disciple saw that it was still shining, that it had not gone out in the darkness. He was probably writing in the darkness of Domitian's reign, when the might of the Roman Empire was pitted against this new faith. In the very forefront of his Gospel, in that time of impenetrable darkness, he put the words of comfort: "The light goes on shining in the darkness and the darkness does not put it out."

A new darkness has covered the earth and our candles have burned out. We need more than ever to hold on to St. John's great words, the darkness does not put out the light that God has lighted. When the Eternal breaks in on us, *that* lasts on. Our transmitters may fail, as happens often with our electrical light and power. We fail to connect with the sources, but all space is still crammed with electrical energy and *that* does not fail. So, too, with

223

the Light of Life. It may not break through for the moment, but the darkness does not put it out. It is the ultimate Reality and it stays on. . . .

The greatest work of the world is done through tiny instruments. The little instrument called "the coherer" makes wireless communication possible. The "transmitter" is essential to the message by telephone. The compass needle may be ever so small but it made Columbus' voyage possible. The hair-spring looks unimportant enough but without it the watch stops. The most stupendous thing, after all, is not the leagues on leagues of measureless space crowded with suns and throbbing with waves of energy; it is rather the fact that a human soul can become conscious and can link up its little life with the infinite Heart and Mind that made the universe. It is not seraphim nor archangels that transmit the light of life. It is mortals like us.

Every day a vast plateau of water is raised in the central ocean many feet above the surrounding water and held suspended until it breaks on the shores and makes our tide. It is lifted by the invisible attraction of the moon—all the wild waters, heaving from pole to pole, rise obedient to that invisible force. In all lands and under all skies, for nineteen hundred years the invisible attraction of the Galilean Life, which brought the light to us, has raised human lives, wherever it has touched them, above the common level of the surrounding life. The conquests of science, the march of history and criticism have not put it out. No, nor has the new wave of pagan darkness put it out. We may, I think, conclude, with the Voice out of the far past, that the light shines in the darkness and the darkness does not put it out.

From *New Eyes for Invisibles,*
pp. 20–21; 23–24.

->>><<<-

I HAVE often come out of a subway train, carrying a heavy suitcase, thinking fondly of the lift the escalator was about to give me, when my hopes have been dashed by a placard announcing that the escalator is not running today. Unfortunately something perverse has happened to our "cosmic escalator," which Victorian optimists believed was certain to carry the human race to unbelievable heights. "It is not running today." If we are to go to great heights it will not be on a "cosmic escalator," it will be rather

Upon the great world's *altar stairs*
That slope through darkness up to God.

The Mind that binds the cluster of the Pleiades and brings forth Mazzaroth in its season is still operating, not only in the region of the firmament, but in the affairs of men and of nations. Emerson used to tell us that if you hold a straw parallel to the Gulf Stream the ocean will flow through your straw. It is a more important fact that as soon as a life comes into parallelism with the Divine purpose God operates to the shaping of history through that life, and the Spirit that was revealed in Christ continues to carry forward the revelation.

In many respects it is easier for us to believe in the continued life and work of Christ than it was for His own disciples. They *saw* and believed. They had the evidence of the senses which we cannot have and there can be no question that the testimony of the senses is very convincing. We, on the other hand, have the overwhelming evidence of nineteen hundred years of Christian victories over the world, the flesh and the evil in man. We do not see all things put under His triumphant feet. His Kingdom is far from completed. But the story of Christ's victories across the centuries is, I think, the most amazing single fact of history.

We have the luminous trail of saints whom Christ has made. In the best of them it seems as though the Life of God was manifestly operating within. The earliest major one of these saints, a man who never saw Christ in flesh, said: "It is no longer I that live, but Christ lives in me." Something like that they all say. They all in one way or another practice His presence in their lives and in their triumphs over sin and over the world. When Francis of Assisi ran away to God it was because he believed that he saw Christ beckoning to him and calling him to rebuild his broken Church. St. Catherine, the dyer's daughter of Siena, kept doing all her life what no woman alone could do. Her strength became the strength of ten, because she had invisible allies. Meister Eckhart in his hard century knew with joy like that of Mary that God brought forth His Son in him. The shoemaker, Jacob Boehme, had the thrill of feeling, in his tender humility, "Christ became what I am and now He has made me what He is." What saved George Fox during those three years of wandering in his leather breeches was his final discovery that "there is One, even Christ Jesus," who could speak to his condition and Who gave him the key that opened all the doors of life. This procession of saints, and millions who "nameless the same great pathway trod," gives us an evidence which a disciple in the upper room in Jerusalem in the first century could not possibly have had.

But perhaps even more impressive, if anything could be more impressive than this luminous trail of saints, is the way in which Christianity has met the crises, the crucial moments, in history, and has led captivity captive—has conquered and more than conquered. I see at certain epochs of history what seems like an emergence, an incursion, of the Divine Life. It seems as though in a marked way and to a peculiar degree the Life of God—again humanly revealed—has broken, like a vernal equinox, into the lives of men and into the stream of history. A new installment of life and power has burst into the world, like a mutation, that changes the old level forever.

I know only too well what a poor old broken world confronts us at the present moment. This is no time for soft and easy optimism. Jeremiah the prophet usually took a dark view of things. He did not expect the leopard to change his spots, or the Ethiopian to go white. He looked for no miraculous panacea—no balm in Gilead—to change the hard conditions. But watching a potter remake a spoiled vessel on his potter's wheel, he suddenly has a vision of reality and in a flash he saw that that is what God does with His world. He does not scrap the marred clay. He remakes what has gone wrong. How often He has done it! What a list it is!

But always the emergence, the incursion, the vernal equinox of the Spirit comes through some human individual or some prepared group. It does not come as lightning out of the sky.

From *The Luminous Trail,*
pp. v–vii.

-->>)<<-

WE are passing through one of the most critical moments in modern history. We have learned how, as Emerson suggested, to hitch our wagons to a star. We tap the forces of the universe for our power and our speed. We turn a button and start our car, light our house, and set our furnace going. We can beat the antelope on the ground and we can outfly the eagle in the air.

But who will show us how to find the eternal springs of peace and joy? Who will help us to draw upon the eternal resources of inward power? Who will take from us our sin and our weakness and make us strong and good? We may hold it as settled that we cannot change the world from ways of war to ways of peace, nor can we rebuild the social order on right lines for future generations, without the influence and guidance and inspiration of vital religion. A world built on purely secular lines would be a world that would fester and spoil and corrupt, as has always happened. We must, above everything else, find our way back to the springs of life and refreshment for the hearts and souls of men.

On a great occasion St. Paul said: "None of these perils unsettles me." Everything indicated dangers of the gravest sort ahead of him. He was starting out on a journey that was to end in Nero's dungeon and finally in a martyr's death. When the actual event was close upon him, and the shadow of it was in sight, he calmly spoke of the peace of God that passed all comprehension as the garrison of his heart and mind.

This complete control over the peril of unsettlement is one of the main miracles of a genuinely religious way of life. Religious faith, when it comes to its true power, does just that miraculous thing for us all. It turns water to wine. It brings prodigals home. It sets men on their feet. It raises life out of death. It turns sunsets to sunrises. It makes the impossible become possible. The master secret of life is the attainment of the power of serenity in the midst of stress and action and adventure.

This principle of calm is, I am convinced, not attained by a method of detachment and withdrawal. We all praise simplicity and the Franciscan reduction of desire but, even so, we cannot reduce desires to zero, and if we succeeded in annihilating desires we should find the values of life also shrinking to naught. No, not that way do we come to the sources of peace and power. The rich and genuine life of calm and adventure comes rather by a new and greater attachment, by the formation of a profounder loyalty and the discovery of a wider reference of interests.

The issue which confronts us is not whether the contemplative life, represented in art by Mary, is the higher way, or the active life, represented by Martha, busy with her dinner. It is not a question of alternatives. It is not a problem of *either-or*. Mary, lost in rapture and doing nothing with it, is not the true figure of the high-powered life. And Martha rushing nervously about, frantic in her haste and hurry, irritated and complaining, is certainly no nearer the true goal of life. Somehow we must get these two half-aspects of life fused together into a vital whole. We want to secure a life which combines contemplation and action, an inward serenity and a spirit of adventure. This union of the two essential aspects is the Quaker ideal—to find the springs and sources of power and then to go forth to the tasks of the world in the armor of Light. . . .

There are deeps in us all far below our ideas. There is in fact a substratum which is the mother-soil out of which all our ideas and purposes are born, as capes of cloud are born out of the viewless air. To feed or to fertilize that sub-soil of our conscious life is far more important than to capture and to organize a few stray thoughts. To discover how to flood with power and to vitalize this fundamental stratum of our being is, after all, to uncover one of the master secrets of life. Just that is what seems to happen to some of us in the hush and mystery of intimate contact with Divine currents, in the living silence of corporate worship.

It is like a ship in a lock. Here the ship is, shut in by great gates before and behind. Its driving engines have slowed down. Its speed has diminished to naught. It is no longer going anywhere. And yet all the time the water is rising underneath the ship, and when the gate in front swings open, and the ship emerges from its period of full stop, it will go out for its journey on a higher level and carry its burden of freight henceforth on a new plane. . . .

There are moments when the walls between the seen and the unseen appear to grow thin and almost vanish away, and one feels himself to be in contact with more than himself. The threshold of consciousness which in our attentive and focussed states of mind bars the entrance of everything that does not fit the business in hand, drops to a different level and allows a vastly widened range of experiences, and we suddenly discover that we can draw upon more of ourselves than at other times. And in these best moments of widened range, when we share the coöperative influence of many expectant worshippers around us, it seems often as though streams of life and light and love and truth flow in from beyond our margins, and we come back to work and business and thought again, not only calmed, rested and made serene, but also more completely organized and vitalized and equipped with new energies of the Spirit.

From *New Eyes for Invisibles,*
pp. 56–61.

→»«←

EACH tested soul has to meet its own peculiar frustrations. All of us who work for "causes" or who take up any great piece of moral or spiritual service in the world know more about defeats and disappointments than we do about success and triumphs. We have to learn to be patient and long-suffering. We must become accustomed to postponements and delays, and sometimes we see the work of almost a lifetime suddenly fail of its end. Some turn of events upsets all our noble plans and frustrates the result, just when it appears ready to arrive. Death falls like lightning on a home that had always before seemed sheltered and protected, and instantly life is profoundly altered for those who are left behind. Nothing can make up for the loss. There is no substitute for what is gone. The accounts will not balance; frustration in another form confronts us. Or it may be a breakdown of physical or mental powers, or peradventure both together, just when the emergencies of the world call for added energy and increased range of power from us. The need is plain, the harvest is ripe, but the worker's hand fails and he must contract when he would most expand. Frustration looks him straight in the face. Well, to achieve a peace under those circumstances is to have a peace which does not follow a normal sequence. It is not what the world expects. It does not accord with the ways of thought and reasoning. It passes all understanding. It brings another kind of world into operation and reveals a play of invisible forces upon which the understanding had not reckoned. In fact, this strange intellect-transcending peace, in the very midst of storm and strain and trial, is one of the surest evidences there is of God. One may in his own humble nerve-power succeed in acquiring a stoic resignation so that he can say:

> In the fell clutch of circumstance
> I have not winced nor cried aloud.
> Under the bludgeonings of chance
> My head is bloody, but unbowed.

He may, by sheer force of will, keep down the lid upon his emotions and go on so nearly unmoved that his fellows can hear no groan and will wonder at the way he stands the universe. But peace in the soul is another matter. To have the whole heart and mind garrisoned with peace even in Nero's dungeon, when the imperial death sentence brings frustration to all plans and a terminus to all spiritual work, calls for some world-transcending assistance to the human spirit. Such peace is explained only when we discover that it is "the peace of God," and that it came because the soul broke through the ebbings and flowings of time and space and allied itself with the Eternal.

Few things are more impressive than the persistent search which men have made in all ages for a refuge against the dangers and the ills that beset life. The cave-men, the cliff-dwellers, the primitive builders of shelters in inaccessible tree tops, are early examples of the search for human defenses against fear. Civilization slowly perfected methods of refuge and defense of elaborate types, which in turn, had to compete with ever-increasing ingenuity of attack and assault. But I am not concerned here with these material strongholds of refuge and defense. I am thinking rather of the human search for shelter against other weapons than those which kill the body. We are all trying, in one way or another, to discover how to escape from "the heavy and weary weight of all this unintelligible world," how to bear the "slings and arrows of outrageous fortune." We are sensitively constructed, with nerves exposed to easy attack. We are all shelterless at some point to the storms of the world. Even the most perfectly equipped and impervious heroes prove to be vulnerable at some one uncovered spot. Sooner or later our protections fail, and the pitiless enemies of our happiness get through the defenses and reach the quick and sensitive soul within us. How to rebuild our refuge, how to find real shelter, is our problem. What fortress is there in which the soul is safe from fear and trouble?

The most common expedient is one which will drug the sensitive nerves and produce an easy relief from strain and worry. There is magic in alcohol and kindred distillations, which, like Aladdin's genie, builds a palace of joy and, for the moment, banishes the enemy of all peace. The refuge seems complete. All fear is gone, worry is a thing of the past. The jargon of life is over, the pitiless problem of good and evil drops out of consciousness. The

shelterless soul seems covered and housed. Intoxication is only one of the
many quick expedients. It is always possible to retreat from the edge of
strenuous battle into some one of the many natural instincts as a way of
refuge. The great instinctive emotions are absorbing, and tend to obliterate
everything else. They occupy the entire stage of the inner drama, and push
all other actors away from the footlights of consciousness, so that here, too,
the enemies of peace and joy seem vanquished, and the refuge appears to
be found.

That multitudes accept these easy ways of defense against the ills of life
is only too obvious. The medieval barons who could build themselves castles
of safety were few in number. Visible refuges in any case are rare and scarce,
but the escape from the burdens and defeats of the world in drink and drug
and thrilling instinctive emotions is, without much difficulty, open to every
man and within easy reach for rich and poor alike, and many there be that
seize upon this method. The trouble with it is that it is a very temporary
refuge. It works, if at all, only for a brief span. It plays havoc in the future
with those who resort to it. It rolls up new liabilities to the ills one would
escape. It involves far too great a price for the tiny respite gained. And,
most of all, it discounts or fails to reckon with the inherent greatness of the
human soul. We are fashioned for stupendous issues. Our very sense of
failure and defeat comes from a touch of the infinite in our being. . . .

In hours of loss and sorrow, when the spurious props fail us, we are more
apt to find our way back to the real refuge. We are suddenly made aware
of our shelterless condition, alone, and in our own strength. Our stoic armor
and our brave defenses of pride become utterly inadequate. We are thrown
back on reality. We have then our moments of sincerity and insight. We
feel that we cannot live without resources from beyond our own domain.
We must have God. It is then, when one knows that nothing else whatever
will do, that the great discovery is made. Again and again the psalms announce this. When the world has caved in; when the last extremity has been
reached; when the billows and waterspouts of fortune have done their worst,
you hear the calm, heroic voice of the lonely man saying: "God is our refuge
and fortress, therefore will not we fear though the earth be removed, though
the mountains be carried into the middle of the sea." That is great experience,
but it is not reserved for psalmists and rare patriarchs like Job. It is a privilege for common mortals like us who struggle and agonize and feel the thorn
in the flesh, and the bitter tragedy of life unhealed. Whether we make the
discovery or not, God is there with us in the furnace. Only it makes all the
difference if we do find him as the one high tower where refuge is not for the
passing moment only, but is an eternal attainment. . . .

A generation ago almost everybody read, at least once, Carlyle's great book on heroes. He gave us the hero as prophet, as priest, as poet, as king, and he made us realize that these heroes have been the real makers of human society. I should like to add a chapter on another kind of hero, who has, perhaps, not done much to build cities and states and church systems, but who has, almost more than anybody else, shown us the spiritual value of endurance—I mean the hero as invalid.

It is the hardest kind of heroism there is to achieve. Most of us know some man—too often it is oneself—who is a very fair Christian when he is in normal health and absorbed in interesting work, who carries a smooth forehead and easily drops into a good-natured smile, but who becomes "blue" and irritable and a storm centre in the family weather as soon as the bodily apparatus is thrown out of gear. Most of us have had a taste of humiliation as we have witnessed our own defeat in the presence of some thorn in the flesh, which stubbornly pricked us, even though we prayed to have it removed and urged the doctor to hurry up and remove it.

What a hero, then, must he be, who, with a weak and broken body, a prey to pain and doomed to die daily, learns how to live in calm faith that God is good and makes his life a centre of cheer and sunshine! The heroism of the battlefield and the man-of-war looks cheap and thin compared with this. We could all rally to meet some glorious moment when a trusted leader shouted to us, "Your country expects you to do your duty!" But to drag on through days and nights, through weeks and months, through recurring birthdays, with vital energy low, with sluggish appetite, with none of that ground-swell of superfluous vigor which makes healthy life so good, and still to prove that life is good and to radiate joy and triumph—that is the very flower and perfume of heroism. If we are making up a bead-roll of heroes, let us put at the top the names of those quiet friends of ours who have played the man or revealed the woman through hard periods of invalidism and have exhibited to us the fine glory of a courageous spirit.

One of the hardest and most difficult features to bear is the inability to work at one's former pace and with the old-time constructive power. The prayer of the Psalmist that his work, the contribution of his life, might be preserved is very touching: "Establish thou the work of our hands upon us, yea, the work of our hands establish thou it." What can be more tragic than the cry of Othello: "My occupation is gone!" So long as the hand keeps its cunning and the mind remains clear and creative, one can stand physical handicap and pain, but when the working power of mind or body is threatened, then the test of faith and heroism indeed arrives.

A man whose life meant much to me and whose intimacy was very precious to me made me see many years ago how wonderfully this test could be met. He was a great teacher, the head of a distinguished boys' school. He was experiencing the full measure of success, and his influence over his boys was extraordinary. He realized, as his work went on, that his hearing was becoming dull and was steadily failing. He went to New York and consulted a famous specialist. After making a careful examination the specialist said, with perfect frankness: "Your case is hopeless. Nothing can be done to check the disaster. You are hard of hearing already, but in a very short time you will have no hearing at all." Without a quaver the teacher said: "Don't you think, doctor, that I shall hear Gabriel's trumpet when it blows!" He went back to his school, learned to read lips, reorganized his life, accepted without a murmur his loss of a major sense, and finished his splendid career of work in an undefeated spirit and with a grace and joy which were envied by many persons in possession of all their powers.

All my readers will think of some "star player" in this hard game of patience and endurance, and will have watched with awe and reverence the glorious fight of some of those unrecorded heroes who won but got no valor medal. The only person who ranks higher in the scale of heroism than the hero as invalid is possibly the person who patiently, lovingly nurses and cares for some invalid through years of decline and suffering. Generally, though not always, it is a woman. Not seldom she is called upon to consecrate her life to the task, and often she gives what is much more precious than life itself. We build no monuments to daughters who unmurmuringly forego the joy of married life, who refuse the suit of love in order to be free to ease the closing years of father or mother, grown helpless; but where is there higher consecration or finer heroism? Men sometimes complain that the days of chivalry and heroism are past. On the contrary, they are more truly dawning. As Christianity ripens love grows richer and deeper, and where love appears heroism is always close at hand. Our best heroes are mothers and wives and daughters, fathers and husbands and sons.

From *Spiritual Energies in Daily Life,*
pp. 3–10; 65–69.

-»>«<-

THERE are moments in the history of the race when some gifted soul sees a *principle of life* which proves to be as universal and eternal as are the axioms of geometry. The principle may, for long periods, drop out of focus and lie unused and forgotten, but if it is one of the essential laws of spiritual life it will be again and again rediscovered and reinstated in its place among the inalienable assets of the soul. Few greater instances of this recurrent discovery of such a principle of life can be cited than the attitude of faith which formed the spring and basis of the Reformation. We are just now in danger of "losing" it again, and for that reason it may be time to revive it "in our ears." *Faith* is so often pitted unfavorably against "reason" and depreciated as a spurious way of discovering truth that it deserves fresh consideration in these days when "demonstration" is in such high favor.

The great note was first struck by an unknown Judean prophet whose message bears the name of "Habakkuk." Nobody knows just when he lived or just what crisis of disasters he was facing when he wrote his little immortal book. It is enough to know that his world was terribly out of joint. The winepress of suffering was working overtime. The ancient mystery of frustrated hope hung over him like an impenetrable cloud. A new trouble trod close upon the heels of the one that at the moment was harassing his soul. The hardest thing to bear was, however, not the agony which his body suffered but the agony that came from the impossibility of finding a clue to the meaning of the ways of God. He felt that he could bear *anything* if he only knew what God meant and could see a divine purpose and function in what was happening. In any case, this prophet proposed to hold fast by his soul's faith that there is a meaning in it all and that there is a divine purpose, however hidden it may be. He resolved to build his watch-tower and wait for the light to break. He will not yield to despair. He will not surrender to the pitiless facts that besiege him round about. He also, like his great successor Luther, says: "Here I stand. I cannot do otherwise." The answer may be postponed; the vision of relief may tarry, but he decides to "wait for it." Then comes the great discovery that *faith itself is the victory*. The life lived in the power of a great faith is its own evidence. The answer which comes to his soul as he waits in his watch-tower is this: "The righteous man *lives* by his faith."

The word which has usually been translated "faith," here in Habakkuk's great declaration more properly means *faithfulness*. It means unswerving loyalty. It is a dependable quality of character that can always be counted on in the shift of events and in the fluctuations of the hour. Whatever else changes, this man stands like a rock amid the drift of desert sand. There he is unmoved in the welter. But the important point to be noted is the fact that his "faithfulness" roots back into his *faith*. He has unswerving loyalty because he has an immense confidence in God. He can stand the universe, because he somehow feels that God is captain of the ship on which he sails. The righteous man then, the man who in the end gets divine approval, is the man who, through his soul's confidence and calm assurance, holds steadily on, in the dark or in the light, and builds his watch-tower above the surface clouds of the present moment. How effective the method is comes out at length in the triumphant words which are worth a whole army with banners:

"Although the fig-tree may not blossom, neither shall there be fruit in the vines; the labor of the olive shall fail and the fields shall yield no food; the flock shall be cut off from the fold and there shall be no herd in the stalls, *nevertheless I will rejoice in the Lord and joy in the God of my salvation, and I will walk in my high places.*" This means that faith helps, in some measure, to create the world of the spirit. It helps to build the refuge and fortress of the soul, where victory is finally won.

Herbert Spencer, in the nineteenth century, laid down as his principle of ethics "conformity of the individual to his environment." Moral progress is measured, according to him, by the adjustment of internal conditions to the external environment in which one lives. The man who is "well adjusted to his environment" has learned how to live. One trouble with Spencer's theory is the ambiguity of this word "environment." Our environment as moral persons is always largely colored and transformed by our point of view, our outlook, our attitude, our frame of mind. No two of us have anywhere near the same "environment." But even if we had a fixed and unvarying environment, who of us feels that he has won a moral victory when he has succeeded in adjusting himself to it? Our real problem is not adjustment of ourselves to our environment, but it is rather the problem of so transforming the environment that in some measure at least it fits our own ideal of what the environment *ought to be.* The real moral hero is not the person who gets *adjusted*—as, by the way, the hard-shelled mollusc has so perfectly done— and who conforms to the conditions of his external environment, but the moral hero is the person who raises the whole level of his world until it conforms, at least a good deal better, to what ought to be.

But, anyway, here in Habakkuk appears a new kind of hero. He will not conform himself to his environment and he cannot reshape his environment to fit his ideal. Nothing he can do will save his olive crop or protect his flock. His world is not safe for cattle raising nor can he *make* it safe. What can he do? He can hold straight on by his faith that God is slowly beating out the answer to his problems and his mysteries. He can erect his watchtower and stand firmly on it until the clouds break and the vision is granted. That is his peculiar heroism and that is his moral victory in a dark moment of history.

His principle of life became the keynote of St. Paul, of the author of the Epistle to the Hebrews, of St. Augustine and of Martin Luther. His torch kept kindling other torches. His cry of *faith* took on many meanings. But through it all the central meaning of the great idea persisted. Faith, for these heroic souls, was never some easy magical solution of life's mysteries, or of a man's salvation. It was first and foremost a determination to hold unswervingly one's confidence and trust in the character and purpose of God. They had a real advantage over the lonely man on his Judaen watch-tower. They had an impressive historical revelation of the Divine character and purpose to inspire them. They had a clue which Habakkuk lacked. They had a beam of light where he had only enveloping darkness. But it must be said, in all honesty, that faith is still, as in the centuries B.C., heroic business and it calls as much as ever for all there is in a man.

Since beginning to write this article, I have been brought into close relation with a present-day situation as hard to bear as Habakkuk's was. A young friend of mine who is the sufferer in the present instance, is facing issues as mysterious, as baffling and as hard to reconcile with the love of God as were the issues in Judea twenty-five hundred years ago. The most perplexing aspect of my friend's heart-searching agony is due to the insistent question whether God really *cares* or not. All the harrowing features of a genuine tragedy are massed together in this new case. *And God does nothing, and He says nothing to relieve the strain.* One's feet go clear down to the bottom of the winepress and all the time the heavens remain as stern as brass. It is God's own affair, and yet He does nothing to support the faith of the person who is suffering in His cause. Is it not strange? It is strange. It always has been strange. It baffled Job. It wrung the soul of many a Psalmist. It sounded Habakkuk to his depths. Even Christ cried out, "My God, why hast *Thou* forsaken me?" It has come from the lips of every "suffering servant" through the ages.

The answer is that there are situations in which natural, brute forces play their role. They cut straight across our wishes and desires; defeat our plans; crush our hopes and seem to be at war with all that is spiritual. The only way God could intervene in such crises and vindicate His cause would be by miracle. He does not work that way. He does not interrupt the course of atoms or the sweep of unfolding events. Those who would find Him must not look for Him as a bringer of supernatural relief when the house is on fire, when the train jumps the rails, or when a dread disease is running its course. God is found, now as of old, by the soul that builds the watch-tower and waits, refusing to surrender to the shadow and the darkness. In quietness there is strength. In the voice of stillness comes His answer. Once more, now as then, faith *is* the victory. The soul of the good man *lives by his faith*. The heart answers, "I have felt." He that endures to the end and will not drop to the lower level is saved. God does not interfere. He does not turn the current of the storm, but He is the Companion of the suffering soul in the storm, and He is in the furnace and in the winepress with the agonizing heart.

From *The Friend*, London, Vol. 68 (1928), pp. 165–167.

-»» «« -

IT seems no doubt a bit of religious aristocratic pride in the midst of the welter of bombed cities and invaded countries and war camps and actual slums and sinking ships and unfed children, to talk of the progress of the soul and the immortal beauty of love, since there are a great many persons in our world whose souls, so far as our minds can see, will make no progress, but in spite of all the temporary darkness and the eclipse of the higher values of life, we must go on interpreting the eternal aspects and the higher laws of the human soul. While we are talking on high-sounding themes it will be well for us, however, to remember that the truest love does not run smooth, but is often blood-red with sacrifice. Our danger, however, is not that we shall talk of love in too exalted terms, but that we shall treat it in too commonplace a fashion. If love is to be the spring and source of the progress of the soul, as Plato and Dante and Emerson and many other geniuses of the race have prophesied, it must have a touch of eternity to it, and it must bring an unwonted splendor to life.

William Law, a very wise guide in all matters which have to do with the progress of the soul, said: "There is but one salvation for all mankind and *that is the life of God in the soul.* You have no true religion but in and by that spirit of love which is God Himself living and working in you. Turn therefore inwards and all that is within you will demonstrate the presence and power of God in your soul."

Life at its best, when the eternal Beauty shines into it, is a radiant affair. John Woolman—dear man—said: "Some glances of real beauty may be seen in their faces who dwell in true meekness." L. P. Jacks of Oxford some years ago wrote a remarkable essay on "The Lost Radiance of Christianity." I am profoundly concerned to have this lost radiance *recovered* and made once more an essential feature of our Christianity. And I am inclined to believe that we shall not see the evidence that there is a genuine progress of the soul until we recover that radiance which was such a striking feature of the Gospels and of the life of St. Francis and the other saints who, like him, "ran away to God."

Lockhart reports, in his "Life of Sir Walter Scott," a conversation in which the novelist said that the pictures of Byron give no idea of the beauty of Byron's face. "The luster," he said, "is there in the pictures, but it is *not lighted up.*" I am eager to find out what lights up the luster and restores the radiance of life. A great cause does it, a great purpose does it, a great faith does it, a great love does it.

Professor W. H. Sheldon has said that "Happiness is essentially a state of going somewhere whole-heartedly." It is equally true of this radiance of life, which is deeper than happiness, that it comes when you are "going somewhere whole-heartedly." But ideas and professions that "lie bedridden," as Coleridge puts it, "in the dormitory of men's souls," do not do it. It is not got by speculating and arguing. Chesterton was quite right when he wrote his lines:

> Oh, we have learnt to peer and pore
> On tortured puzzles from our youth,.
> We know all labyrinthine lore;
> We are the three Wise Men of yore
> And we know all things but the truth.

The greatest things in the world are not reached by argument. Some experiences of life come like a vernal equinox, or like the radiance of sunrise, and there is no longer any need of argument; you are in the presence of an immutable fact of life.

Pascal had a transforming experience which colored all the rest of his life. He expressed it in broken gasps of joy, written at the time of the experience and sewed into his coat, to be found after his death: "Certainty, joy, certainty, feeling, sight, joy, joy, joy, tears of joy." He had here an installment of life come into him, like the fragrance of Mary's ointment. Unfortunately he held a theory of human life which did not encourage the expression of radiance, and this exuberance of joy was discovered only after Pascal's death. Too often it has been the inscription on the tombstone that has announced the triumphant note of life and not the lighted luster on the face during life-time.

The Kennebago Mountains are visible in the far horizon of my home in Maine, but they come into sight only when the wind is northwest and has blown the sky clear of fog and mist and cloud. Then there they are, in all their distant purple glory. But we know that they are there all the time, when the wind is east or south, though we cannot see them, and we say to our visitors, wait until the wind comes round and blows from Saskatchewan, and then you will see our mountains which are over there in our far skyline! Some persons' luster lights up like that only when the wind is in the right quarter. I am pleading for a type of life that is sunlit and radiant, not only in fair weather and when the going is smooth, but from a deep inward principle and discovery which makes it lovely and beautiful in all weathers.

I went many years ago, in London, to visit Baron Friedrich von Hügel, who was at that time one of the foremost philosophical thinkers in Europe, and the leading interpreter of mystical religion in the world. It was a momentous event in my life to talk freely with this extraordinary man of the matters that meant the most to me of anything in the universe, but the most memorable feature of the visit came as I was saying good-by. He said to me, "Before you go I want to tell you of the four conditions of life which must be fulfilled before anyone can be canonized a saint in my Church (the Roman Catholic). He, or as is more often the case, *she* must have been throughout life loyal to the Faith of the Church. In the second place the person must have been heroic. He must have faced danger and difficulty in a magnanimous and unconquerable spirit, and have done what seemed impossible for a person to do. In the third place, the person who is to rank as a saint must have been the recipient of powers beyond his ordinary human capacities. He must have been the organ of higher forces than those which appear to belong to human nature as such, so that an element of the miraculous gets expressed through his life and deeds. And, finally, in the fourth place, through good report and evil report, through prosperity and the loss of it, in the mountain top moments and in the dull round of everyday life, he must, she must, have been radiant." The old philosopher and mystic stood up in front of me, half a head taller than I was, and he raised his hands as high in the air as he could reach and said: "They may possibly be wrong about those first three conditions, but they are gloriously right about that fourth condition—a saint must be *radiant*."

I suppose very few of my readers will be canonized, and the writer will certainly not be, but if we can have the beauty of the Lord our God upon us, the grace of Christ with us, and sunlight and joy in our hearts, we shall in so far demonstrate the progress of the soul and we shall reveal at least one trait of the saint.

From *The Radiant Life*,
pp. 1–5.

→»)«‹-

(This is the story of one of Rufus Jones' greatest sorrows and of the way he met it.)

ISAIAH was gloriously right when he said, "A little child shall lead them." I know that that is so. My life has been led and guided on its way by a child. I have waited until I had reached an advanced age to tell the story of this child, for it was too intimate and sacred to speak of easily at an earlier stage. But it seems right to do it now, for it belongs here. I have been writing about saints. They are of many types. St. Paul called all the members of his churches "saints." They were not perfect. Many of them were far from perfect. *Saint* for him was a hopeful, gentle word. It expressed a faith, a hope, an aim, an attitude of direction, rather than an attainment. The boy I am writing about here never had a chance to arrive at a goal. He left me when he was only eleven years old, but his life was so full of promise, the attitude of direction was so marked, that I am convinced he belongs in my list here. Only one twenty-seventh of the range of ethereal vibration is visible in our spectrum. We see only a tiny fraction of the colors of our universe. But we see enough to know that it is a world crammed with beauty. I only saw enough of this boy's life to know that it gave the promise of expanding beauty, which was to be realized otherwhere, not here, where I could see it with my present eyes.

The birth of this son in midwinter of 1892 was one of the supreme events of my life. He was named Lowell, after my beloved poet. I took him in my arms from the doctor—which would not be allowed now in a modern hospital—and felt an unutterable emotion of joy and wonder. It is impossible to tell what makes a father's emotion so unique, so overwhelming. He has not suffered, as the mother has. It is not quite fair for him to have such a thrill of joy. But there it is, and it cannot be helped. It is a fusion of thanksgiving and joy, of awe and wonder. Here is a vital part of one's self starting out on a new momentous career. There is ground enough for awe and wonder. But here was something more than a vital part of one's self. It was something from God, trailing clouds of glory, breaking into the world. It was a creative act of God as much as any act "in the beginning." I have always loved Pompilia's words in "The Ring and the Book," and they became more full of meaning than ever, as I held this child of mine:

> I never realized God's birth before—
> How He grew likest God in being born.
> This time I felt like Mary, had my babe
> Lying a little on my breast like hers.

I never got away from this divine miracle. There was a light on this child's face which I did not put there. There were marks of heavenly origin too plain to miss. Poets admit that the child trails "clouds of glory from God Who is our home," but they spoil it all by predicting that the glory will quickly "fade into the light of common day." It was not so with this child. A child looking at a beautiful object was told that it would soon be gone. "Never mind," he said, "there'll be something else beautiful tomorrow." The "light" kept growing plainer and more real through the eleven years he lived here on earth with me. It never became "common day." His little mind was keen and alert from the very first. The first thing I did when I had him in my arms was to carry him up a flight of stairs, as I said jokingly, "This will give him a climbing spirit!" Anyhow, that is what he always had. He picked up words at an astonishingly early period. "Clock" was his first word, because he was somehow fascinated by the round face of our clock, and at once he began shouting the word whenever he saw similarities to the clock in other objects. When I held him up to see the full moon, rising in the east, he shouted, "clock!"

But his supreme fascination, which came very early and lasted as long as he lived, was at the sight of a flower. He exhibited this strange thrill of joy at the sight of any and every flower. It was so marked that it seemed like an original bent or *trope,* which the little mind had brought with it. It was a plain marking. During the summer before he was born his mother had spent all her free time collecting and analyzing flowers which abound in vast quantity and variety in the Kennebec Valley in Maine, where we were living at the time. She had lived that summer surrounded with flowers and with a passionate enjoyment of them. In some strange way this passion had gone by a process too subtle for analysis into this new-born child. If one wanted to see a heavenly light break and radiate over Lowell's face all one needed to do was to hold out a flower to him—any flower would do it. I shall have more to say later of this flower passion. A little child enjoying an unexpected pleasure smiled up toward the sky and said, "Thank you, God." That is the way Lowell felt with each new flower.

Each triumph of my little man in his early stage of adjustment to space and time gave me a constant thrill. His achievement of food assimilation, his extraordinary tendency to imitate sounds and movements—"as if his whole vocation were endless imitation"—his methods of self-transportation, his fear of darkness and the long list of attainments recapitulated not only those I made as a child, but the unfolding story of human civilization as well. Here it all was before my eyes in miniature. From the first, and always, he and I seemed to go together in a remarkable way. We fitted at every point like young lovers. In fact we fell in love with each other from the start. It seemed like a mystical union. Beyond words and even beyond thoughts we loved and understood and thrilled with joy in each other's presence. It seemed as though our inner being somewhere touched within and interfused, so that even when we were separated by space we were still inseparable. There was a vibrating chord that stretched between us. He found God as naturally and with the same enthusiasm as he found beauty in flowers and everywhere in his world. He has forever convinced me that God is as real to the child as visible objects are. I have just heard of a child who was busy drawing a picture. Some one asked him what he was doing, "I am making a picture of God," he said. "But you can't do that," he was told, "for nobody knows what God looks like." "They will know when I get this picture done," was his confident reply. The great poets have always been saying that the child knows. Here it was before my eyes. Bible stories always charmed him. It was primarily for him that I wrote my "Stories of Hebrew Heroes," which two generations of children have read. He took sheer delight in the lofty English style of description in the Bible passages, which were suited for a child, especially the chosen Psalms. He loved the silence of our periods of worship in the home, and he very early entered with real appreciation into the congregational hushes of our Quaker Meetings. I am convinced that children have a sense of Presence in these times of intense community hush. Lowell formed a beautiful group of little friends who played Quaker Meeting together, and after attending a Quaker marriage, he and a little playmate with charming innocence took hold of hands and said the Quaker marriage ceremony together! All the way through these eleven years he belonged to the invisible Church and was a child of the Kingdom of Heaven. A friend of mine saw a little boy flying his kite which had gone up out of sight. "How do you know you have got a kite up there?" my friend asked the boy. "Cause I can feel the tug on the string," the boy said. There was some sort of inner tug on the soul of my boy which made God always real to him.

When he began school at four he took at once to the steps which drew out his unfolding mind. Poetry, at first of a very simple type, and later poetry of the greater type, fascinated him almost as much as flowers did. Edward Lear and Stevenson, and Whittier's "Child Life," were his early favorites, but he very soon had a long list of beloved poets which we read together. He had a natural ear for the melodious and for rhythm. When he was five, on Christmas Eve, he sang the whole of Phillips Brooks' "Little Town of Bethlehem" without any book to guide him. The summer Lowell was five we spent some time in my old home in South China, Maine. I took him with me on an errand. We had the old farm horse and were riding in a high-seated wagon. As we were riding along he saw some beautiful chicory flowers growing near the schoolhouse yard. "Oh, Daddy, let me get some of those flowers," he cried. I should have let him go for them himself, but instead I stupidly got out to get them for him. I left the reins hanging on the seat, not dreaming that this old plug of a horse might be dangerous to leave. But just as I reached the flowers I heard Lowell scream. I looked to see the horse starting off on a gallop with this precious boy alone on the wagon seat. I prayed with all my soul, but I ran as vigorously as I prayed. With the greatest sprint of my life I dashed after the flying wagon, by a leap far beyond my normal powers—"doing what I couldn't"—I sprang into the back of the wagon, climbed over the seat, recovered the reins, pulled in the running horse and saved the day. I can still feel the emotion swell within me.

One of the most fortunate features of this summer's visit was the fact that Lowell got the chance to know and come under the spell of my Aunt Peace—the saint who had guided my early steps in the pursuit of light and truth. In some strange way, beyond diagnosis, this heavenly-minded woman knew by a higher instinct—a Light within—how to guide a boy without his knowing at the time that he was being guided. She left a permanent touch of influence on Lowell, as on me.

It was not the custom in his day, in primary schools, as it is now, to start children writing poetry. He would have taken naturally to it, as he did to music. He began taking violin lessons at an astonishingly early age. That and the game of cricket must be mastered early, if they are ever to be mastered, and Lowell was determined to be an expert both with the violin and the cricket bat. It always leaves me with a deep pathos when I see his violin or his cricket bat lying unused. The time came all too soon when I had to be both father and mother to this dear boy, and then the depth of fusion became even greater, and our lives grew together from within in a way that does not often happen. What I did for him cannot be known, but I live to say no human being could have done more to teach me the way of life than he did. He helped me to become simple and childlike, gentle and loving, confident and trustful. When I talked with Mahatma Gandhi, he made me think of Lowell. It was the same simple, naturally loving spirit in both of them. And so this boy of mine belongs among the transmitters.

When he was eight he went to the Friends Boarding School in Providence, Rhode Island, while I was studying at Harvard. I spent every other week-end at the school and we went off Saturday afternoons hunting for flowers in the wonderful grotto by the Seeconk River. Here in this beloved school he was thrown intimately with the remarkable botanist, Thomas Battey, who had also been my inspiring teacher. They went off together on frequent trips to the woods and they came back laden with spoils. From this time on Lowell knew the Latin botanical names of all his flowers, and it was then that he began to form his herbarium. At about that period we were on a visit at the home of James Wood at Mount Kisco, New York. Lowell came in one day with an armful of wild flowers; James Wood asked him the names of them. He gave the popular name and the botanical name of every flower in the collection. The following spring he brought in here at Haverford a violet which had been found on the first day of March. I have hunted each March first ever since and have never been able to find one. With him they seemed to know each other! Here at school in Providence he formed beautiful friendships and made progress in every aspect of life. I took him to Harvard for a week-end. I asked him what he would like to do Saturday forenoon, while I had lectures. "Oh, I want to see the glass flowers in the Harvard Museum." I left him the whole forenoon. When we finished lunch I asked him what he would like to do in the afternoon. "I want to spend the afternoon with the glass flowers—the man that made them is certainly a wizard, father."

In the summer of 1901, just after the year of school was over, I was to go to England to lecture in the Scarborough Summer School. I decided quite rightly to take Lowell with me. He was taken, while we were on the steamer, with a desperately bad bronchial cold, with a terrifying cough. Two Roman Catholic Sisters on the steamer had seen us together, had been struck by the boy, and when they heard that he was ill, they came to me and asked if they might bring his meals and stay with him while I went to meals. All through the voyage they took care of us as though we belonged to their flock, and they left on his mind the fragrance of angel visitors. He learned thus early that both Quakers and Roman Catholics might be God's dear children. Then, on landing, followed three wonderful weeks in the home of John Wilhelm Rowntree, another saintly life, who, like Aunt Peace, left on the mind of this sensitive boy an impression of the beauty of holiness, joined with the joy of happy living, which never lost its effect on him. He played new, and before unheard of, games with the Rowntree children, and he returned with the added riches of many new friends and many new flowers. I told him how Linnaeus had fallen on his knees and thanked God for its beauty the first time he saw English gorse. But he was hardly prepared for the glory of the broom (Genista) in flower, and for the unparalleled sight of the heather on a Yorkshire moor.

I cannot remember that I ever punished Lowell. This was not due to an easy theory that vigorous discipline is intrinsically wrong. It was due to the fact that another method worked and worked better. If I ever did punish him it was something slight, like the punishment my mother had from her father. He gave her one stroke with his silk handkerchief. But it impressed her powerfully and she never needed another indication of disapproval. Lowell was very quick to catch my attitude. We talked over situations together with their moral implications. Our friendly intercourse and trust in one another kept him from wanting to take lines of action which he knew I would not like. It was a striking instance of life guided by loving regard and wise insight rather than by fear. I overheard him once talking with a group of playmates, when each one was telling what he wanted to be when grown up, and Lowell said when his turn came, "I want to grow up and be a man like my daddy." Few things in my life have ever touched me as those words did, or have given me a greater impulse to dedication. What kind of a man was I going to be, if I was to be the pattern for my boy!

One incident which happened while we were in England shows that he hardly knew what punishment meant. We were invited to dinner in a home where there were a number of boys, two of whom were near Lowell's age. These two boys were disorderly at table and were sent away and made to stand in different corners of the room while we ate. On the way home Lowell said, "Did you ever see anything like that, father? Just think how they must have felt." I know quite well where the rod is spared the child is sometimes spoiled, and I know, too, that fond fathers are not always conscious of when their child is "spoiled." But it was the universal testimony of Lowell's play-mates, of their parents, and of his teachers, that he was a normal, happy, unspoiled boy. His loving, responsive spirit, his enthusiasm in living, his joy in beautiful things, and his unqualified faith in me guided him much better than the severity of a rod could have done.

All too soon this boy, "by the vision splendid on his way attended," came to an end here on earth where I could see him. He had diphtheria in the spring of 1903. He was given anti-toxin and recovered, as far as we could see, completely. In July I went to England to lecture in the Quaker Summer School, which was to be the opening of the Woodbrooke Settlement at Selly Oak, near Birmingham. Lowell was to stay at his grandmother's home in Ardonia, New York, with a very efficient Friend who was to be caretaker and companion. He was always happy at Ardonia, with aunts and cousins, and we left feeling very comfortable about him. But the night before landing in Liverpool I awoke in my berth with a strange sense of trouble and sadness. As I lay wondering what it meant, I felt myself invaded by a Presence and held by Everlasting Arms. It was the most extraordinary experience I had ever had. But I had no intimation that anything was happening to Lowell. When we landed in Liverpool a cable informed me that he was desperately ill, and a second cable, in answer to one from me, brought the dreadful news that he was gone. When the news reached my friend, John Wilhelm Rown-tree, he experienced a profound sense of Divine Presence enfolding him and me, and his comfort and love were an immense help to me in my trial. Philip Wicksteed, the great Dante and Wordsworth scholar, gave me unique help in that early darkness, and he became one of my guides to St. Francis of Assisi, and to the triumph of love.

There had mysteriously come to Lowell an attack of paralysis which affected his speech and his breathing. He seems to have fully realized that he could not live long, and he wrote on a slip of paper: "Give some of my books to Philip and Norris"—two of his dearest friends at Haverford. His little friends and playmates later joined together and raised a memorial fund and finished and furnished "The Lowell Jones Reading Room" in the Boys School at Ramallah, Palestine. Lowell's picture hangs in this attractive room, and Arabic boys have carried on a happy memory of him.

All of a sudden, as the end came, he raised his hands in wonder and got voice enough to say, "Oh, Mother," as though they had found each other in the world that is Real, for this boy undoubtedly belonged to the King-dom of God. Julian of Norwich, who never had a child, said: "To me was shown no higher stature than childhood." I knew exactly how Emerson felt when he wrote *Threnody,* when he had lost his boy:

There's not a sparrow or a wren,
There's not a blade of autumn grain,
Which the four seasons do not tend
And tides of life and increase lend;
And every chick and very bird,
And weed and rock-moss is preferred.
O ostrich-like forgetfulness!
O loss of larger in the less!
Was there no star that could be sent,
No watcher in the firmament.
No angel from the countless host
That loiters round the crystal coast,
Could stoop to heal that only child,
Nature's sweet marvel undefiled,
And keep the blossoms of the earth,
Which all her harvests were not worth?

I know now, as I look back across the years, that nothing has carried me up into the life of God, or done more to open out the infinite meaning of love, than the fact that love can span this break of separation, can pass beyond the visible and hold right on across the chasm. The mystic union has not broken and knows no end. Lowell had here only eleven years of happy joyous life. The victory that comes through the long years of struggle in a world full of hard choices could not be his. He was not to have the chance, "with toil of heart and knees and hands, through the long gorge to the far light" to form his character and to do his life work; but who knows what chances there are for transplanted human worth to bloom, to profit in God's other garden? As certainly as God lives there is more to follow after this brief span of preparation ends. Those who are only potential saints here—"probable" saints—may very well become full-fledged shining ones, when God has brought the beginning to its complete fulfillment. When my sorrow was at its most acute stage I was walking along a great city highway, when suddenly I saw a little child come out of a great gate, which swung to and fastened behind her. She wanted to go to her home behind the gate, but it would not open. She pounded in vain with her little fist. She rattled the gate. Then she wailed as though her heart would break. The cry brought the mother. She caught the child in her arms and kissed away the tears. "Didn't you know I would come? It is all right now." All of a sudden I saw with my spirit that there was love behind my shut gate.

Yes, "where there is so much love, *there must be more.*"

From *The Luminous Trail,*
pp. 153–165.

⇒⇒ XII ⇐⇐

Who Are the Quakers?

XII

THE Quaker Society is still a small body and it presents a seemingly feeble front for the age-long battle of Armageddon. It is a tiny band of laborers for the task of building a spiritual civilization. But this is a matter in which *numbers* are not the main thing. The vital question, after all, is whether this small religious Society here in the world today is a living organ of the Spirit or not. Is it possessed by a *live* idea? Is it in the way of life? Has it found a forward path toward the new world that is to be built? Is it an expansive, or a waning, power? It has stood scorn and brutality; it has weathered the beatings and buffetings of a hostile world; it has surveyed its own blunders and stupid divisions. When now the world has become kind and friendly toward it, and is even eager for it to *prove* its divine mission, can it make a significant contribution to the truth and life and power of the Christianity that is to save and redeem the world? ...

No one knows the weaknesses and limitations of the Quaker movement more clearly than I do. I have no illusions. I have looked its history full in the face. I am acquainted with all the symptoms of its present ailments. But I am not writing now in order to tell that part of the story. I am concerned here to show what the Quaker movement has taken as its line of life and what it still hopes and believes its mission to be.

There will always be diversities in the Christian Church. It will never be possible to attain complete uniformity in thought or in forms of worship or in ways of interpreting religious history, nor is that desirable. There are characteristic varieties of mental type. Our outlooks are different. Our needs are different. Our range of thought and experience is different. We should as individuals belong, if possible, to a religious group, a spiritual family, that best fits our needs and aptitudes. We should not all be fused and merged into one uniform mould in one vast structure. We should have our denominational homes and we should worship where we find ourselves in most sympathetic accord with others. But our narrow *isms* should vanish. Our sectarian spirit should die out. Our rivalries and jealousies should cease. And we should all contribute to the one growing, expanding Church of the Spirit, which is being builded through the ages "for a habitation of God."

The Quaker Society is one of these spiritual families with definite characteristics. It offers a denominational home of a specific type. It fits, and is congruous with, a well-known and well-defined mental outlook and habit of thought. It emphasizes certain very important aspects of religion. It cultivates a type of worship which seems to many vital and spiritual. It maintains a spirit and method of human service, which are greatly needed in the world today. It exhibits a warm and intimate type of inward religion. It is broad, inclusive and tolerant. It cares intensely for religious experience and discounts those aspects of religion which are argumentative, speculative and divisive. It has preserved a good degree of evangelical fervor, without becoming seriously entangled in the network of theology that often goes with the doctrinal word "evangelical." It has kept pretty close to the central meaning of the Incarnation, the definite breaking in of God into the course of history, the coming of eternity into the midst of time, in the form of a living, visible human-divine Person, through whom all life on its highest levels is to be interpreted. But it discovers no temporal *end* to that Life here in the world. The Christ who was a visible presence in Galilee and Judea is just as certainly alive and present now.

> The healing of His seamless dress
> Is by our beds of pain;
> We touch Him in life's throng and press,
> And we are whole again.

The Friends are essentially Johannine in their religious faith and outlook. Their great religious words are found in the Fourth Gospel. They are *light, truth, life, love, spirit, way.* They take the message at Jacob's well as the heart of their faith: "God is Spirit and they that worship Him must worship Him in spirit and in truth." They find their loftiest hopes expressed in the words: "I am the resurrection and the life; he that believeth on me, though he dies, yet shall he live; and whosoever liveth and believeth on me shall never die." They look out on the future with their expectation grounded on the saying: "When He the Spirit of truth is come, He shall guide you into all truth." Many of my readers, who will perhaps approve of these affirmative and vital features, will at the same time very likely miss something in this type of Christianity. They will feel that it is partial and one-sided. It will perhaps not appear to them to be complete and universal, wide and catholic enough to be a faith for the whole race. I shall not attempt to meet that criticism. The facts must be as they are. If there are other essential aspects of religion which the Quakers leave out of account, they must be looked for in other denominational families where they are stressed. Those who compose the Quaker family do not feel the need of them. They are satisfied with a few simple and vital realities. . . .

What the Friends were concerned about, with a concern that was absolutely sound, was that the autonomy of the soul should be protected and safeguarded. They had seen enough, and more than enough, of outside compulsion in religious matters. It had been thought of too long as something in the possession and control of a historic institution, something infallibly preserved and held and something to be transmitted ready-made to the new recipient. It was this theory that the Quaker challenged and denied in behalf of the inherent rights of the soul. The soul itself, as even Carthaginian Tertullian admitted, "when it comes to itself, as out of a surfeit, or a sleep, or a sickness and attains something of its natural soundness, speaks of God," and has an experience to tell. This theory of the soul was, of course, not absolutely new. It did, however, run flatly counter to the main current of the Reformation. It was positive heresy in the ears of the followers of Luther and Calvin, and it had no standing with the guardians of orthodoxy anywhere. It seemed out of line with the general prevailing conception of the "fall." It met the pessimism of depravity with a rival optimism about human potentiality. The Puritan saw in man a wreck like that of a ship hopelessly stranded on a reef or jagged rock. The Quaker saw in him a wreck, if wreck at all, like that of the buds in spring, burst from within by the warm sun, after having been tightly sealed all winter against sleet and storm, wrecked indeed, and by the push and power of a deeper, larger life working within and preparing for vast future possibilities.

We have here, then, a type of Christianity which begins with experience rather than with dogma. Luther, again, took this position in his great battle-documents which were written in the years that followed the nailing up of his Theses. His saving *faith* is an inward attitude based upon first-hand experience. It is "an active, powerful thing," "a deliberate confidence in the grace of God," which makes a man "joyous and intrepid" and ready to die for it "a thousand deaths." But as the Reformation proceeded, the old dogma of the Church assumed an ever-increasing importance and in the end doctrine was raised to a status which overpassed anything known in the Mediæval Church. In fact, the acceptance and maintenance of sound doctrines became the essential condition of salvation. *Faith* ceased to be an active, powerful attitude of will; it became synonymous with "belief." The Church was built up around its doctrine and it took on the aspect of a fort or garrison constructed to defend its saving doctrine. This position became an obsession. Christian bodies divided and subdivided over abstruse points of belief. Wars were fought. Nations were wrecked. Humanity was forgotten. The spirit of the divine Founder was ignored in the determination to maintain at all costs the "sacred" decision of some synod. The way of life inaugurated by the Crucified weighed as almost nothing in comparison with the only true theory of the atonement which some man had formulated.

George Fox called all these formulated beliefs "notions." He pointed out that they could all be believed, adopted, held and defended without cleansing, purifying or transforming one's heart in the very least. They were thundered from pulpits and received with "amens," but the lives of the affirming congregation seemed to him but little altered thereby. These things appeared to him to occupy a similar position to that which circumcision occupied in St. Paul's mind and which "works" held in Luther's thought. One could carry all these matters through to the very end and still be the same unchanged person. "Not circumcision, but a new creation," is St. Paul's demand. "Not works, but a discovery by faith that God is for us" is Luther's message. "Not the holding of notions, but an inward transforming experience of God," is George Fox's word of life.

The important point is that one must begin with something *vital*, and not with something merely formal and forensic. The essential transaction is not outside but inside. We want to get across from an old self to a new self, from an old way of living to a new way of living. It often, perhaps usually, involves a change of ideas. We cannot ignore here the crucial significance of right thinking. Many a person fails to be "saved," to get to his feet on the highway of salvation, because he is tied up with a muddled system of thinking. He goes on "believing what isn't so." He is trying to live on what is in fact a stock of errors about the eternal nature of things, and he cannot "prosper" as he would if he knew the truth and had the freedom and power of it. Fox, and the Friends who have followed him, have always stood like adamant for the everlasting significance of *truth*. They do not encourage slip-shod thinking as though it made no difference. They induce no one to suppose that there is some inward magic which will save us from the effects of calling black white in matters that have to do with the soul's welfare.

What they disapprove is the tendency to set up as standards of faith and as essentials of salvation ancient doctrines which have been adopted in controversial gatherings, which deal often with issues very different from those *alive* in our day, and which carry on the mental outlook and intellectual attitudes of centuries long past and outgrown. Religious truth must grow like all truth. It must spring out of living experience. It must fit the convictions and aspirations of the time. It must be current coin. Whatever is proved and verified is thereby orthodox. We owe immense debts to past centuries in which heroic souls fought their valiant fight for the truth and passed it on to us.

But their loyal devotion and their glimpse of truth do not settle our issues or relieve us from personal decision and present-day action. No manna for the soul can be permanently kept over, and discoveries of truth or light cannot be "passed on" in sealed containers.

Experience, then, is the Quaker's starting-point. This light must be *my* light, this truth must be *my* truth, this faith must be my very own faith. The key that unlocks the door to the spiritual life belongs not to Peter, or to some other person, as an official. It belongs to the individual soul, that finds the light, that discovers the truth, that sees the revelation of God and goes on living in the demonstration and power of it. For this there is no substitute. One can be saved with but very little theology, but no one can be saved who does not personally *want* to be saved, who does not himself *intend* to be saved and who does not meet the grace of God with an inward swing of *affirmation.* . . .

If any one supposes that Friends have inclined to be "humanists" and to assume that man is so inherently good that he can lift himself by his own belt into a life of consummate truth and beauty, he has not yet caught the deeper note of the Quaker faith. Friends have always exalted Christ. They have been as eager as any Christians to know the facts of the gospels and to have sound, clear knowledge of the events in the life of the Jesus of history. They have been very desirous to see vividly and effectively that wonderful person who lived and preached and healed, and helped and loved and died and rose again. They have not usually blurred or slighted the outward life lived in the frame of time and space. But, like St. Paul, they are most concerned with the inward Christ. He is the source of their life and power. The Quaker poet, John Greenleaf Whittier, has finely expressed for the whole fellowship what He means as a living presence:

> Warm, sweet, tender, even yet
> A present help is He;
> And faith has still its Olivet,
> And love its Galilee. . . .

The Quaker way of worship is organized to cultivate this deeper and diviner aspect of life. But there are other features of life no less important than worship and occupying a far larger proportion of the day and week. The atmosphere and climate of one's ordinary daily life, the outlook and expectation, the central ambition of the person's real life—those are the things which in the long run largely settle what kind of person one is to be. There are certain mental states which lock up our lives with restraints, fears and inhibitions. There are other states and attitudes which liberate us, release our forces and send us forward conquering and to conquer. Resolves and determined purposes, formed at the center of the inner life, are mighty energies, and even day-dreams and the subtle mental stuff of our reveries play a more important role in the drama of our lives than we usually are aware of. In any case, the persistent habits of thought, the dominant ideal aims, may be counted as the major factors in making a person the type of being that he becomes.

In all the best generations of Quakerism, the ideal aim and the controlling expectation of the wiser members have been to live the simple life. It is, of course, a vague and indefinable term. It is not a magic phrase by which we can do just the opposite of the miracle of Aladdin's lamp, and suddenly leap from the extravagance of palatial living to the quiet Eden of a one-roomed cottage, with bark dishes and wooden spoons. The simple life does not begin outside, with the house or the spoons. It begins inside, with *the quality of the soul*. It is first and foremost the quality of sincerity, which is the opposite of duplicity or sham. Emerson's famous line, "What you *are* stands over you the while, and thunders so that I cannot hear what you say," makes the idea pretty clear. The fountain must be right, if we want the water to be clear. Unclouded honesty at the heart and center of the man is the true basis of simplicity. The tone of a bell is settled by the quality of the constituent metal, and, if that is wrong in stuff and mixture, you will not get a good bell by putting on a coat of fine paint.

This kind of simple life will call, among other things, for an attitude of meekness and humility. But those traits are always consistent with manliness and dignity. The meek person is not a Uriah Heap; the humble person is not a doormat. To be "meek" is to have a true, honest estimate of your life—it is to see you yourself as you are, without any artificial inflation. All one needs to do, if he means to be "humble," is to keep a constant contrast in mind between himself as he now is and that larger, truer, richer potential self which he all the time feels hidden away within himself. Perhaps this is what is meant by "the white stone with a new name written on it, which no man knoweth *save he that hath it*." It involves not merely honesty and sincerity in all the relationships with one's fellow men, but it calls also for utter clarity of spirit in all one's relationships with God. It is extremely easy to be insincere in prayer, to say words which have no *intention* behind them, to strain for high-sounding phrases which, however, do not carry a freight of real meaning. The highest reach of sincerity is surely to be found in the resolve of soul to maintain an unsullied *honor* before God and to be in His sight what we *seem* to be. That has been persistently, I believe, the honest aspiration of the serious-minded Quaker.

This trait of simplicity has been very clearly in evidence in the Quaker aversion to creeds and formulations of doctrine. The Friends have not been rebels in their attitude toward the great central truths of Christendom. They have usually preserved a profound evangelical spirit and devotion. But they did not want to have their lives or their faith complicated by the wholesale adoption of words and phrases coined in other centuries, colored by the battle-temper of ancient issues and incapable today of the same meaning which they originally bore to their formulators. They find it difficult to be absolutely honest and sun-clear when they undertake to use these inherited statements of bygone ages. Such phrases do not truly interpret the heart's deepest meanings. They engender controversy and strife. Instead of unifying Christendom, they divide it. Instead of forming into one irresistible array the spiritual forces of the world, they tend to form groups of contending partisans —opposing each other instead of turning to conquer the evil and darkness of the world. But the essential difficulty is the inner difficulty of maintaining one's moral honesty and sincerity. The words by which we express our deepest faith must be not only rich with the experience of the saints and martyrs of the past, but they must also interpret for us the living, present truth of our time; they must be consistent with all we have proved and verified, and they must be tested by our own soul's experience. The Quaker means this by his aim at simplicity. Few things are more needed today than this plain, simple note that religion, on its upward-reaching side, is just joyous companionship with God—with God who is nearer than Abraham realized when he talked with Him at his tent door, or Jacob dreamed when he saw Heaven at the far end of a ladder. . . .

It is a mistake to call Quakers "non-resisters" or "passivists." They are neither. They do not face any giant evil with a passive attitude. They seek always to organize and to level against it the most effective forces there are. They know as well as anybody does that instincts and passions are not changed by miracle and that peace cannot prevail where injustice and hate are rampant. They seek to do away with war by first doing away with the causes and occasions for it; that is, by removing the fundamental grounds from which war springs, by eliminating the roots and seeds of it in the social order, and by forming an atmosphere and climate that make war impossible. This means, of course, that peace-making is "big business."

The forerunners of the Quakers had for some centuries before George Fox been opposed to war. The Waldenses were strict and scrupulous in their refusal to fight or to take life in any way. Many of the small heretical sects before the Reformation had similar views on these matters. The Anabaptists were divided in their conclusions about the right of a Christian to bear a sword and they varied in their practice, though there was a large wing of the movement that refused utterly to have any part in war. The influence of Erasmus, the greatest of the humanists, upon the scattered groups of spiritual reformers was very profound. He discounted the value of dogma and theology and turned instead with freshly awakened interest to the original teachings of Jesus. Every page of the New Testament, he declared, "speaks of little else but peace and concord; and yet the whole life of the greater portion of Christians is employed in nothing so much as the concerns of war.... It were best to lay aside the name of Christian at once, or else to give proof of the teaching of Christ by its only criterion, brotherly love." It was no doubt the rediscovery of the message of the New Testament that swung Erasmus so strongly against the spirit and methods of war. This note of opposition to war, which receives its most powerful expression in the great scholar's *Querola pacis,* from which I have quoted above, recurs again and again in his writings. He was one of the major shaping influences in the life and thought of the spiritual reformers. They held his view of the freedom of the will; they shared his revolt from theology; they returned with him to the primitive teaching of Jesus, and they felt as he did about the prevailing evils of society and about the wickedness of war. Gentleness, love, grace, light, truth and the forces of the Spirit are their armory. They had no fixed propaganda. They quietly and simply taught a way of life with which war was entirely incompatible. "What will Christ say," Jacob Boehme asks the ministers of his day, "when He sees your apostolic hearts covered with armor? When He gave you the sword of the Spirit, did He command you to fight and make war, to put on the sword and kill?"

George Fox gives us no clue by which we can trace the origin and development of his own position toward war. His outlook and attitude are in every particular similar to the outlook and attitude of these predecessors, but he never quotes them and he supplies no positive evidence of direct correspondence with them. The influences which shaped his mind in this direction were almost certainly subconscious influences, though his constant absorption with the New Testament was without question one of the leading forces that set his thought into antagonism with war. His earliest positive reaction is the famous response which Fox made while in Derby jail to the Commissioners who proposed to make him the captain of a troop of soldiers in the Commonwealth Army. "I told them," he says, "that I lived in the virtue of that life and power that takes away the occasion of all wars." ... "I was come into the covenant of peace which was before wars and strifes were." It was a remarkable position for a young man to take and it was oddly enough expressed. The "covenant of peace" into which he had come was almost certainly in his mind the life of the Spirit. He felt that he was raised to the nature and type of the new Adam and was forever done with the ways of the Adam who fell, and it seemed to him that the new and higher life entailed a spirit and method of life which were essentially Christlike. It is a way of life that practises love and forebearance. It seeks to give rather than to get. It conquers by grace and gentleness. It prefers to suffer injustice rather than in the slightest degree to do it. It wins and triumphs by sacrifice and self-giving. It spreads abroad an atmosphere of trust and confidence and proposes to prepare the way for a new world by creation of a new spirit—which is essentially the spirit of the Cross. If everyone lived thus, there would be "no occasion of war" but "a covenant of peace."

That is the birth of the Quaker "testimony" for peace. Fox laid down no rules for his followers. He formulated no prohibitions. He was easy and lenient toward those who were in the army or the navy and who neverthless wanted to become "Children of the Light." He always left them free to "follow their light." He seems to have felt sure that their inward guidance would eventually bring them to "the covenant of peace" which he had found in his own way. There is an interesting tradition that William Penn asked George Fox whether it was right for him to continue his custom of wearing his sword, and that Fox answered, "Wear it as long as thou canst"; i.e., wear it until conscience makes it clear that a sword is not consistent with Christian life and profession. The early Friends in Fox's lifetime did extremely little to clarify and interpret their position any further in this matter. Fox himself frequently uses the phrase, "Our weapons are spiritual, not carnal." That may be taken, I think, as the substance of the Quaker position in the first generation. They were not absolute "non-resisters," but they put their faith and confidence in the gentler forces of the Spirit. On one occasion, when a man rushed at him with a naked rapier, threatening his life, Fox looked at him unmoved and calmly said, "Alack, poor creature, what wouldst thou do with thy carnal weapon? I care no more for it than I would for a straw." There was a certain power in his undisturbed face, a conquering quality in his manner which enabled him to meet rage, brutality and cruelty and triumph over them. When the Cambridge "scholars" tried to pull him off his horse in their rough, rude sport, he says, "I rid through them in the Lord's power and they cried, 'he shines, he glistens!' " An address of Philadelphia Yearly Meeting in 1774 very well expresses the ground and attitude of Friends in this first stage. "Through the influence of the love of Christ in their minds," it says, "they ceased from conferring with flesh and blood and became obedient to the heavenly vision, in which they clearly saw that all wars and fightings proceeded from the spirit of this world which is at enmity with God, and that they must manifest themselves to be the followers of the Prince of Peace by meekness, humility and patient suffering." . . .

But a still more important positive note began to emerge by the middle of the nineteenth century, a note which has not died out and please God never will die out in the hearts of the Quakers. They began to see that it was not enough to stand out for the personal privilege of renouncing war and of living a peaceful life as an individual. They passed over from the mere claim of a privilege to the sense of a weighty obligation. They awoke to the discovery that no man can either live or die unto himself. They came to realize how closely tied into the social fabric we all are. Our noble word obligation means just that. Taken out of Latin and turned over into English it becomes "tied-in-ness." Anyone who is intending to claim his own right to walk the path of peace must take also his share of the heavy burden of trying to build a world in which the gentler forces of kindness, love, sympathy, and coöperation are put into function.

John Woolman had seen that "the seeds of war have nourishment" in the daily lives of men in so far as they encourage luxury and unnecessary worldliness. The spirit of love, therefore, if it is to be effective, must operate not only in war-time, but in those important peace-stretches between wars as well. In short, those who propose to hold aloof from fighting and claim the privileges of peace must become devoted *peace-makers*. This is not to be construed to apply alone to those who bring wars to an end, to diplomats and treaty-makers, nor does it mean in any exclusive sense those who make public peace addresses or who sign petitions or who "post o'er land and ocean without rest" to attend peace conferences and conventions. It applies rather to a deeper and more continuous service of living an everyday life which is "in the covenant of peace." It means a home-life which exhibits the sway and dominion of love practised in the domain of the family life. It means a neighborhood life which makes love prevail between man and man, and between woman and woman. It means a business life which translates and interprets, as much at least as one individual can do it, the principles which underlie the sway and kingdom of God. The Friend had intended to live apart. He went his own way, maintained his standing as one of a "peculiar people," worshipped in isolation from the rest of the community and showed little readiness to share with others his life, his experience or his ideals. If society was "in a mess" it was not his fault. If men stupidly went to war and wasted their substance and had their heads blown off, it was something for which he was not responsible. Gradually, however, this deeper sense of corporate life and responsibility began to dawn upon the more sensitive of the Quakers. A new spirit was born. Other things came to seem more important than hat-brims and bonnets, the problems of garb and speech, the height of gravestones, and the *patois* of this little Zion. They came out of their quietism and their petty concerns to face the issues of a larger world. They awoke to their responsibilities as citizens, as heads of business, as Christian men. They became magistrates, they stood for

Parliament, they went to work to make their operatives comfortable and happy. They did the work of peace-makers in a multitude of ways which were much more important than holding peace meetings. They widened out their vision and began to think in international terms. . . .

A prominent preacher said in the stress and strain of the Great War that he could imagine Christ sighting down the barrel of a rifle aimed at the enemy opposing the Allies and then firing it, and he further believed that if He were in the world to-day he would have called His followers to this fight. Well, Friends do not believe *that,* and they cannot be so swept off their calm faith in higher forces that they ever will believe it. They have not been as united on this absolutist peace position as some of us could wish and they have not been as effective in making their *idea* of life clear and attractive to men as they might have been. But this may perhaps be honestly and humbly said, that the sound and solid kernel of the Society of Friends can under all conditions and circumstances be counted on as purveyors of peace and as peace-makers both in peace-time and war-time. They will not fight nor be entangled in the mechanisms of war. They will be calm and brave and heroic. They will not dodge their spiritual responsibilities, they will make heavy sacrifices to transmit their love, they will die if it will make their truth and faith dearer, but they will not endorse war-methods or support them or be themselves a voluntary part of a system that is engaged in carrying on war.

It may well be said that the world is not yet ready for this advanced idealism, that Christ Himself was filled with apocalyptic hopes, that He was proposing a program for a new dispensation, not for this present mixed world. That may all be as it may be. But in any case, there ought to be a world like this one for which Christ lived and died. And that kind of a world will never actually come unless some of us take the vision and the hope seriously and set to work to make it real here on this very earth. It will be said again that these dreams and hopes are visionary and impractical—even Christ Himself, with all His spiritual power and divine authority, failed to "change human nature," came up against the thick bossed shield of fixed habit and ancient custom and ended His beautiful life in dark defeat and ignominious death. The answer is that He has been changing human nature ever since, that His Cross has become the most decisive factor in human history, and that it appears to be a better venture to die for love and truth and an ideal world than to live along the grooves of fixed habit and ancient custom and the old stupid compromise. The world will at least be better off if there is a Christian group, even a small one in England and America, resolved to live for these hopes, for this way of life, to bear their clear testimony for peace and love at any cost and at any price, and ready, if the last supreme sacrifice is demanded, to die for that faith and for that vision.

From *Faith and Practice of the Quakers,*
pp. 13–16; 43–47; 50; 89–92;
103–107; 113–115; 120–122.

I CANNOT tell you what the future of Quakerism is to be. No mortal knows. I *can* tell you, however, what has made the Quaker movement spiritually significant in the past and I can predict with some certainty what line of development would secure it as an important creative future. I believe that the truths and ideals which the Quaker leaders discovered and which the past two hundred and fifty years have tested and verified are still vital with unfolding power and are well adapted to meet the spiritual needs of this strange and confused time of ours and the future that is to emerge from it.

What are those truths, principles and ideals which lay at the heart of Quakerism of the past and which must form the core and marrow of any great constructive Quakerism of the future?

One of the most important of them has to do with the essential nature of religion. Our Quaker founders and the pillar Friends of all periods have insisted that religion is and must be rooted and grounded in personal experience. It has to do with life and character. It is a continuation of God's work of making man. Life—our human life—comes to its true glory and joy and power only when man responds to the revelation of God and opens his nature to God as the flower does to the sunlight. It is not possible to live by bread alone.

> This life were brutish
> Did we not sometimes have intimations clear of wider scope,
> Hints of occasion infinite to keep the soul alert
> With noble discontent and onward yearnings of unstilled desire.

Eternity has been put in our hearts and we can never be all that we were meant to be until the upper part of our nature is fed and brought into full function. Religion, then, is a way of living which raises human life to its true spiritual height and makes fellowship with God as much a part of our normal activities as breathing or digestion are.

Religion being thus a personal experience is vastly more than conforming to established views and practices. Bad men in all ages have done this and have notwithstanding continued to be bad men. Devils, says the apostle James, believe and are scared, but that does not transform them into good angels—they remain devils in spite of their belief. The heart and fiber of religion lie deeper down, far below these formulations of thought which are expressed in words, or in what the early Friends called "notions." Husbands do not become good husbands by promising to be loving and faithful when they take the solemn marriage vow. If in the great venture of life they prove to be good husbands it will be because they possess a certain deep-lying spirit and character that makes them true, affectionate, self-sacrificing and dependable. Wives are not good wives just because they promise on a certain day to be good. Very bad wives have made that lofty promise. The good ones are good because they have a beautiful nature formed within them, which holds on through every crisis, which makes them a perennial joy and blessing to their fortunate companions and which enables one to count on them as he counts on gravitation and sunrise. So, too, the essential feature of religion is deeper than words or testimonies. It springs out of those first-hand convictions and experiences that form, shape and control thought and action and all that concerns living. To be religious is to be a wholly different kind of person from one who is not religious. Religion is an experience that alters the whole background and outlook of life and affects all human relations both toward God and toward man. Religion consists, therefore, not so much in what you say as in what you *are*. It can no more be picked up and put on from the outside than the rhythm of your heart's pulse can be.

This fundamental conception of religion has been one of the great shaping forces in the lives of those who are behind us and who have passed on the torch to us. If we wish to build for the future and to have a living place in the spiritual work of the world we must not, we dare not, let go of the central principle. To turn from a basis of life and experience and to offer the world a religion which centered around statements of belief, declarations and creeds would be to pass from a religion of first-hand power to one of second-hand power and it would mean furthermore that we should at once fail to speak to the deeper need of our age and should miss the chance of being spiritual and prophetic guides, as our ancestors in the past assuredly were.

The next great central principle has to do with the essential nature of God. The Quaker discovery of the real nature of God was of course not absolutely original with them. As a matter of fact it was a rediscovery rather than discovery. Those men and women of the Commonwealth era who disturbed the peace of all Conformist Churches and of all Laodicean Christians did not claim to be innovators. They merely cut through the theological maze and tangle of the centuries and went back freshly to the supreme revelation of God, made in the person of Jesus Christ. They re-experienced the God whom He revealed. They could say with thrilling joy, "I have found my God. I have met my Saviour." They saw, as St. Paul and St. John had seen long before, that God is a spiritual Being, not remote and absentee but here with us. This is His world and He is here in it. We no more need to go somewhere else to find Him than the fish needs to soar to find the ocean or the eagle needs to plunge to find the air. This discovery of theirs that God is within and close as breathing formed their main message. Their truth was often put in terms of contemporary phraseology which needs to be freshly re-translated into the quick and living words of our time, but there was no doubt about the mighty fact that they were in vital contact with those divine energies that build the world and regenerate the souls of men.

Not only did they freshly announce the real presence of God among men as an inner, penetrating, vitalizing Spirit, they re-discovered the loving character of God as Father. They refused to accept the current pictures of God which made Him stern and hard and arbitrary, a sovereign Lord with rights that must be satisfied, a Judge insisting on exact legal justice. They leaped to the full height of the new revelation. They took it as settled that in nature and character, in heart and will, God is like Jesus Christ—really like Him. He does not wait for accounts to be squared, He does not stand on His sovereign rights, He cannot be conceived in terms of justice. He is a God of grace—"There's a wideness in God's mercy, like the wideness of the sea." ...

The world with its load of tragedy and its burden of sin and sorrow needs to be brought back home to the God and Father of our Lord Jesus Christ. There has been a widespread revolt against the semi-pagan and mediæval accounts of God which have too long passed as Christian. We need again to proclaim the God of all patience and tenderness, who suffers long and is kind, who pursues with a love that never lets go, who gives Himself in the uttermost self-sacrifice, as Christ's Cross has forever revealed.

A Quakerism that sounds that truth clearly, sincerely and vividly has a future and will meet a great response. There is always a tendency in the world to lower the thought of God, to bring Him down to our level and to conceive Him in terms of our human ideas and passions. It ought rather to be our mission as Friends to "draw the portrait by the living Face," and to help our age to pass from man's God to God's God as He has revealed Himself in that one Face which

> Far from vanish, rather grows,
> Or decomposes but to recompose,
> Becomes my universe that feels and knows.

Our third central principle has to do with the essential nature of man. The Quaker movement at its birth was a strong surge away from the Calvinistic conception of man. "There is something of God in man," George Fox declares in almost every sermon and epistle. He was as conscious as anyone ever was that man goes wrong, that he has evil propensities, traits, tendencies and habits which are unspiritual and sinful, but he profoundly believed that man—every man—was made for God and was created for a lofty destiny. Christ and not the fallen Adam seemed to him as to St. Paul to be the head of the race, the true type of humanity and he saw every person in the light of his infinite possibilities. "I came up through the flaming sword," he triumphantly says, "into the paradise of God and was in the condition Adam was in *before he fell.*" That experience is open to every man and the power to "come up through the flaming sword" lies within the reach of everyone, because the Seed of God is in the soul of man as the supreme possession of his being.

This was one of the most thrilling of all the Quaker discoveries and it gave the early Friends the ground for their new estimate of the worth of man. They felt once more, as had been felt in Galilean days, that man was unspeakably precious; not man in the abstract, but the concrete Johns and Peters and Marys. Friends became the champions of every cause that would liberate and lift man into his true life and enable him to realize his full possibilities. They became the opponents of every system and institution that tended to keep man from the complete possession of himself as a free person, made for growth and expansion.

They flung themselves against the stupid fashions of the time and the meaningless etiquette of their age because they thought these things degraded man and made him a fashion puppet, when he ought to be a dignified human being. They attacked the terrible penal system then in vogue because it degraded man and was constructed on a false conception of human nature and of remedial conditions. They raised their voice more clearly than any other body of Christians had ever done against war. There were various reasons for this new note of protest against one of society's most ancient systems but the outstanding reasons lay in their new and revolutionary estimate of the worth and dignity of man. He was not made to be gutted with a bayonet, he was not redeemed by Christ to be blown into little pieces by explosive shells, he was not granted relation and fellowship with the Spirit of God to be afterward drilled and dragooned into a brutal instrument of human destruction or to be hardened and depraved in camps and barracks. They resolved absolutely to live by a different spirit from that which made war possible and they settled the matter forever with themselves that, come what would, they at least would have no part in a system which seemed to them at complete variance with all that God had revealed of His own nature and of men's worth and destiny as potential sons of God.

They went still further with their high faith in man. They believed that Negroes should not be held as slaves, because they too had divine possibilities in them and that Indians should be treated with the same respect as other men, for in red men too there was something of God. The man who was down, the individual who suffered anywhere from the tyranny of a wrong system, found a friend and defender in these Quakers who, though not warriors, were nevertheless fighters. They began the long campaign for the rights and privileges of women. George Fox found people in his day who said that women had no souls, any more, they added, than geese had! He replied, Mary said, "My soul doth magnify the Lord," which she could not have done if she had not had a soul! He insisted not only that women had souls, but that they had bodies also which must be respected, that they must be treated as persons and given their full chance at life and for the fulfillment of their divine mission.

In fact one does not reach the core of the Quaker position until he recognizes that it is the very crown and pinnacle of man's mission—i.e., man's and woman's mission—to reveal God, to be organs of the Spirit. I doubt whether anybody has made a greater discovery than this one, that God is of such a spiritual nature and character that He can reveal Himself through responsive, dedicated, human lives. There is nothing more important to believe than *that*, to know it and to accept it as the early Christians did and as the early Friends did.

Here then is another opportunity for Friends to become heralds of a vital truth and leaders in a noble venture, impressive enough to call out all our daring spirit. We have too often conceived of religion as a way of safety— safety first—a method of guaranteeing our own peace and assurance. The Quakerism of the future, if it is to have any future, must be self-forgetful, concerned for other ends than safety. It must be daring like Columbus, brave like Luther at the Diet, ready for venture and experiment like St. Francis of Assisi and as passionate and eager to relieve suffering and to advance the Kingdom of God as was our own John Woolman. Our war-shattered world cannot be rebuilt, our selfish and commercial age cannot be saved from its poor, thin self and prepared for service to others until the infinite worth and preciousness of men becomes the active spring and motive in the lives, both of capitalists and laborers, of church people and those of no church.

We Friends have a heritage which fits us, or ought to fit us, to be in the vanguard as propagators of this shining principle. William Schaefer, the poet, seeing our widespread work of relief in Europe and touched by the fact that we included in our care and love those who had fought against us, asks eagerly: "Are you they that should come or must we look for another?" We undoubtedly stand forth in the eyes of most European countries as the representatives of these great constructive ideas of life and of modern society. Professor Harnack said to me the other day: "First came the war, then came our terrible hunger, then came the Quakers, and I consider your work of love one of the greatest exhibitions of the essential nature of Christianity that has been made in all Christian history."

I need hardly tell you that we are very far from having attained any of these ideals. There were many among us who did not see their way to challenge the war spirit and who felt that they must take their part, as others were doing, in what they then believed a war to end war. There are many among us who have not been able to get free of the commercial spirit, many who go along with the fashions and etiquette of the time. There are perhaps some that are hearing me today who do not even share this ancient Quaker conception of the nature of God or of the worth of man and his divine possibilities. In any case there are many of us who have several generations of Quaker ancestors behind us who do not practice in any high degree these truths and principles for which our valiant forerunners suffered and died.

Most of us are not sufficiently lighted up, kindled with our fathers' faith and fired with an intensity of purpose which makes us hundred horse-power persons, as those early Quakers were. We have been weakened by pitiful divisions; we have slowed down and become stagnant with forms and habits; and we have wasted much precious energy contending about issues which are foreign to our main line of action.

But we have not yet lost our chance. We can if we *will*, complete what our founders so well began. We can once more demonstrate the powers of a religion born of the soul's first-hand experience. We can let others thresh old straw and rise up ourselves to proclaim God as Christ has revealed Him. We can, if we so desire, be matched with this difficult hour and meet the desperate issues of this floundering epoch with an optimistic message of man's real nature and destiny which we propose to exhibit by practising it. . . .

A great book appeared a few years ago which divided religions into two specific classes. One class the writer called Religions of Authority, the other class he called the Religion of the Spirit. Religions of Authority claim absolute sway over the individual; they are arrayed in dim magnificence of ancient tradition; they possess an august and imperial organization; they have awe-inspiring sacraments and they speak out of a background of infallibilities. The Religion of the Spirit does not depend for its power upon organization. It does not pride itself upon any external claims. It talks little of infallibilities. It begins in the human soul like a tiny grain of mustard seed, but it expands like swiftly growing yeast and it works from individual to individual like invisible molecular forces, "stealing in through the crannies of the world like so many soft rootlets, or like the capillary oozing of water, yet rending the hardest monuments of man's pride if you give them time." It, too, has authority but it is a different kind of authority. It is like the authority which beauty has over the rapt beholder, or that truth has over the mind convicted by it, or that goodness has over the moral will of the good man or that a mother's love has over a son who has discovered the meaning and value of love. Its source of power is inward, its authority also springs from within the soul. It counts not upon the driving forces of tradition nor upon the splendor of its external structure. It rests its hope and faith entirely upon the irresistible might of the living Spirit of God revealing Himself in man's soul and working triumphantly forward by the contagion of truth and goodness.

There can be no doubt in which of these two classes the Quakerism of the future is to be found. Religions of Authority have had their day. Their knell was sounded at the Diet of Worms when Luther said, "Popes have erred and Councils have erred. I hold to the word of God. Here I stand. I cannot do otherwise, God help me. Amen." Or when George Fox challenged the priest in Nottingham Church in this fashion: "No, the revelation of God is not confined to the past—the day still dawns and the day-star rises in our own hearts." The organization is not the primary thing. The individual soul responsive to the Spirit of God, reverently moving forward as the Light leads—that is primary. That is Quakerism. And that way of life has a future as surely as God has.

From *The American Friend*, Vol. 9 (1921),
pp. 679–682 (Old Series, Vol. 28).

-»)«-

WE are familiar with the peace-time pacifist—"done with war forever"— who swings over and becomes a fighter as soon as his country is at war. He finds *this* war different from any other one, and the "issue" now one that calls on every true man to support his country with undeviating and unquestioning loyalty. In my long life I have seen determined pacifists go down in a crisis like nine-pins before a well-aimed ball. It is a situation one can well understand. In the abstract almost everybody hates war and its methods. If one sits down in a cool, calm frame of mind, especially if he is a professed Christian, he is pretty sure to line up mentally, so long as the world is at peace, against almost everything that war involves.

But there comes a sudden change in the cosmic weather. The sky darkens.

There is a noise of battle and trumpets rend the air. As the Psalmist puts it, "War rises up against us and foes come on to eat up our flesh." The issue shifts suddenly from the abstract to the vivid concrete. Everything now is "different." All the values of life appear to be at stake. Civilization hangs on the issue of arms. Theory yields to realism.

> Theory thinks fact a pooty thing
> An' wants the banns read right ensuin';
> But fact wun't no-wise wear the ring,
> 'Thout years o' settin' up and wooin'.
>
> Theory is jest like a train on the rail,
> Thet, weather or no, puts her thru without fail,
> While fact's the old stage that gits sloughed in the ruts
> An' hez to allow for your darned ifs and buts.

The ultimate issue turns out in the end to be in the main a question of the soul's highest loyalty. The highest loyalty is a slow creation, formed in the face of many rival loyalties, and one hardly knows until the testing crisis comes which is to be the *supreme* loyalty. The tragedy of loyalties is one of our greatest human tragedies, for one cannot usually follow one supreme loyalty without going back on some other to which his spirit clings.

It is often asked why we Quakers come so near as we do to being unanimously devoted to peace, even in wartime, and why so many of our youth stand firm in their pacifist faith when others who had been equally anti-war-minded shift over and go out with the war forces.

The answer is in essence that we have been committed and dedicated as a people for three hundred years to a great experiment with a fairly definite way of life, which is flatly incompatible with the method and practice of war. The Quaker's supreme loyalty—after years of "settin' up and wooin'"—is to that way of life which has peace as its essence. It is not merely objection to war and refusal to take a person's life that characterize the "experiment," though those are both very real attitudes. It is a high resolve to manifest a spirit of love and to exhibit a type of life, which if they became general among men would make war unnecessary, and even impossible. The whole basis of the "experiment" is positive; not a negative halt. We sometimes use the phrase, "conscientious *objector*," but it does not truly express the heart of the position.

The first Quakers, and especially their founder, George Fox, who formed his view of life in the midst of the Civil War in England, took the Galilean way of life very seriously. They were inaugurating a new movement in the spiritual life of the race—a new stream of spiritual life. They proposed to have done forever with dead abstractions about Christianity, to take it out of a Book and then translate it into the dynamic language of life and action. If it was true and real, then for them it had to be *acted*.

They furthermore held the explosive faith that Christ was not only raised from the dead on Easter Day, but that He was now and henceforth a living presence, re-living His divine life in men, in sensitive and responsive souls, and writing His New Testament for the new age in men's lives. A new type of loyalty came to birth in these people's hearts. That way of Christ—the way of love and sacrifice—came to be the very breath of their lives. They struck at everything which held men in slavery of mind or body to effete inherited systems of the past, and they set out to attempt the creation of a new social order by faithfulness to the guiding Spirit revealed in their souls. It meant for them that a person who is potentially a child of God and a revealing place for the divine purpose must be treated as precious and sacred, as ancient temples were held by their devotees, for to them persons were thought of literally as possible temples of the ever-present Spirit of God.

The experiment, then, which these people, themselves persecuted and harried, started in the world was an experiment to see whether love and gentle forces would work in place of the harsh, cruel and brutal methods which had always held the field. They refused to make distinctions between "high class" and "low class" people. They were "levelers," but they proceeded to "level up" instead of "levelling down." They undertook to recognize a divine worth in persons who were down and under. They wiped out, or at least forgot, the differences of color, or the accidents of race and class. They struck at customs and systems that were built on sham and insincerity. They cried out against inhuman forms of punishment and outdated social habits that had endured because it had not occurred to anyone to challenge them and propose a better way.

It was obviously quite natural for them—with their determination to practice Christ's way of life, with their ideals about the preciousness and the divine possibilities of persons, and with their decision to stand out against every inherited custom that treated persons as things—to refuse to take part in wars and carry on that ancient way of the cave man of securing rights. They felt about war as Tolstoy wrote in his "Confessions" that he felt about the execution of a man which he had witnessed: "No theory of reasonableness can justify this deed and, though everybody from the creation of the world has held it to be necessary, *I know it to be unnecessary and bad.*"

The years grew into centuries—all of them centuries crowded with wars, including the French and Indian Wars, which ended the empire of France in America, the Revolutionary War and the Napoleonic Wars—and through all those years of strife successive Quaker generations went on with their experiment. They inaugurated a "holy experiment" in government in Pennsylvania, they governed Rhode Island for a hundred years, they reformed prison systems and were in the forefront of the long crusade against American slavery.

Finally the torch set aflame in the seventeenth century was passed on to our hands in this stormy century, and we found their age-long experiment committed to us. It is an essential feature of a spiritual movement that it shall not slavishly copy the ideas and systems and methods of the past, but rather that the new generation shall capture the spirit of the founders, shall be the inheritors of their faith and vision and passion, and then transmit the ideals and central experiment of the movement, re-thought and freshly wrought, to fit the demands and the inner climate of *the new age that has come.*

That meant that we who had the turn of responsibility come upon us twenty-five years ago had to repossess our spiritual possessions and reshape the experiment with this inherited way of life in terms of our time. We were as sure as our forebears were that war was the wrong, the irrational, way to settle international issues, that men made in God's image, with their divine possibilities as persons ought not to be turned into targets for machine guns and T. N. T. bombs, or made themselves to become bombers; that this whole inherited system from barbaric ages was "unnecessary and bad."

But at the same time we knew that the one impossible course for us was to refuse all responsibility for the tragedy that was enveloping the world. We could not withdraw into some safe and quiet retreat and assume that this tragic situation was no affair of ours. The world tragedy, with its series of cumulative blunders, was a common tragedy for which we were all in our degree to blame, and in the agony of which in some measure we were all bound to bear a share. We wanted to show our faith in action, and to make the experiment, which seemed to us a holy one, *work;* to demonstrate its value as a way of life even in war-time. The American Friends' Service Committee, with its twenty-five years of creative service of love and constructive work, is our contribution to this experiment which our forefathers inaugurated.

It is of course inadequate, because it does not prevent wars from occurring. The worst one in history has come while we were doing our best to prevent it, and to demonstrate another way of handling the issues of life. But it is a fact that if this experiment of ours of carrying love and service right into the areas of war and hate could be expanded, widened out to include for instance all the persons who belong to the Church of Christ, it would probably end war and make possible a new kind of world.

We took large bands of youth to France in 1917 and rebuilt the villages in the Marne Valley which had been destroyed in the Battle of Marne, and there we rehabilitated the wrecked families.... We stayed after the war was over and rebuilt the villages of the Verdun District.... We brought cows into Vienna to get milk for the children. We brought in coal for the hospitals and helped life to start afresh in that desolated city of two million people.... We fed the German children whom the blockade had starved—more than a million of them—and we carried the feeding on for four years.... We helped the Serbians rebuild their destroyed homes. We helped the Polish peasants plow their abandoned fields, and we stayed with them and fought the typhus epidemic.... We carried food to Russia in their great famine, and we remained after the famine was over to organize clinics for their children.... We fed children of the unemployed and depressed soft-coal miners in West Virginia, Kentucky, Ohio and Pennsylvania, and worked out plans for rehabilitating their families.... We cared for the children of Spain on both sides of the battle-lines during the civil war.... And we have been in the south of France ever since the fall of Paris, doing everything in our power to care for underfed children and others in these hard months of their supreme tragedy.

This is only a brief catalogue—bound to miss the human faces—of the experiment with this way of love and service in times of war and its aftermath of suffering and agony. Would anyone who had seen its healing effects, who had felt its warmth of love and fellowship, who had fathomed the spiritual depth of its way of life, want those who had engaged in it to go back on it, give it up, surrender the mission and return to the methods of war and join the fighting forces of the country? I think the answer is NO.

There is no doubt about what Woodrow Wilson thought. I have his word of approval and blessing in his own handwriting. Hosts of men and women in all walks of life have supported the experiment not merely by letters of appreciation, but by generous contributions of money, which have made it possible to carry on the experiment effectively. If we failed in our faith and gave up our experiment, if we took the world's way of "saving" civilization with guns and tanks and bombing planes, these men and women, who have counted on us and believed in our belief, would feel that we had gone back on them. But what would be our most poignant feeling of failure would be the sense that God would be missing us at our post.

If there should be no spiritual volunteers in this crisis of human history to bear testimony to the truth and splendor of this brave way of life for which Christ lived and died, then the final victory of arms by the successful bombing of cities and sinking of fleets and destruction of armies can hardly save the faith of the ages. Somebody must love it enough and be enough dedicated to it to refuse to compromise or to count the cost, or to argue about what might happen if something else isn't done. When the priceless jewel of the soul is at issue, you do not argue or hesitate, or halt between two opinions. You say, "I cannot do otherwise. God help me. Amen."

From *Survey Graphic*, August, 1942.

->>)<<-

WE have grown familiar during the last score of years with the accumulation of economic reasons against war, and we have followed with interest the congresses and conferences that have piled up and driven home these impressive economic arguments. They, however, generally, if not always, end with a caveat, or hedging clause, to the effect that "peace at any price" is no part of the intention and is not implied in the argument.

The Quaker idea is fundamentally different from this economic idea. The Quaker is not primarily concerned with the question whether war pays or does not pay for the people engaged in it; whether it succeeds in its aim or does not succeed. The Quaker flatly insists that it is absolutely and eternally wrong morally, that Christianity and war are utterly incompatible. He does not blame or judge others—and they are vastly in the majority—who think differently; but for himself the light of his truth is clear, and he cannot see otherwise.

This position goes back to and is grounded in the Quaker's idea of the nature of human personality, for this is the tap-root of all Quaker idealisms. There is something divine, something of God, in every person. The eternal passion of God, the whole redemptive story of the gospels, gets its significance in the tremendous fact that man and God belong together, are meant for each other and that beings like us are potential sons of God. To become a person, in the real sense of the word, is to awake to the consciousness of the divine relationship, to feel the inherent possibilities of sonship with God, to draw upon the inexhaustible supplies of grace, to enter into the actual inheritance of this divine-human privilege and to live in it and practice it.

But this process of realizing the possibilities of life, this mighty business of becoming persons, can go on only in an atmosphere of human love and fellowship, and in an environment of coöperation. Great as is the influence of the divine operation in the realization of this higher life of man, it is forever conjoined with human assistance and with human elements. Men cannot come to their spiritual stature, they cannot realize their potential nature, in a social atmosphere of hate and anger, when they are occupied with killing men like themselves. In that inward climate, the higher impulses and the diviner contacts are weakened or missed altogether and the truer ideal of manhood is frustrated and defeated. Even if war paid in territory and in commerce, it would still be an impossible hazard for a people, because it checks and blocks the whole business of the higher life of man, it interferes with all the essential processses that go to the making of spiritual personality.

For one who has found his way through Christ to the full meaning of life, to the real worth of man, to the inestimable ministry of love and brotherhood, war is simply impossible. It is no longer a question of expediency. With the Quaker view of life one cannot engage in killing men, whatever may be involved in the refusal.

Through pain and struggle the world has slowly discovered the immense possibilities of democracy. We are just at the dawn of a real human emancipation. Vast processes of liberation are at work. Human rights, quite undreamed of when the Declaration of Independence was written, are gradually being won and enjoyed by common men and women. Social transformations are well underway which some day will bring new heavens and a new earth.

But war interferes with all these social undertakings; it postpones the realization of all ideals and human hopes. Pledged as he is to the advancement of human emancipation and to the achievement of a society which furnishes and guarantees richer and fuller and freer opportunities of life, the Quaker opposes all war and war methods because he believes they defeat this supreme business in which the best men and women are engaged.

Holding such views of man and of life, partaking of a kingdom in which war is flatly an impossible course, what is the Quaker's business and mission in a world organized as ours is today? One of the first things that is laid upon him is the business of making his idea of life, his grasp of Christianity, clear and luminous to men. He should simplify it, strip it of outgrown phraseology and make it march with quick, vital human interpretation. He should then be ready to take unflinchingly whatever amount of suffering is involved in his truth, and he should verify it in its length and depth by going all the way through with his faith, even at the uttermost cost; for no prophet-visions of life can ever be wrought into the fabric of the everyday world except through the patient suffering of those who are privileged to see.

It becomes, further, a very essential part of his business, as George Fox, the Quaker founder, saw, to live in the virtue of that life and power which does away with the occasion for war. That is, if Quakerism is to be anything more than an empty abstraction and the name for an ideal in a vacuum, the Quaker is bound to practice a kind of life that abolishes the spirit that leads to war—the spirit of avarice and covetousness, tendencies of suspicion and hate, actions of injustice and selfishness. He must exhibit, hard as is the call, a life that puts his ideas of God and man, of divine and human interfellowship, of love and self-giving, full into play. He must weave his idea into the visible stuff of daily life.

Then he must be gentle and tenderly respectful toward all Christians who feel the stern necessity of continuing the world-old way of settling differences and of working out national issues. It is never safe to assume the role of special favorite or sole guardian of truth, or remnant of the elect. Other Christians are also serious and honest, sincere and conscientious, and possessed of their profound convictions; and the Quaker, in holding on the way which seems sun-clear to him, must avoid all reflection upon the motives or the Christian loyalty of other faiths.

And whether in times of war or times of peace, the Quaker is under peculiar obligation to assist and to forward movements and forces which make for peace in the world and which bind men together in ties of unity and fellowship. In times of war, every avenue of loving service, of heroic devotion, of self-forgetful ministry should be entered, that the Quaker may vie with the soldier in his blood-red loyalty and devotion to his cause.

The moment war is over, and in times of peace, those who hold this high and steady faith in God and man must not be content to conduct mild and lukewarm peace meetings and to issue commonplace resolutions— "helpless as spilled beans on a dresser," as Hosea Bigelow puts it. They must take a thoroughly virile and robust part in the work of creating higher national ideals and in forming a truer public sentiment, and a healthier social atmosphere. There must be no withdrawal from the complicated life of the world into any of the subtle forms of cloistered piety. Religious ideals must be interpreted and reinterpreted in terms of present-day thought; the ties of human sympathy must be linked up and woven in between all classes of men; every opportunity must be seized for directing and perfecting methods of public education, and for raising the moral tone and quality of the press; and a full share of responsibility for the character of local and national government must be taken up and borne with the same fidelity that the Quaker has always shown to the inner voice in matters of intimate, personal duty.

A peace-testimony is, thus, a heavy undertaking, and calls for all the courage and all the sacrifice of a battlefield, though the "weapons" are of a vastly different sort from Krupp guns and Mauser rifles.

From *The Quaker Peace Position,* a pamphlet,
pp. 1–4.

⇾ XIII ⇽

Why Believe in Immortality?

XIII

O NE striking effect of "naturalism" on the modern mind has been the disappearance, or at least the weakened hold, of faith in immortal life. No one quite knows in a particular case why his faith in a future life has oozed away and vanished. It has not usually been dislodged by argument, certainly not by any proofs. *Eternal* life somehow does not seem to fit the kind of world one finds left to him by current interpretations. The hope of a great future life has grown dim, the expectation of it has waned away. To a great many persons this vision of relief from the hard present facts has ceased to count vitally. It no longer figures as an inward resource in a day of sorrow and frustration. It cannot be reckoned on as a dynamic for noble living. The modern person has grown "weak in futurity." The "spell of eternity" is not for him. It may well be surmised that no other one change of outlook has so profoundly affected the life and thought of this generation as has this blight of temporality that has thus fallen upon it. If a new day of faith is to dawn for this age it will almost certainly have as its morning star a new-born expectancy in the conservation of the supreme value of personal life.

Meantime, the main effect of this general tendency has been a prevailing pessimism of mind about the significance of life. There are not so very many persons who are thoroughly committed to an intellectual academic theory of "naturalism." And the number of practical men who *consciously* accept secularism with finality as a creed of life is perhaps not so very large. The trouble comes from the fact that a powerful "drift" of suggestion, sentiment, and habit carries along a multitude of persons who have no explicit creed or theory of things, but who go with the push and trend of the secular current. There is extremely little serious and severe thinking behind secular modern drifts. They are not the result of profound thinking but rather of thin and superficial living. Hosts of persons join the rush just because there is a rush. They exhibit an attitude of "frantic immediacy" because "frantic immediacy" is a contagious state of mind. They join the speed throng because *speed* is a temporary substitute for direction. They discount "spiritual realities" because popular writers make such realities seem absurd and they suppose "science" has proved them to be unreal. The

277

entire "drift" *runs* on extremely little intellectual motor-force. Its havoc is altogether out of proportion to the stock of mental power which is supposed to give it momentum.

The prevailing confusion of life and thought is almost exactly parallel to that which occasions a "run" on a thoroughly sound and reliable bank in a time of financial depression. Everything is uncertain; fears are abroad; panic is contagious; loss of nerve follows; rumor starts doubts. If in that state of mind anybody questions the solvency of a given bank and starts a suspicion of its soundness, the "run" on its resources begins. Nobody waits to get an accurate report on its assets. Fear and imagination exaggerate the liabilities.

That panicky state of mind is a fair illustration of the present-day attitude toward the spiritual assets of human life. These assets have been challenged or doubted or pronounced unreal on a quite inadequate consideration of the inexhaustible grounds on which they rest. In the "drift" of secular living and naturalistic formulations, in the rush and hurry with no time for meditation and restoration, in the weariness and the disillusionment that come from the failure of enthusiastic adventures and yeasty ideals, there suddenly seems to be nothing in the far visions and the fond hopes that buoyed up and supported those of an earlier time in their endurances and in their adventurous pilgrimages. Like the naïve little child who blurted out the truth that the king was naked when all the sophisticated people were expressing their amazement over his invisible suit, so this frank and honest generation, not seeing anything where those before them saw a world of invisible realities, announce the nakedness of life and the bankruptcy of its spiritual assets.

It seems cold and unpromising to describe this secular drift of the time with its futilities without offering any remedy for it. But there are no quick and easy solutions for states of mind and ways of life that are bound up with a dominant and prevailing type of civilization. One can urge a return to "the simple life," or one can advise the strained and frantic hurrier to insist on periods of hush and silence and meditation. But these expedients are all short of the mark and they leave the world-confusion still unsolved. In some way we must discover how to acquire more adequate interior resources to live by and we must set our faces toward a transformation of our civilization by processes of education and influences of religion.

From *A Preface to Christian Faith in a New Age,*
pp. 15–18.

I AM considerably disillusioned over *arguments* for immortality, or, for
that matter, for any of our supreme value-aspirations. We shall of course
not stop arguing or searching for proofs. God forbid! As long as we
continue to have minds of our type, which include logical capacity, we
shall search and reason and argue and endeavor to prove the realities which
are essential to the loftiest kind of life. A dour Scot on his deathbed heard
that the minister was coming to pray with him. "But I dinna want onybody
tae pray wi' me," he said. "Wull," his wife said, "then he'll speak words of
comfort tae ye." "But I don' want tae hear words of comfort." "What do
ye want then?" asked his wife. "I want tae *argue* wi' him."

That expresses a striking trait of the *homo sapiens*. But it is rather
pitiful to discover how thin and weak are the logically formed cables which
the greatest minds have flung across the chasm between the here and the
hereafter, for the construction of the bridge we need for complete logical
assurance of travel heavenward. Nobody has put the fact of our ignorance
more clearly, or in more beautiful phrase, than has Emerson in his essay
on Swedenborg: "The secret of heaven"—by which he means immortal life—
"is kept from age to age. No imprudent, no sociable angel ever dropped an
early syllable to answer the longings of saints, the fears of mortals. We should
have listened on our knees to any favorite, who, by stricter obedience, had
brought his thoughts into parallelism with celestial currents and could hint
to human ears the scenery and circumstance of the newly parted soul."
That negation of facts is put as well as it can be put. Nobody will improve
on the grandeur of Emerson's paragraph. But he did not stop with the
negation, and the human race through the centuries has never stopped, and
never will stop, there. His brief and positive addendum is that the scenery
and circumstance of the newly parted soul "must tally with what is best
in nature. It must not be inferior in tone to the already known works of
the Artist who sculptures the globes of the firmament and writes the moral
law. It must be fresher than rainbows, stabler than mountains, agreeing
with flowers, with tides and the rising and setting of autumnal stars.
Melodious poets shall be as hoarse as street ballads when once the penetrating
keynote of nature and spirit is sounded—the earth-beat, sea-beat, heart-beat
which makes the tune to which the sun rolls, and the globule of blood, and the
sap in trees."

In a certain sense this addendum of Emerson's is "argument," not an
unemotional calm statement of fact, like his previous sentences. But if one is
to "argue" at all, this structural form of Emerson's argument is undoubtedly
pointed in the right direction. If there is any rational ground for expecting
immortal life, it must be looked for in the prophetic structure of the world

we already have on our hands, it must tally with the best we know, and especially with the moral significance of man's inmost being, and with the upward curve of the historical process, for there is an upward curve. We are so made that we should find the world not only *intolerable*, but unintelligible as well, if it carried in its structure no indication of significant finality, no promise of increasing purpose, no moral meaning in terms of the creative results of its processes. We may not go quite as far as the prophet Amos did when he tells us that he saw God forever holding a plumb-line in His hand, which means that there is a principle of moral gravitation, as universal as the principle, whatever it is, that holds the world together and that twice each day raises the tumultuous ocean, heaving from pole to pole, in our well-known tides. But all our wisest prophets in all ages have insisted that the universe is built on moral lines, is an intelligible world—going somewhere— and can be counted on to meet and answer the hopes it has raised in the minds which it itself has produced.

Pascal, who is one of these wise prophets, declared that we should not be seeking for the supreme realities if we had not already, at least dimly, found what we are seeking. We do not have appetites and cravings for what we have not already tasted. And it may well be that the universe that has planted in us aspirations and longings for the adequate fulfillment of life on new and higher levels has already formed in its moral and spiritual structure the provision for the realization of all the hopes it has raised. We take our solid ground and we stake our hopes on the fact of the grandeur and the nobility of the human spirit when it comes out of its torpor and really finds itself. We may well trust the inevitable permanence of character.

We are obviously at the moment passing through an era of depressed hopes. The faith of our generation in the moral and spiritual structure of the universe, and its confidence in the promise of increasing purpose, have dropped to a low level. Our age does not feel the thrill of moral grandeur which profoundly moved Kant, and which made Wordsworth write the lines of his "Ode to Duty":

> Thou dost preserve the stars from wrong;
> And the most ancient heavens, through Thee, are fresh and
> strong.

We cannot subscribe today to Tennyson's optimism, and we read Emerson's Essay on "Compensation" with a sense of wonder that any wise men could have believed that the universe was so sensitive to moral issues and so loaded with spiritual purpose. But in a happier era, when sanity returns, as it will do, and we once more begin building the Kingdom of love and truth, instead of watching the *débâcle* of ancient civilizations, we, or our children, will once more thrill with hopes and expectations, and will find it easy to believe that the universe carries in its structure a *nisus* toward significant finality, though we shall still have our doubts of the imminence of the millennium. In 1913 George Santayana wrote: "The spirit is not dead in the lull between the seasons of steady blowing. Who knows which of them may gather force presently and carry the coming age steadily before it?" ...

One of the greatest mysteries in the world is the mystery of the origin and destiny of our type of mind. We who have this *nous*-type of mind, as Plato called it, not only know, but have the unique experience of knowing that we know, of knowing ourself as the knower of objects. We look before and after, which means that we can recover the past that is gone. We can anticipate the future, which does not exist except for our minds. We can bind past and future together in a momentous duration, out of which by our decision of will a new and unique event emerges, which would not be there but for us. We can *see* not only what is there for senses, but we can *see* "what ought to be," whether it *is* or not. We carry within us an august moral dominion over events. This means, I think, that we have a pedigree which does not stem wholly from the biological order, is not inherited from flat-nosed baboons, and is not explained by atoms or genes, or any vibrating stuff of the earth's crust. Heraclitus was right when he said: "You can never discover the boundaries of the soul by travelling in any direction." And Emerson was sounding a companion note when he said: "The philosophy of six thousand years has not searched the chambers and magazines of the soul." We shall not recover our faith in immortality until we rediscover the moral and spiritual grandeur of the spirit-mind in us—the *nous* which links us to a *noumenal* universe,

> Not matter, nor the finite-infinite,
> But this main-miracle, that thou art thou,
> With power on thine own act and on the world.

At least we carry something within us that *might be* immortal, that is worth transmission to a more permanent sphere, and that *ought* to "bloom to profit otherwhere." ...

What we need, and all we need, for the recapture of imagination and for the recovery of the spell of immortality is a more genuine apprehension of the true nature and interior depth of spirit in man, and a more vivid sense of the reality of God as Spirit. If the ultimate Reality of the universe is an Over-World of Spirit, as the greatest minds that have ever lived have thought to be the case, and if the most unique thing about us is, not our bipedality or body-form, but our possession of self-consciousness and the power to transcend time and space and to originate creative action, we already belong to a World of the eternal type, or at least may belong to it. We are essentially

already great amphibians, built in our inmost structure to be the denizens of
either of two worlds, as well suited for the Over-World as for this world down-
under. George Santayana said once with his usual insight: "Whoever it was
who searched the heavens with a telescope and found no God would not have
found the human mind if he had searched the brain with a microscope."

The form and manner of our life after the cocoon of cellular tissue has
fallen away we cannot further conceive. We have so far been using brain
as our medium—sometimes adequate for our purposes and sometimes woe-
fully inadequate. This is adapted to fit only the world down-under. If it is a
highly good one it is destined to be preserved in a bottle of alcohol; if it is
a common one it is destined to return to the dust of the earth's crust. We
cannot perdure and go on in our higher World with a form and medium for
the essential personality which is only suited for a world of matter in space-
time. The secret of that new "form and medium" is strictly kept. So, too, is
the secret of every significant *mutation* kept until the mutation arrives; nevertheless the mutation occurs. So, too, is the secret kept how the hereditary
traits of the generations behind him, and his own marvellously adapted form,
come with the new-born child into the here over the infinitesimal bridge of a
cell of protoplasm. The secret is kept how a voracious caterpillar emerges
into a gorgeous butterfly delicately flitting in the air from flower to flower
for the drops of honey. We can only say as St. Paul did: "God gives it a
body as it pleases Him," even as He giveth to each form of life its body well
adapted to its peculiar environment. We may, with Browning's *Grammarian,*

> Throw on God (He loves the burden)
> God's task to make the heavenly period perfect the earthen.

We find ourselves brought up at last against a problem before which all
the other problems of life fall back to a secondary place. Has this universe
a single story to it, or is it a world of two levels? Is it a world strictly confined to time and space and matter, or is it a world which includes as well a
realm of spiritual realities of a higher order, where what begins on the first
level is carried on, completed and fulfilled? If the one level, the single story,
is all there is to it, then all the problems over which the amateur theologians
contend seem to me to be futile questions. It comes back, after all, to a
single vital issue. Is the God whom we invoke, in actual fact, GOD, or only
an imagined reality that we have "fulminated" out of our agitated minds
to dispel our fears and to argue about? If God is GOD which means in other
words, Spirit, Life of our lives, Love at the heart of things, the over-arching,
under-girding Source of all that is eternally Real and True and Beautiful
and Good, then we already have a two-storied universe with a Home in it

for all we love and a Garden in it greater than Eden, where transplanted human worth *will* bloom to profit otherwhere. This faith at least may "call home our hearts to quietness."

From *The Radiant Life,*
pp. 109–114; 135–137.

→»«←

WE do not assume immortality just because we want it. It rests upon the moral consistency of the universe, upon the trustworthy character of the eternal nature of things. The moral values which are revealed in fully developed personality are certainly as *real,* as much a fact of the universe, as are the tides or the orbits of planets. If we can count upon the continuity of these occurrences and upon our predictions of them, just as surely can we count on the consistency of the universe in reference to spiritual values. If there is conservation of matter, there is at least as good ground for affirming conservation of moral values. If biological life can pass over the slender bridge of a microscopic germ-plasm and can carry with itself over that feeble bridge the traces of habit and feature, the curve of nose and the emotional tone of some far-off dead ancestor, and all the heredity gains of the past, may we not count upon the permanence of that in us which allies us to that infinite Spirit who is even now the invisible environment of all we see and touch?

It is not a matter of reward or of "wages" that concerns us. It is not "happy isles" or care-free "Edens" that we seek, not "golden streets" and endless comfort to make up for the stress and toil of the lean years here below. We want to find the whole of ourselves, we ask the privilege of seeing this fragmentary being of ours unfold into the full expression of its gifts and powers. The new period may be even more strenuous and hazardous than this one has been—still we want the venture. We ask for the culminating acts that will complete the drama, so far only fairly begun. It must be not a mere serial, or straight line, existence; it must be the opening out and expansion of the possibilities which we feel within ourselves—new dimensions, please God.

I am not wrong, I am sure, in claiming that this postulate, this rational faith in the conservation of values, is an asset which death has revealed to the race. The shock of death has always made love appear a greater thing than we knew before the baffling crisis came upon us. It has, too, by the same shock of contrast, awakened man to the full comprehension of the moral sublimity of the good life. Kant maintained that the sense of the sublime is due to the fact that when we are confronted with the supreme powers of nature we then become aware of something unfathomable in ourselves, and feel that we are superior to the might of the storm, or the mountain or the cataract. Nowhere is this truer than when man—man in his full, rich powers —is confronted by death. Instead of cringing in fear, he rises to an unaccustomed height of greatness and is utterly superior to death and aware of some quality of being in himself which death cannot touch. It is just then in that moment of seeming disaster and dissolution that a brave, good man is most triumphant and ready to burn all bridges behind him in his great adventure.

From *Spiritual Energies in Daily Life,*
pp. 123–125.

—>>)<((—

SOME time ago a gentleman was crossing this continent in the train when at one of the stations on the road a mother got on with a little girl. The little girl sat in the seat with the gentleman and soon they were good friends, talking as though they had always known each other. The traveler said, "It will be only another hour before you reach your city and get off the train." "I wish we would never reach the old city," the girl said; "I hate to get there." When she was asked why she felt so, it appeared that she was moving with her mother to a new home and she had overheard her mother say that it was too bad for her little girl to leave the school where she had just learned her alphabet, for now she would have to "begin all over again." The little girl took that to mean that she would have to learn a new alphabet in the new town and that the old alphabet she had painfully learned would be of no more use. The man kindly explained to her that he had often been to the city where she was going, and that they all used the same alphabet she had just learned and that she could go right on from where she had left off in her old school.

There are some things that last on. They are just as good in one place as in another. They grow richer and more precious with the years. They are as eternal as God is. They will abide yonder as truly as they have endured here, for they are eternal values. Nothing can be more important than the discovery and the cultivation of these indispensables. . . .

There is something in the fundamental nature of man which sends him out *beyond himself.* At first "the beyond" is sought in space; later "the beyond" is found to be within himself. Man's spirit is over-finite. He always transcends what he has before his consciousness. He transcends himself. He looks before and after and lives *for what is not yet.* He looks down on his thoughts and acts, and judges them in the light of an ideal. It is this deeply-lying trait of "a more yet within him" that gives man his sense of wonder, mystery, awe and sublimity in the presence of stupendous things and momentous experiences such as birth and death.... I am insisting here that man was from the first the kind of being that could not be satisfied with anything short of immortal life.

Socrates and Plato were the first persons to think through and systematically to express the implications of man's inner life and thus to put the faith in a continuing life on a new and higher level. There seems to be no doubt that Socrates possessed an intense faith that death is not an evil but a good. He met the verdict of death from his judges with the words: "The hour of departure has arrived, and we go our ways—I to die and you to live. Which is better only God knows." And in the last moments of his life in prison, before he drank the poison, he told his friends that a man about to die ought to be of "good cheer about his soul," for "the prize is fair and the hope is great," and "the venture of death is a glorious one." It is to Plato, however, his loftiest disciple, that we owe the weightiest philosophical arguments for immortality which the ancient world presented. We pass over here in Plato from a mere dim hope of survival to a reasoned faith in immortal life. Plato was the first person to put the ground of faith in immortal life squarely on the fundamental nature of the soul and on the moral values revealed through personality. His argument as it is formulated in the *Phaedo* seems to us now antiquated and ineffective, but Plato's *Dialogues* nevertheless reveal a point of view which is still vital and convincing. There is in man, he holds, an inner center of reality which is inherently linked up with a divine and supersensuous world from which he has come and to which it indissolubly belongs. The supreme values of the deeper universe—beauty, truth, love and goodness—have their home and habitat in our souls as well as in the eternal nature of this deeper world of reality. We are in it and of it now and forever, for nothing physical and temporal can destroy that whose intrinsic nature is eternal. The soul that has become an organ of beauty, truth, love and goodness, which are eternal realities, is itself thereby an eternal and abiding reality and no longer doomed to the fate of things which belong to the world of time and space.

> Hence in a season of calm weather
> Though inland far we be,
> Our Souls have sight of that immortal sea
> Which brought us hither,
> Can in a moment travel thither,
> And see the Children sport upon the shore,
> And hear the mighty waters rolling evermore.

Immortal life for Plato attaches essentially to the supreme spiritual values of life.

An early Christian writer (2 Tim. i. 10) declared that Christ has "put down death and brought life and immortality to light." It is a great claim to make but it is at the same time profoundly true. He raised the belief in immortality to a level so much higher and to a conviction so much more intense that we date our faith in the future life, as we do our centuries and our calendar, from His coming. The faith rests primarily on the fact that He exhibited a life which embodied and revealed eternal life here in the midst of time. He showed "the power of an endless life" and He convinced His followers that death had not ended His life, but that through death He had risen to a new and greater mission and destiny.

The important thing, however, in Christ's revelation of immortality is not the fact that life goes on after death. Mere "going on" might not be very desirable—to some it would be terrible to go on forever the same poor old self. What Christ does is to announce and demonstrate a new kind of life, a new order of life which is essentially "eternal life." The phrase, "eternal life" is peculiar to the Fourth Gospel, but the *truth* of eternal life is everywhere implicit in the synoptic accounts. "Life," as Jesus uses it, means life in its eternal or absolute sense. "Eternal" is not to be taken primarily in a quantitative sense, to signify mere endlessness. It is rather a life of new dimensions, life raised to new capacities—the full opening out of life Godward. By a birth from above, the soul partakes of the Life of God and enters upon a type of life as inexhaustible as His life is and as incapable of being ended by physical catastrophes.

From *The New Quest*,
pp. 62–63; 163–166.

Books Written by RUFUS JONES

Eli and Sybil Jones: Their Life and Work.
  Philadelphia, Porter and Coates, 1889. 316 pp.
Practical Christianity. Essays on the Practice of Religion.
  Philadelphia, J. C. Winston Company, 1899. 250 pp.
A Dynamic Faith.
  London, Headley Brothers, 1901. 103 pp.
The Message of Quakerism. Two Addresses.
  London, Headley Brothers, 1901. 30 pp.
A Boy's Religion from Memory.
  Philadelphia, Ferris and Leach, 1902. 141 pp.
Social Law in the Spiritual World. Studies in Human and Divine Inter-Relationship.
  Philadelphia, J. C. Winston Company, 1904. 272 pp.
The Double Search. Studies in Atonement and Prayer.
  Philadelphia, J. C. Winston Company, 1906. 124 pp.
Quakerism and the Simple Life.
  London, Headley Brothers, 1906. 38 pp.
The Abundant Life.
  London, Headley Brothers, 1908. 67 pp.
Quakerism: A Religion of Life.
  London, Headley Brothers, 1908. 48 pp.
Studies in Mystical Religion.
  London, Macmillan and Company, Ltd., 1909. 518 pp.
Little Book of Selections from the Children of Light.
  London, The Swarthmore Press, 1909. 89 pp.
Selections from the Writings of Clement of Alexandria.
  London, Headley Brothers, 1910. 86 pp.
The Quakers in the American Colonies.
  London, Macmillan and Company, Ltd., 1911. 603 pp.
Stories of Hebrew Heroes.
  London, Headley Brothers, 1911. 160 pp.
Spiritual Reformers in the Sixteenth and Seventeenth Centuries.
  London, Macmillan and Company, Ltd., 1914. 362 pp.
The Inner Life.
  New York, Macmillan Company, 1916. 194 pp.
St. Paul, the Hero.
  New York, Macmillan Company, 1917. 172 pp.
The World Within.
  New York, Macmillan Company, 1918. 172 pp.
The Story of George Fox.
  New York, Macmillan Company, 1919. 169 pp.
Religion as Reality, Life and Power.
  Philadelphia, W. H. Jenkins, 1919. 45 pp.
The Remnant.
  London, The Swarthmore Press, 1920. 163 pp.
The Nature and Authority of Conscience.
  London, The Swarthmore Press, 1920. 75 pp.
A Service of Love in War-Time. American Friends' Relief Work in Europe, 1917–1919.
  New York, Macmillan Company, 1920. 284 pp.

The Later Periods of Quakerism.
  London, Macmillan and Company, Ltd., 1921. 2 vols.
The Boy Jesus and His Companions.
  New York, Macmillan Company, 1922. 189 pp.
Spiritual Energies in Daily Life.
  New York, Macmillan Company, 1922. 179 pp.
Fundamental Ends of Life.
  New York, Macmillan Company, 1924. 144 pp.
The Church's Debt to Heretics.
  New York, G. H. Doran Company, 1924. 255 pp.
The Life and Message of George Fox, 1624–1924. A Tercentenary Address.
  New York, Macmillan Company, 1924. 31 pp.
Finding the Trail of Life.
  New York, Macmillan Company, 1926. 148 pp.
The Life of Christ.
  Chicago, American Library Association, 1926. 28 pp.
Religion and Life.
  Shanghai, Association Press of China, 1926. 73 pp.
The Faith and Practice of the Quakers.
  London, Methuen and Company, 1927. 181 pp.
New Studies in Mystical Religion.
  New York, Macmillan Company, 1927. 205 pp.
The New Quest.
  New York, Macmillan Company, 1928. 202 pp.
Trail of Life in College.
  New York, Macmillan Company, 1929. 201 pp.
Some Exponents of Mystical Religion.
  New York, Abingdon Press, 1930. 237 pp.
George Fox, Seeker and Friend.
  New York, Harper and Brothers, 1930. 224 pp.
Pathways to the Reality of God.
  New York, Macmillan Company, 1931. 253 pp.
A Preface to Christian Faith in a New Age.
  New York, Macmillan Company, 1932. 206 pp.
Mysticism and Democracy in the English Commonwealth.
  Cambridge, Mass., Harvard University Press, 1932. 184 pp.
Haverford College. A History and an Interpretation.
  New York, Macmillan Company, 1933. 244 pp.
The Trail of Life in the Middle Years.
  New York, Macmillan Company, 1934. 250 pp.
Re-Thinking Religious Liberalism.
  Boston, The Beacon Press, Inc., 1935. 26 pp.
The Testimony of the Soul.
  New York, Macmillan Company, 1936. 215 pp.
Some Problems of Life.
  Nashville, Cokesbury Press, 1937. 214 pp.
The Eternal Gospel.
  New York, Macmillan Company, 1938. 235 pp.
The Flowering of Mysticism; the Friends of God in the Fourteenth Century.
  New York, Macmillan Company, 1939. 270 pp.
A Small-Town Boy.
  New York, Macmillan Company, 1941. 154 pp.
Spirit in Man.
  Stanford University, Stanford, Calif., Stanford University Press, 1941. 70 pp.
The Vital Cell.
  Philadelphia, Book Committee, Religious Society of Friends, 1941. 27 pp.
The Shepherd Who Missed the Manger.
  Garden City, N.Y., Doubleday, Doran and Company, 1941. 28 pp.

New Eyes for Invisibles.
New York, Macmillan Company, 1943. 185 pp.
The Radiant Life.
New York, Macmillan Company, 1944. 154 pp.
The Luminous Trail.
New York, Macmillan Company, 1947. 165 pp.
A Call to What Is Vital.
New York, Macmillan Company, 1948. 143 pp.

Books Edited by RUFUS JONES

George Fox, an Autobiography. Edited with an introduction and notes by Rufus M. Jones.
Philadelphia, Ferris and Leach, 1903. 2 vols.
Religious Foundations. Edited by Rufus M. Jones.
New York, Macmillan Company, 1923. 144 pp.
The Church, the Gospel and War. Edited by Rufus M. Jones.
New York, Harper and Brothers, 1948. 169 pp.